Minorities in the Contemporary Egyptian Novel

Edinburgh Studies in Modern Arabic Literature
Series Editor: Rasheed El-Enany

Writing Beirut: Mappings of the City in the Modern Arabic Novel
Samira Aghacy

Autobiographical Identities in Contemporary Arab Literature
Valerie Anishchenkova

The Iraqi Novel: Key Writers, Key Texts
Fabio Caiani and Catherine Cobham

Sufism in the Contemporary Arabic Novel
Ziad Elmarsafy

Gender, Nation, and the Arabic Novel: Egypt 1892–2008
Hoda Elsadda

The Unmaking of the Arab Intellectual: Prophecy, Exile and the Nation
Zeina G. Halabi

Post-War Anglophone Lebanese Fiction: Home Matters in the Diaspora
Syrine Hout

Nasser in the Egyptian Imaginary
Omar Khalifah

Conspiracy in Modern Egyptian Literature
Benjamin Koerber

War and Occupation in Iraqi Fiction
Ikram Masmoudi

Literary Autobiography and Arab National Struggles
Tahia Abdel Nasser

The Arab Nahḍah*: The Making of the Intellectual and Humanist Movement*
Abdulrazzak Patel

Sonallah Ibrahim: Rebel with a Pen
Paul Starkey

Minorities in the Contemporary Egyptian Novel
Mary Youssef

edinburghuniversitypress.com/series/smal

Minorities in the Contemporary Egyptian Novel

Mary Youssef

EDINBURGH
University Press

Edinburgh University Press is one of the leading university presses in the UK. We publish academic books and journals in our selected subject areas across the humanities and social sciences, combining cutting-edge scholarship with high editorial and production values to produce academic works of lasting importance. For more information visit our website: edinburghuniversitypress.com

© Mary Youssef, 2018

Edinburgh University Press Ltd
The Tun – Holyrood Road
12 (2f) Jackson's Entry
Edinburgh EH8 8PJ

Typeset in 11/15 Adobe Garamond by
Servis Filmsetting Ltd, Stockport, Cheshire

A CIP record for this book is available from the British Library

ISBN 978 1 4744 1541 5 (hardback)
ISBN 978 1 4744 1542 2 (webready PDF)
ISBN 978 1 4744 1543 9 (epub)

The right of Mary Youssef to be identified as author of this work has been asserted in accordance with the Copyright, Designs and Patents Act 1988 and the Copyright and Related Rights Regulations 2003 (SI No. 2498).

Contents

Series Editor's Foreword	vi
Acknowledgements	ix
Note on Transliteration and Translation	xi
Introduction: Historical Transformations: Framing a New Consciousness in the Contemporary Egyptian Novel	1
1 History and Representations of Otherness in Idris ʿAli's *al-Nubi* and Bahaʾ Tahir's *Sunset Oasis*	42
2 Reading Cosmopolitanism in Yusuf Zaydan's *Azazeel* and Muʿtazz Futayha's *Akhir yahud al-iskandariyya*	67
3 The Irrecuperable Heterogeneity of the Present in ʿAlaʾ al-Aswani's *The Yacoubian Building* and *Chicago*	98
4 Heart Deserts: Memory and Myth between Life and Death in Asharaf al-Khumaysi's *Manafi al-rabb* and Miral al-Tahawi's *The Tent*	124
Epilogue: New Directions	158
Bibliography	189
Index	199

Series Editor's Foreword

Edinburgh Studies in Modern Arabic Literature is a new and unique series that will, it is hoped, fill in a glaring gap in scholarship in the field of modern Arabic literature. Its dedication to Arabic literature in the modern period, that is, from the nineteenth century onwards, is what makes it unique among series undertaken by academic publishers in the English-speaking world. Individual books on modern Arabic literature in general or aspects of it have been and continue to be published sporadically. Series on Islamic studies and Arab/Islamic thought and civilisation are not in short supply either in the academic world, but these are far removed from the study of Arabic literature qua literature, that is, imaginative, creative literature as we understand the term when, for instance, we speak of English literature or French literature. Even series labeled "Arabic/Middle Eastern Literature" make no period distinction, extending their purview from the sixth century to the present, and often including non-Arabic literatures of the region. This series aims to redress the situation by focusing on the Arabic literature and criticism of today, stretching its interest to the earliest beginnings of Arab modernity in the nineteenth century.

The need for such a dedicated series, and generally for the redoubling of scholarly endeavour in researching and introducing modern Arabic literature to the Western reader, has never been stronger. Among activities and events heightening public, let alone academic, interest in all things Arab, and not least Arabic literature, are the significant growth in the last decades of the translation of contemporary Arab authors from all genres, especially fiction, into English; the higher profile of Arabic literature internationally since the award of the Nobel Prize for Literature to Naguib Mahfouz in 1988; the growing number of Arab authors living in the Western diaspora and writing both in English and Arabic; the adoption of such authors and others by mainstream, high-circulation publishers, as opposed to the academic publishers of the past; the establishment of prestigious prizes, such as the International Prize for Arabic Fiction (the Arabic Booker), run by the Man Booker Foundation, which brings huge publicity to the shortlist and winner every year, as well as translation contracts into English and other languages; and very recently, the events of the Arab Spring. It is therefore part of the ambition of this series that it will increasingly address a wider reading public beyond its natural territory of students and researchers in Arabic and world literature. Nor indeed is the academic readership of the series expected to be confined to specialists in literature in the light of the growing trend for interdisciplinarity, which increasingly sees scholars crossing field boundaries in their research tools and coming up with findings that equally cross discipline borders in their appeal.

During the months of January and February of 2011, Tahrir Square in downtown Cairo acquired international fame, fronting in news bulletins of all genres of media across the globe, and invoking reverence in the corridors of the UN, in the White House, Downing Street, the Élysée, and many other seats of power. It was a glorious moment in the history of modern Egypt, when hundreds of thousands of the Egyptian people congregated in Tahrir Square between January 25 and February 11 demanding and finally achieving, at the expense of many hundreds of their lives, the overthrow of the autocrat Hosni Mubarak and his corrupt regime. Regardless of what happened in the five years since 2011 and the failure of the uprising, and the eventual return of the military to power with much loss of the freedoms gained in its aftermath, Tahrir Square and the popular uprising for which it became a focal point has gained an iconic status in contemporary Egypt.

Egyptian events of 2011, and the Arab Spring in general, may have taken world politicians by surprise, but not quite as many of Egypt's intellectuals, including novelists. For popular revolutions to happen, a "new consciousness" needs to have been fermenting for a while, an increasing awareness of the failings of the status quo coupled with an aspiration to something different. Invariably literature plays a core role in fomenting such "new consciousness," and it is up to literary historians and critics to look back after the event and trace the beginnings of this new consciousness in the literary products of the decades leading up to a momentous historical change. This is what this timely study attempts to do, bringing scholarship up to speed with the contemporary socio-political scene. It may be too early to study how the events of the 2011 uprising have been reflected in literature. Indeed, this literature may be still in the making. However, it is not too soon to look, as this study does, for the premonitions of the "new consciousness" in the literature of the decades leading up to the uprising. The novels constituting the backbone of this study were written in the twenty-first century, that is, in the ten years preceding the uprising, and all deal with communities marginalised on account of their difference and their minority status. "Tahrir Square" was the crucible and the moment that provided all communities in Egypt, however different, with a voice, a sense of entitlement, of being part of the larger whole, with a stake in what was happening. It is as if the fiction under study here was a herald for that moment: its "prophetic soul," to use an apt phrase from Shakespeare's *Hamlet*.

Professor Rasheed El-Enany, Series Editor,
Emeritus Professor of Modern Arabic Literature,
University of Exeter

Acknowledgments

This book would not have been possible without the absolute support I have received throughout my studies and career path from the loving and caring people I am surrounded with. Special acknowledgments go to my parents, whose unconditional love and faith in me have inspired me to complete the research task at hand. I would also like to exclusively acknowledge my daughters for their benevolent understanding of and support for "Mama's work," without which I could not possibly have completed this book. My daughters' faces have been the highlight and motivating source of any long day I spent researching and writing. Wholehearted thanks to Lydia and Sophia.

To my friends and colleagues, whose continued advice, generous help, inspiration, and keenness on my success have been indispensable to the completion of this study, I express my utmost gratitude. Special thanks go to Nancy Um for her constant encouragement, the numerous hours she spent on reading my writing drafts, and her incredibly valuable feedback. To Andrew Scholtz, my senior colleague and mentor, your generous input, guidance, and unselfish support have not only made the completion of this manuscript possible, but have inspired me to grow and develop as a scholar and a participating member in the Department. Many thanks go to Kent Schull, Miral al-Tahawi, and John Starks for their relentless encouragement and keenness on my success.

I gratefully acknowledge the support and generosity of New York State and the United University Professions Joint Labor-Management

Committees for granting me the Dr Nuala McGann Drescher Affirmative Action/Diversity Leave Award. This award has provided me with ample time to complete my book. I would also like to acknowledge Binghamton University's efforts to support its junior faculty, especially with the Harpur College Dean's Research Semester Award for junior faculty as well as the Institute for Advanced Studies in the Humanities Fellowships. Both supporting opportunities have been necessary for my professional development and the completion of this manuscript.

My notable gratitude and special thanks go to the editors, editorial board members, and staff in the area of Middle East Studies at Edinburgh University Press; but most expressly to Rasheed El-Enany, Series Editor of the Edinburgh Studies in Modern Arabic Literature, and Nicola Ramsey, the Commissioning Editor for Middle East Studies. Rasheed and Nicola's support for my book, since it was an idea and a proposal, has been invaluable for its completion and for propelling it through the different publishing stages. Special thanks to you, Rasheed, for your constructive suggestions and critical feedback on the earlier drafts of the manuscript, without which the substance of this study would not have culminated in it making its desired contribution. My special thanks go to my two peer reviewers, whose valuable reviews and recommendations made the publication of this book possible.

Note on Transliteration and Translation

My transliteration of Arabic words in this book adheres to the transliteration guidelines of the *International Journal of Middle Eastern Studies*, by which Arabic words and phrases are transliterated with diacritics as well as with ʿ*ayn* (ʿ) and *hamza* (ʾ) insertions. Titles of books and articles, personal names, place names, and names of political parties and organizations are also transliterated according to the same guidelines, but without diacritical marks. The spellings of Arabic words found in Merriam-Webster, such as "sheikh," are used as they appear there, except for the insertion of ʿ*ayn* (ʿ) and *hamza* (ʾ). Names of Arab authors and political figures who are known to English-speaking audiences are transliterated on first mention, but thereafter I refer to them by the familiar English spelling of their names. For example, the first mention of the former Egyptian President Jamal ʿAbd al-Nasir, is fully transliterated, but thereafter I use the familiar English spelling of his name, Gamal Abdel Nasser, or simply Nasser. The names of Arab critics who publish their scholarship in English are not transliterated. Instead, the English spellings of their names as they appear in their English publications are used. Examples include Samia Mehrez and Sabry Hafez.

Titles of all Arabic novels are transliterated on first mention. If a novel was translated into English, I immediately provide the English translation title along with the publication date, and use that English title thereafter: for example, *al-Khibaʾ* (1996; *The Tent*, 1998). For the sake of harmonizing the spelling throughout, characters' names within the English-translated novels are also transliterated on first mention, but thereafter their spellings as they appear in the English translation are used. If a novel was not translated into English, I immediately provide my English translation of the title in this form: *al-Nubi* (2001, "The Nubian"), then continue to use the Arabic transliteration for its title throughout. Characters' names in untranslated novels are also written in the transliterated form throughout the book. At times, the spellings of characters' names in Arabic transliteration are identical with their spellings in the English translation.

Introduction
Historical Transformations: Framing a New Consciousness in the Contemporary Egyptian Novel

Identifying a New Consciousness

This book identifies and explores an important recent trend in contemporary Egyptian novels, particularly since the turn of the millennium, that presents Egyptian society—from antiquity to the present—as fundamentally heterogeneous, which is to say, as consisting of several groups based on imagined and lived differences in race, ethnicity, religion, culture, language, and gender. While many of the novels in question depict indigenous and immigrant ethnic and religious groups during modern colonial and post-independence times, some venture to portray these groups' status and life conditions in historical periods that precede the arrival of Arabo-Islamic rule, going back in time to as early as the Egyptian Demotic period (BCE 664–641 CE). I argue that these novels depart from the confined and relatively monolithic picture of the nation-state, and exhibit a new consciousness, a new critical sensibility towards difference and the multiplicity of identities that compose Egypt's population today and contribute to its complex history, all amid political, socio-economic, and cultural instabilities.

This is not to say that, prior to this new consciousness, the Egyptian novel failed to engage with the issue of difference and practices of differentiation and exclusion from homogeneously constructed political, social, and cultural national paradigms. On the contrary, since its emergence as a genre at the beginning of the twentieth century, the Egyptian novel has foregrounded difference and asymmetries of power, but predominantly across an axis of class, and, from the 1970s onward,[1] gender. Building upon this foundation of addressing persistent inequalities across class, gender, or the combination of these,[2] the newest phase in the development of the Egyptian novel broadens the purview of difference to underscore the cultural experiences of marginalized identities at the intersections of race, ethnicity, religion, gender, language, and class. Their diversely inclusive scope of representation responds to persistently uniform political and cultural imaginaries and exclusionary practices within Egypt that continue to overlook and/or exacerbate the marginalization of certain groups, most discernible of which are racial, ethno-religious, and women minorities. As will be underlined in this study, acts of marginalization and practices of exclusivism have continuously been inflamed by the current local and regional instabilities and rising neocolonial interventions.

I call this new trend within contemporary Egyptian novels the "new-consciousness novel,"[3] as it aspires to what Edward Said describes as the "decentered consciousness" that postcolonial cultural and intellectual efforts demonstrate to subvert constituencies and ideologies of dominance and essentialism (Said 1985: 105–6).[4] The new-consciousness novel likewise displays an expansive cultural purview that is grounded in anti-dominant and counter-essentialist depictions of Egypt's heterogeneous society. Its representational scope includes, for example, the North African indigenous population of the Amazigh in *Wahat al-ghurub* (2006; translated as *Sunset Oasis*, 2009) by Bahaʾ Tahir (b. 1935); the Nubians in *al-Nubi* (2001, "The Nubian") by Idris ʿAli (1940-2010), and in *Dawwamat al-shamal* (2007, "Northern Whirlwinds") by Hasan Nur (b. 1940); Bedouins in *Manafi al-rabb* ([2013] 2015, "God's Exiles") by Ashraf al-Khumaysi (b. 1967) and the Bedouin woman in *al-Khibaʾ* (1996; *The Tent*, 1998) by Miral al-Tahawi (b. 1968); the indigenous and immigrant Jewish populations in *Akhir yahud al-iskandariyya* (2008, "The Last Jews of Alexandria") by Muʿtazz Futayha (b. 1987); and Coptic Christians in *ʿAzazil* (2008; *Azazeel*, 2012) by Yusuf Zaydan (b. 1958), and in *Istasiyya*, 2010 by Khayri Shalabi (1938–2011). Constructs of difference are intensified in *ʿImarat yaʿqubiyan* (2002; *The Yacoubian Building*, 2006) by ʿAlaʾ al-Aswani (b. 1957) because of its presentation of an exhaustive and almost encyclopedic portrayal of Egyptian groups sharing a common destiny. *Shikagu* (2007; *Chicago*, 2007), also by al-Aswani, and *Bruklin hayts* (2010; *Brooklyn Heights*, 2011), by Miral al-Tahawi, depict Egyptian experiences of migration to the USA and feature diverse characterization and the interfacing of local and global settings. The writers of these novels, who do not themselves necessarily belong to the groups they depict, rewrite the Egyptian past with racial, ethnoreligious, and women communities as active participants. They create an assemblage of distinctive cultural experiences by portraying members of a given group in interaction with one another, with other groups, and with the global community at large, rather than in isolation. This interactive and dynamic portrayal is anchored to a new, "decentered" consciousness that disrupts essentialist perceptions of the self and the other and calls into question claims to cultural purity in a global age.

The spectrum of representation of marginalized communities in Egypt is not intended to be exhaustive or comprehensive. My selection of texts is based primarily on the degree to which each focuses on the portrayal of the experiences of existing marginal groups in Egypt: no attempt is made to focus on particular groups, or on authors of any particular status or background. As such, the selection is not restricted to works by writers who belong to the minorities they creatively portray in their works, such as the late Idris ʿAli, a Nubian writer writing about Nubians' plight and displacement in the second half of the twentieth century in *al-Nubi*, or Miral al-Tahawi, a female Bedouin author representing a young Bedouin woman's struggle with the cloistering and suppression of her physical and emotional needs in *The Tent*. In fact, the study deliberately includes a diverse group of novels and of writers such as Zaydan and Tahir, who are not members of the minorities they creatively represent in their respective works, *Azazeel* and *Sunset Oasis*, with the aim of expanding the analytical and critical framework used by Gilles Deleuze and Félix Guattari in their seminal book *Kafka, Toward a Minor Literature*. Their study prominently situates Franz Kafka's writing and its politics in the then new literary category of minor literature,[5] which, they explain, breaks from preexistent generic identifications and requires the opening up of new critical perspectives and reading tools. However, it delimits minor literatures to those written by minorities such as the Jews of Prague and blacks in the USA (Deleuze and Guattari 1986: 16–17).[6] This study broadens that limited scope of minor literature and purposely examines a diverse group of novels and writers to evince a hidden totality and uncovered unity under what might appear to be discordance and difference; for the analysis of such a group of diverse novels reveals a shared textual code that emanates from a new consciousness brought about symbolically by their writers as individual acts in order to disrupt essentialism and "possessive exclusivism" (Said 1985: 106). This new consciousness, articulated by means of literature, simultaneously creates a space for and is created by a community of difference. Said articulately warns lest postcolonial cultural and intellectual work lapse into "parochial dominations and fussy defensiveness" when claims to exclusive insider's experience and knowledge in the name of "fragmentation and specialization" are made (ibid. p. 107). In addressing "the problem of the division of labor," he refers to the issue of

> whether in identifying and working through anti-dominant critiques, subaltern groups—women, blacks, and so on—can resolve the dilemma of autonomous fields of experience and knowledge that are created as a consequence. A double kind of possessive exclusivism could set in: the sense of being an excluding insider by virtue of experience (only women can write for and about women, and only literature that treats women or Orientals well is good literature), and second, being an excluding insider by virtue of method (only Marxists, anti-Orientalists, feminists can write about economics, Orientalism, women's literature). (ibid. p. 106)

The application of Said's view undergirds the shared premise of difference in the novels I study in two distinct ways. First, it foils restricting the act of writing about marginal groups to writers and critics who have the insider's experience and knowledge. Second, it highlights the creativity with which these novels freely represent marginalized experiences in Egypt without subscribing to any prescribed political or social agenda. The multiplicity of creative perspectives included in this book's selection of texts underscores the fact that the fields of experience and knowledge pertaining to this new genre are neither autonomous nor reserved to insiders alone. Rather, this corpus includes texts that adopt marginalized positions with the aim of bringing them to the fore of the literary imaginary, and of creating what Kwame Appiah calls a "perspectival shift" (Appiah 2006: 77).[7] Additionally, the present selection serves as an antidote to the critical establishment's treatment of works addressing marginal populations as something separate from the larger whole of Egyptian literature. An example of this differentiating stance is manifest in the predominant critical categorization of literature by/on Nubians as *"tayyar al-adab al-nubi"* (stream of Nubian literature) (Hasan 2010),[8] a separation that was strongly rejected, and considered mere *"kasal naqdi"* (laziness of literary criticism),[9] by Idris ʿAli (ibid.).[10]

Before I proceed to an analysis of the historical conditions that underlie the rise of the new-consciousness novel, it is important to note that this trend is firmly taking root in the larger Arabic literary tradition, especially since some of these novels have been awarded the prestigious International Prize for Arabic Fiction. Tahir's *Sunset Oasis* and Zaydan's *Azazeel* won the prize in two consecutive years, 2008 and 2009 respectively. Furthermore, al-Tahawi's *Brooklyn Heights* was shortlisted for the same prize, whereas Shalabi's *Istasiyya* and al-Khumaysi's *Manafi al-rabb* were longlisted. Although ʿAlaʾ al-Aswani's *The Yacoubian Building* did not win any prizes—it was only longlisted for the International Dublin Literary Award in 2006[11]—it was a best-seller for five consecutive years, the highest level of popularity ever achieved by a contemporary Arabic novel.[12]

The Emergence of a New Novelistic Genre

Michael McKeon argues that the novel as a literary genre is a historical category whose evolution is directly aligned with the context in which it is created (McKeon 2000a: 1). The Egyptian novel, with its changing features, continuously invites its critics to develop historically reflexive methodologies that help us to analyze and interpret these works and their mediatory role in formalizing and articulating historical moments. Fredric Jameson observes that the importance of the idea of genre lies in its relational function, which "allows the coordination of immanent formal analysis of the individual text with the twin diachronic perspective of the history of forms and the evolution of social life" (Jameson 1982: 105).[13] This study seeks to fulfill the critical task of identifying an emergent genre in contemporary novelistic production in Egypt through examining its homologies with and disjunctures from other novels; my aim is to understand the developments within Egyptian culture and society, especially in the tumultuous past few decades. In so doing, I bring to light some of the strands that have been missing from past treatments of the larger complex of Egypt's cultural and literary history.

In the following section, I situate the new-consciousness novel in Egypt's novelistic production by following three necessary steps. First, I reveal its historical underpinnings by reviewing the socio-political and cultural context from which it arose. Second, I demonstrate how this new genre can be distinguished from other novelistic production by reviewing examples of antecedent novels in order to understand what socio-political and cultural conditions these newer works reevaluate. Third, I detect what this new, homological body of novelistic production shares in terms of formal and semantic features, and what it achieves as a corpus.

Historical Transformations

The work of critics such as Samia Mehrez, Richard Jacquemond, and Sabry Hafez, whose extensive research examines the correlation between the state and the history of intellectualism and cultural production in Egypt, has largely informed my own critical endeavor. In addition to reviewing these critics' insights into Egyptian culture, I draw upon Michael McKeon's historical approach to understanding the emergence of new genres, the novel in particular, whose development he roots in the precarious epistemological and cultural conditions of seventeenth-century Europe. The rise of the new-consciousness novel in Egypt is, to a similar degree, situated in the socio-political-cultural tumult the country has undergone for the past few decades, and the application of McKeon's historical approach yields critical insights into contextual factors conditioning the emergence of the genre in question. By examining narrative patterns in the literature of early modern Europe, McKeon demonstrates that narrative forms and content subvert their literary traditions as well as the surrounding social establishments. On the literary plane, he identifies the generic instability that gave rise to the novel and associates it with changes in how truth is conveyed in narrative. In the same way, McKeon identifies the vacillation within the social structure at the time, and links it to changes in people's perception and signification of virtue, or in his words, changes in "attitudes toward how the external social order is related to the internal, moral state of its members" (McKeon 2000b: 383).[14]

McKeon demonstrates how new genres break from tradition by adopting antithetical positions, which, over time, "lose their way" and generate new "counter-critiques." The resulting "counter-critiques" evoke the earlier traditions that were initially refuted (ibid. pp. 384–97), and thus present a dialectical process of subversion, counter-subversion, and synthesis. This dialectical process demonstrates "how conceptual categories, whether 'literary' or 'social,' exist at moments of historical change: how new forms first coalesce as tenable categories by being known in terms of, and against, more traditional forms that have thus far been taken to define the field of possibility" (ibid. p. 383). McKeon writes:

> the very capacity of seventeenth-century narrative to model itself so self-consciously on established categories bespeaks a detachment so sufficient to imagine them *as* categories, to parody and thence to supersede them. And with hindsight we may see that the early development of the novel is our great example of the way that the birth of genres results from a momentary negation of the present so intense that it attains the positive status of a new tradition. But at the "first instant" of this broader dialectical reversal, the novel has a definitional volatility, a tendency to dissolve into its antithesis, which encapsulates the dialectical nature of historical process itself at a critical moment in the emergence of the modern world. (ibid. p. 396)

McKeon's dialectical model attends to three significant principles crucial to any understanding of how genres are born: how genre unsettles the surrounding established social and generic categories, how it is the result of "a momentary negation of the present," and how it has "a definitional volatility, [and] a tendency to dissolve into its antithesis" by the very nature of the dialectical process of historical change.

In light of McKeon's theory, it is safe to say that new social movements and novelistic genres acquire fluidity in their dissolution into earlier traditions, and thus complicate efforts to distinguish them antithetically from precursors. Egyptian writer and journalist Husni Hasan notes that intellectual and novelistic writing challenges, as well as being challenged by, its precursors in the process of historical change. He describes a similar dialectical reversal that Egyptian avant-garde thinkers and novelists experience when they write against the socio-cultural and literary grain:

> What [was] a crying out, an upheaval, a convulsion, the broken gasps of rebellion against intellectual conformism when it began, has tended over time to let itself come to rest with other forms of tradition, falling asleep in the cradle of its own aesthetics. What was once introduced to us as the dawning of freedom, as a necessary revision and as an authentic act of rebellion has been transformed in the twilight of the century into just a new literary institution that has added itself to those that preceded it.[15] (Husni, quoted in Jacquemond 2008: 220)[16]

In spite of the underlying challenge in locating where the contextual socio-political and cultural categories of the new-consciousness novel collide or converge, I will delineate the points of their disjuncture or conflation in the process of historical transformation in the following section.

Changes in the Socio-political and Cultural Realms

The dialectical reversal process of historical change in the form of subversion and counter-subversion is well illustrated in the socio-political and cultural transformations that occurred in Egypt after independence in 1952. Although many of the writers of the new-consciousness novel were born after that time, the wavering policies of the nascent postcolonial Egyptian state, spearheaded by its military-officer presidents, are key to attempts by novelistic authors to negate the present and create a "new" literary tradition. In the political arena, the two heavyweights of Egypt's modern formation governed in succession: Jamal ᶜAbd al-Nasir (simply known in the West as Nasser) and Anwar al-Sadat (Sadat). While the two shared military training, they were inspired by divergent European nationalist ideologies. On the one hand, Nasser implemented anti-imperialist strategies when he "combined pan-Arabism with pan-Islamism and pan-Africanism"[17] (Young 2001: 190) and allied himself with the former Soviet Union during the Cold War, launching an experimental "Arab deist socialism with autocracy" (ibid. p. 190). Sadat, on the other hand, ventured into a "romance with imperialism" (Tucker 1978: 4),[18] as well as into a long process of "de-Nasserization" (ibid. pp. 3–9),[19] by which he strategized to liberalize the Egyptian economy[20] and democratize in rhetoric, rather than in practice, intellectual life and the political sphere.

Following the same pattern of adopting disparate political and economic policies, the two presidents approached the intellectual and cultural spheres differently. They either courted or neglected cultural-intellectual elites when needing to influence public opinion, especially during the difficult times of war or when implementing controversial policies. In his seminal work *Conscience of the Nation: Writers, State, and Society in Modern Egypt*,[21] Richard Jacquemond explains the complex relationship between Egypt's political and cultural histories as resulting from the state's fluctuating policies towards its intelligentsia and writers. On the one hand, Nasser adopted state patronage strategies leading to the creation of the Ministry of Culture and the General Organization for Culture Palaces, entities supporting writers and journalists with the expectation that they would themselves support the state and promote its policies. Sadat, on the other, retracted from that state support strategy, leaving room for younger writers, who previously had struggled to gain access to the public by publishing their works in state-funded cultural venues, to find alternative publication series. Although the substitute publishing venues were not funded by the state, they gained popularity among avant-garde writers at the time and included the influential literary journal *Gallery 68* (Jacquemond 2008: 15–23). Nevertheless, conflicts between avant-garde writers and the state arose due to Sadat's attempts at de-Nasserization. His regime called for (albeit in flatulent oratory) the liberalization and democratization of the economic and socio-political spheres, a state approach that marginalized non-conforming intellectuals (ibid. p. 24). As Jacquemond observes, Sadat's abandonment of intellectual and cultural production allowed "relative professional and ideological autonomy from the state's commissions" (ibid. p. 24).

Alongside the clashing modern political and economic formations in Egypt, Islamism also emerged as another distinct national culture that developed at the hands of a literate and elite group. Anissa Talahite explains the counter-hegemonic foundation of Islamic resurgence at the turn of the twentieth century. She writes:

> Although . . . calling for the need to adapt Islam to the demands of modern life, the leader of the Islamic Reformist movement, Jamal al-Din al-Afghani [1838–97] . . . and Muhammad Abdu [the Egyptian religious scholar and jurist, 1849–1905], stressed the importance of religion in the spiritual life

of a nation and the necessity to find strength in one's own cultural and spiritual heritage. Speaking against the cultural alienation threatening Arab societies, al-Afghani argued that reforms could only come from Islamic roots and not from superficial imitation of European ways. (Talahite 2007: 40)[22]

However, as much as Islamist groups, especially the Muslim Brotherhood, gained popularity, they were banned by the Egyptian government in 1948 and after independence by Egypt's consecutive military presidents, who continued obstinately to suppress Islamist activism and deemed it a nationally unsettling counterculture.

During his rule from 1981 to 2011, Hosni Mubarak understood the ramifications of Nasser's defiant, yet popular economic, political, and cultural decisions, but also witnessed Sadat's divergent and unpopular strategies, as well as his failure in handling opposition. As a result, Mubarak's decisions, as illustrated below, reflect his socio-political and cultural compromise, yet they also led to an unyielding monopolization of political power by the military and the police. This semi-directionless compromise was the manifestation of what Galal Amin refers to as "the soft state" (Amin 2011: 9),[23] by which Egypt was a mere "bystander" when there was a massive political crisis in the Arab region: this phenomenon is clearly illustrated in the case of Egypt's reaction to the massacre of Palestinian and Shiite Lebanese refugees at the Sabra and Shatila refugee camps in 1982 and in Egypt's mercurial political relations with other Arab countries over Iraq before and after the Gulf War of 1991 (ibid. pp. 9–10). More strikingly, after Egypt had made multiple political and economic concessions to global powers, especially the USA and Israel, "Arab states gradually discovered that they lost Egypt as a leader, mentor, and mediator in inter-Arab conflicts" (ibid. pp. 14–15). On the economic plane, as Amin notes in his book *Madha hadatha lil-thawra al-misriyya* (*What Happened to the Egyptian Revolution*), the problems stemming from the irresponsible application of liberal economic policies—launched by Sadat and continued by Mubarak—were intractable, while the administrative body of the state was largely dysfunctional due to the corruption infiltrating its ranks (Amin 2013: 45–53).[24]

On the cultural plane, at the beginning of his rule Mubarak gradually abandoned the conventional officers' ruthlessness in repressing Islamists, particularly the Muslim Brotherhood[25] and the seekers of the establishment of a theocratic state as long as their activism was delimited to the social and cultural spheres (Ajami 1995: 77).[26] At the same time, according to Jacquemond, the state was also disengaged from the literati because it did not have the means to financially support them in their intellectual and creative endeavors. So, Mubarak's regime granted freedom of expression to the press and freedom of ideological allegiance to the intelligentsia, whatever those allegiances have been, local, regional, or international (Jacquemond 2008: 25–6).[27] By the early 1990s, the cultural sphere was "fragmented" (ibid. p. 26) between two ideological polarities: the secularist liberals and the religious conservatives. The state, in turn, did not recoil from exploiting that divide in order to affirm its monopoly on power (ibid. p. 28). With the growth of extremism within the Islamist stream of thought, and with the inability of institutional Islam to combat that surge by itself, the state had recourse to Nasser's leftist and Arabist mobilization of intellectuals, who, by that time, also needed the state's "political protection in order to contain the growing interference in the cultural field by men of religion" (ibid, p. 26). As Jacquemond puts it:

> From this point onward, the chapter of Sadatism was definitively closed, and a system similar to that which had operated under Nasserism reappeared, at least on the surface, with the authorities now posing as supposedly impartial patrons of the cultural field, integrating all the various groups, schools, and tendencies within the state apparatus, while also attempting to manipulate these groups' internal conflicts for their own ends. (ibid. p. 26)

Alongside the conflicting political, cultural, and ideological trends in Egypt, there have been parallel discordant formations in the social realm. McKeon's investigative model seeks to understand the demise of one social order and the rise of another in early modern Europe by tracking how the exterior societal order can be indicative of the inner moral status of the society's different members.[28] Similarly, examining the recent changes within the Egyptian social order provides a deeper understanding of what the new-consciousness novel attempts to scrutinize in Egypt's social life. In 1952, the revolutionary Free Officers delivered the country from its corrupt king and pledged social and economic reforms. Egyptian state-controlled media, especially television and newspapers, ensured that they were depicted as elite, virtuous individuals, faithful to the modern cultural and national ideals of sovereignty and equality. This propaganda mobilized popular sentiments in the officers' favor. It is worth noting that this mobilization of pro-military popular sentiments resurrected momentarily, first after the ouster of Mubarak and later after that of Muhammad Mursi (hereafter Morsi), the first elected Egyptian president from the Muslim Brotherhood (2012–13), when articles and photos of people in Tahrir Square appeared in national newspapers with the demonstrators shouting pro-military slogans. For example, *al-jaysh wal-shaʿb yadun waḥida* ("The army and the people are one hand")[29] is a memorable slogan, shouted out by demonstrators in 2011 at the sight of military helicopters and military guards and their tanks entering Tahrir Square.[30]

The Islamist national culture in Egypt defended a set of values based on traditional Islam and a homogeneous, sacred community, and appealed to a different social order that both rejected the hierarchy of the officers' regime and celebrated a horizontal and collectivist structure grounded in the possession of and adherence to the tenets of Islam and the goal of reviving its heritage. Egyptian literary and cultural critic Samia Mehrez recounts, in her timely work of 2008, *Egypt's Culture Wars*, how in 2001 innovative cultural production and freedom of speech were subject to obstruction and suppression by both government executive powers and Islamist politicians, who gradually rose to power in the 2000 and 2005 Egyptian parliamentary elections. Mehrez recounts how in 2001 the then "newly elected parliamentary deputy and Muslim Brother Gamal Hishmat submitted a request to the Minister of Culture Faruq Husni to ban three novels published by the General Organization for Cultural Palaces [GOCP] because according to Hishmat, they present 'explicitly indecent material amounting to pornography'" (Mehrez 2008: 14).[31] In agreement with Hishmat's disapproval of the works, Mr Husni dismissed Muhammad al-Bisati, the editor of the cultural ministry publishing agency Literary Voices, and his managing editor, the poet Jirjis (Girgis) Shukri, as well as the head of the GOCP. In defending his decision, the Culture Minister saw his role as "the guardian of societal morality," challenged "anyone who could allow his sister, his wife or his daughter to read such indecencies," and also reminded "intellectuals that Egypt is not

Europe" (ibid. p. 14). This decision was hailed by the Islamists who opposed the publication of such literary works and who "concluded that 'the minister has repented'" (ibid. p. 15).

Dissent regarding the confiscation of rights and freedoms, political, social, and cultural, had been brewing long before the demonstrations in 2011 in Tahrir Square, where men and women from all backgrounds, creeds, and ages collectively voiced their discontent with the then current hegemonic conditions pulling them in the direction of one socio-political-cultural polarity or another, without heeding the pluralism and multidimensionality of their composition. The clamor of their dissident voices was united in a single demand for reform. But these nationally marked mass demonstrations in Tahrir did not erupt without precedent. In fact, they were sparked by the multiple waves of protest and attempts at change and reform that had taken place before them in the new millennium. Mehrez writes:

> On 16 June 2005, Egyptian writers, artists, journalists, and other pro-reform and democracy advocates gathered at the Journalists' Syndicate in downtown Cairo to commemorate the death of Sheikh Imam Issa, the blind composer and singer, who put to music the political protest poems by leading vernacular poet Ahmad Fuad Nigm . . . On this politically charged occasion, on the eve of the Egyptian presidential elections of September 2005, Nigm read the founding statement of the Writers and Artists for Change movement that, only two weeks earlier, had joined the ranks of a host of pro-reform groups and movements that had mushroomed in Egypt to protest against yet another six-year mandate of President Mubarak. (ibid. p. 1)

The movements Mehrez refers to include *Kifaya* ("Enough"), the Popular Campaign for Change, the Youth for Change Movement, human rights activists, and others.[32] They all "primarily demanded the end of Mubarak's rule and opposed the possible succession of his son, Jamal. They also called for democracy, equality, transparency, the right to protest, freedom of literary artistic and academic work and the refusal of all forms of censorship and intimidation" (ibid. p. 1). Mehrez states that "[f]or this nascent movement, political freedom *is* cultural freedom and no regime can claim to be democratic without according freedom of opinion and expression in all fields of knowledge and creative endeavor" (ibid. p. 1).

The conflicting ideological and political trends in contemporary Egypt as represented in the given examples of Nasserist, Sadatist, Mubarakist, and Islamist attitudes towards the literary and creative realms demonstrate how each singularly adopted stance emerges in refutation of its historical predecessor. It does so by coopting the ideological principles its predecessor intended to reverse and, thus, conflates approaches and ideas with earlier historical stages. The concurrence of these conflicting socio-political and cultural practices has heightened tension and competition over the field of power between the two predominant national entities, the army's postcolonial state and the religious authorities. In other words, the "two-part pattern of reversal" (McKeon 2000b: 384) of reformation and counter-reformation is well illustrated in the historical shifts Egypt underwent in the second half of the twentieth century: The parts in question, which constitute the structure of the conflicting socio-political and cultural manifestations in Egypt, give rise to one another and base their value and power systems on antagonistic grounds.

The new consciousness I identify in contemporary novelistic production inheres in a nascent national culture that negates the concurrent exclusive and authoritarian national ideologies and practices, that is, the autocratic and the theocratic. Unlike its predecessors, it is not spearheaded by the literati alone, whose united voices in the 2005 protests, as Mehrez describes, "seemed to come only from the past, reproducing the state's official 'Enlightenment' discourse about the nineteenth-century *nahda* while parading icons of the dead—Taha Hussein, Umm Kalthum, Salah Jahin, among others and chanting Ahmad Fuad Nigm's political poetry of the 1970s" (ibid. p. 6). I argue that the new consciousness manifests itself in the heterogeneous clamor of the twenty-first-century novel, heralding the cacophony of voices heard in Tahrir Square. This cacophony consists of the dissident voices of *Kifaya*, Youth for Change, and artists, journalists, writers, and academics merging with the voices of the Egyptian people from all walks of life in a united discordance. Their conjoined voices negate the claim that the possession of virtue and morality is confined to those who adhere to a particular political, cultural, or religious program, and consequently refuse a social order that is based on political, intellectual, or religious status. In this sense, the nascent historical consciousness exhibited in the literary text and in Tahrir Square calls for our attention to the historical moment as well as to people's assumption of agency to shape their own historical moment and societal values.

Review of Antecedent Novelistic Production

As illustrated with the dialectical process, the socio-political and cultural movements in Egypt's recent history, rather than neatly succeeding one another on the basis of definitively disjointed principles, are shown to converge. The changes in novelistic production in Egypt correlate with their counterparts in the socio-political and cultural spheres and acquire definitional volatility in their own turn. Yet, the Egyptian establishment of literary criticism overlooks the unstable nature of novelistic writing, and does so due to its insistent categorization of novelistic writing on the basis of definitive aesthetic breaks and lines of separation between different generations of writers.[33] Jacquemond contends that it is more accurate to drop the conventional generational divides that organize Egypt's contemporary literary history, because "symbolic struggles within the subfield of the novel have tended not to take the form of collective confrontations between schools, groups, or tendencies supporting opposing aesthetic norms" (Jacquemond 2008: 216). He goes on to say that, unlike poetry, which tends to be defined "mainly according to *form*, about which there is no consensus ... the novel ... [is] defined according to *content*, in other words according to the fictional character of narrative, and this is largely agreed upon" (ibid. p. 216).[34]

In the history of novelistic production in Egypt, inaccurate though it is to claim that nascent novelistic writing definitively disjoints itself from its precedents, it is also misleading to argue that the novel can be defined solely on the basis of its content and fictional character. Mikhail Bakhtin asserts that "in the study of verbal art we must overcome the divorce between an abstract 'formal' approach and an equally abstract 'ideological' approach. Form and content in discourse are one" (Bakhtin 1981: 269).[35] Thus, while novelistic writing is identified in terms of its content, which is directly related to the social life it aesthetically reflects and comments on, it utilizes formal features that effectively articulate its narrative content by creatively assigning new meanings and ideas to the repertoire of language and its signs. It will, then, be inaccurate to say that the new-consciousness novel marks a complete thematic and formal break from its predecessors. Rather, it should be seen as an expansion of them. The new-consciousness novel constitutes a new novelistic genre largely because of its distinctively expansive perspective on difference and heterogeneity in Egyptian society, a perspective that is delivered in its distinctively heteroglossic and polyphonic formal features. In other words, the new-consciousness novel presents in its discourse an aesthetic of communal difference in unity, one whose united form and content enunciate what seems to be a discordant hybrid of polyphonic utterances.

As was mentioned earlier, the new-consciousness novel succeeds a long tradition of treating the fundamental inequalities within Egyptian society in novelistic form. Egyptian novels have been broadly categorized on the basis of their ideological and historical preoccupations, which are generally perceived to be either modern/nationalist[36] or postmodern/postcolonial.[37] Novels tied up with nationalism are usually associated with the colonial period and are known to mobilize anti-colonial resistance by evoking a sovereign nation that has been in existence from time immemorial. The national identity that they conjure up partakes in a singular historical narrative, whether that is based upon agrarian, Pharaonic, or Arabo-Islamic Egypt. During the time of colonial rule and the *ancien régime*, novelists Muhammad Husayn Haykal (1888–1956) and Tawfiq al-Hakim (1898–1987) were preoccupied with the distressed Egyptian peasantry in their respective works, *Zaynab*, 1914 (*Zainab*, 1989) and *Yawmiyyat naʾib fi-l-aryaf*, 1937 (*Maze of Justice: Diary of a Country Prosecutor*, 1947). Similarly, Yahya Haqqi (1905–92) in *Qindil umm hashim*, 1940 (*The Saint's Lamp*, 1973) is concerned with the experience of a traditional family in urban Cairo after being introduced to modern science and its conflict with their cultural and religious practices. These writers mainly directed their social and ideological concerns towards a racially and religiously homogeneous Egypt that suffered from colonialist rifts and the sweeping advent of modernity. Their works exemplify the intellectual and cultural outlook of the *nahda* era,[38] whose literary portraits seem, as Laila Lalami puts it, "schizophrenic" and unable to surmount entrapment in tradition during modern pursuits (Lalami 2009: xv).

Jeff Shalan argues that "the modern Arabic novel developed in conjunction with a specifically nationalist mode of thought, and that it was instrumental not only in the dissemination of that thought, but in its very formation as well" (Shalan 2002: 213).[39] He attests to the difficulty of dealing and the reluctance to deal with untangling the relationship between ideological formations and cultural production, and the correlation of such formations and production with social transformations (ibid. p. 215). Yet, he successfully illustrates the "organic" relationship between the rise of nationalism and the emergence of novelistic writings in Egypt. This he does by examining two pioneering Egyptian novels, Muhammad Husayn Haykal's *Zaynab*, 1914 and *ᶜAwdat al-ruh*, 1933 (*Return of the Spirit*, 1990), by Tawfiq al-Hakim, as key cases. He writes:

> it is almost invariably from the field of culture that proponents of nationalism first posit an idea of the nation as an organic entity, one which pre-exists its geopolitical formation. Whether it be language, territory, race, religion, ethnicity, the presumed historical continuity of a people, or any combination thereof, which serves as the organic and unifying principle of the nation, the idea itself typically takes shape in and is transmitted by way of cultural system. (ibid. p. 212)

Since Haykal and al-Hakim are among the most influential Egyptian intellectuals during the culmination of nationalist sentiments and identities, Shalan examines how in these novels they express the cultural systems and beliefs behind the territorialist national ideologies emerging among Egyptian elites. Their novels demonstrate a writing of nation (ibid. p. 216) that is exclusive to elitist male-engendered ideologies, but simultaneously invoke a common ancient Egyptian past rooted in and practiced by its peasant community. Shalan describes such writing as a "claim to a national entity and identity distinct from Islam and from the Arab lands and peoples of the East" (ibid. p. 220). While Haykal's novel presents an exposé of the poor and repressive life conditions of peasants and women, he denies his peasant and women characters any political agency or right to self-determination. In Haykal's nationalist vision, the freedom to reform ailing traditions and to determine one's own and others' destinies seems to exist only in the minds—and not in the actions—of educated, wealthy males like *Zaynab*'s main character, Hamid. Hamid empathizes with the ever-vibrant peasants who work on his father's farmland for a meager wage, and is impressed by their communal lifestyle. Nonetheless, he remains ambivalent towards his role in effecting any change in their miserable conditions (ibid. pp. 216–32).

As the title of al-Hakim's novel, *ʿAwdat al-ruh* (*Return of the Spirit*), suggests, it invokes the ancient Pharaonic myth of Isis and Osiris, in which Isis collects the parts of the dead body of her husband, Osiris, from all over the land of Egypt and resurrects him. Allegorically, al-Hakim's vision of the Egyptian nation is inspired by this mythical motif of awakening the communal soul of the Egyptian people. According to Shalan, al-Hakim attempts, unlike Haykal, to locate this spiritual reclaiming of power first in women characters like Saniyya, and second in the inherent solidarity of the Egyptian peasantry since Pharaonic times, a process observed by Muhsin, the novel's main character, during his visit to his father's farmland in the countryside. Still, in both cases we are dealing with an attempt to shift this awakening spirit away from the "conflicting" and "egotistical" male desires that have been corrupted by materialism and urban life. At the same time, Shalan writes that al-Hakim's "strategy of displacement" of Egypt's regenerative power shifts from women to peasants in order to finally return it to Egypt's cultural elites, who are able to visualize the unity of the nation through the combination of art and myth. Shalan notes that "these two texts not only represent the dominant focus and trajectory of the nationalist thought of the period, they also provide valuable insight into the rhetorical appeal, as well as the ideological limits and contradiction, of the territorialists' nation-building project" (ibid. pp. 236–47).

As illustrated above, two distinct ideas clearly reject the subordination of the Egyptian peasantry and identify it as the impetus behind the national imaginary. The first involves progressing towards the future by invoking the achievements of ancient Egyptian civilization and through the timeless, socio-economic functionality that its agrarian culture offers. The second illustrates revolution against feudalism and the remnants of Ottoman superiority, as seen in Muhsin's rebellion against his proud Turkish mother and his feudalist father after the father denies his peasant roots. Shalan's thorough and insightful analysis of these seminal works evidences how Haykal and al-Hakim took upon themselves the task of revealing the truth of the socio-economic conditions of the Egyptian peasantry under feudalism. However, in their preoccupation with imagining the aspiring nation-state, their works conjure up a romantic picture of the Egyptian countryside and idealize its agrarian communal life. It is, however, a picture starkly devoid of possibilities that could alter that monolithic stability and traditional harmony of Egyptian society and politics. This portrayal leaves peasant as well as women characters with no agency or right to self-determination.

Before I provide examples of the novelistic writing that emerged in the late 1960s, '70s, and early '80s—a time period during which national demoralization prevailed due to the Egyptian army's loss of Sinai in the June 5 war in 1967—it is important to note that Najib Mahfuz (Naguib Mahfouz) (1911–2006), with his long career span, had at the beginning of his career produced works that leaned thematically towards the anticolonial project and the uncertainty created by the sweeping onset of modernity. For example, his trilogy masterpiece, *Bayn al-qasrayn*, [1956] 1983 (*Palace Walk*, 1990), *Qasr al-shawq*, 1957 (*Palace of Desire*, 1991), and *Al-Sukkariyya*, [1957] 1972 (*Sugar Street*, 1992), is set in Cairo during British colonial rule and reveals the obscurities of a seemingly traditional society falling into rupture and moral decay. It portrays a middle-class merchant and corrupt father named Sayyid ʿAbd al-Jawwad, who lives a double life: a conservative, tyrannical one with his family and a hidden, immoral one with mistresses. Anissa Talahite observes that his son, Kamal ʿAbd al-Jawwad, "a largely autobiographical character, embodies the tension between the old and the new" (Talahite 2007: 44). At the beginning of the trilogy, Kamal believes in revolutionary nationalism and traditional Islam as "asserted truths," but gradually transforms into an uncertain thinker. "As one of Mahfuz's characters remarks, religion used to be the way of asserting truths but now there is 'a new language, which is Science and there is no way of asserting truths, great or small alike, except in this language'" (ibid. p. 44).

Several influential writers in Egypt's modern literary history contributed to the novelistic production in the late 1960s, '70s, and early '80s. Among them are Idwar al-Kharrat (1926–2015), Sunʿallah (Sonallah) Ibrahim (b. 1937), and Jamal (Gamal) al-Ghitani (1945–2015). The majority of these writers' works exhibit disenchantment with the nationalist fantasies that their predecessors' novels are anchored to, and thus depart from the idealized countryside setting of agrarian Egypt. Their works are often set in Cairo or Alexandria to underscore the popular spirit of uncertainty, if not despair, among city dwellers, made distraught by persistent regional wars, increasing class differences, atrocious socio-economic conditions, and lack of political and social reforms. Furthermore, the urban setting epitomizes the spatial flux of modernity, in which tension between traditional life and values, embodied in the constant influx of immigrants from Egypt's peripheries to its metropolises, and the incessantly transforming urban life, embodied in city dwellers' restless lifestyles, are highlighted.

In *Waqaʾiʿ harat al-zaʿfarani*, 1976 (*The Zafarani Files*, 2009), al-Ghitani employs a dual narrative technique that merges third-person narration with official reporting style. The omniscient narrator has access to the secret lives of a multiplicity of men and women living in the Zaʿfarani alley in Cairo and provides the reader with this privileged access to their inner thoughts, bedroom conversations, and secret sexual affairs. At the same time, the novel is loaded with reportorial-style narration of social and cultural peculiarities and humor that would never otherwise appear in an actual official report. Each household has its own, unique dynamic based on its residents' oftentimes debased social conditions due to obscure past occupations and activities. Examples of the lives of the Zaʿfarani microcosm include: the sexually impotent *ʾusta* (master) ʿAbdu, the experienced driver, and his sexually demanding, financially independent wife, Buthayna; Rummana *al-siyāsī* (the political), the former political detainee; and the former sergeant in the ousted Egyptian King's court, Salam, who mourns the lost glory of the past (although it was not his own). Other humorous and therefore entertaining residents of al-Zaʿfarani alley include Farida *al-baydāʾ* (the white), whose yelling at her husband Husayn *raʾs al-fijla* (the radish head) does not bother neighbors, al-Tikrilli, the procurer, and Kirsha, the owner of al-Daturi café, where those who live in the Zaʿfarani alley and their likes outside of it share their concerns. These individuals' differences are manifest in the way they fight in their homes and loudly proclaim their discontent to neighbors from their windows. These overt dissonances are united when Sheikh ʿAtiyya *al-mabrūk* (the blessed) casts the spell of sexual impotence indiscriminately on the alley's residents. The novel's microcosm of the Zaʿfarani's lives highlights the urban fragments of the lower working class, discarded by the Egyptian state in the 1970s. The novel is thus primarily preoccupied with revealing the urban working class's atrocious socio-economic and cultural conditions and does not underscore other dimensions of difference or underlying inequalities.

Sunʿallah (Sonallah) Ibrahim's *al-Lajna*, 1981 (*The Committee*, 2003), written during Sadat's rule, portrays in a Kafkaesque style the absurdity of bureaucracy and political oppression in Egypt, tools the Egyptian state uses to stifle popular dissent. The anonymous protagonist undergoes multiple ambiguous, yet humiliating tests and trials at the hands of the strange-looking and nameless members of a high committee. In his painstaking attempts to impress them and appease their scrutinizing facial expressions, he takes off his clothes, belly dances, and discusses the biggest capitalistic achievement of the twentieth century, which he claims to be the Coca Cola industry and the feminine shape of its bottle. But while he is performing all these seemingly inconsequential farcical acts, he exposes the economic and cultural hegemony of the USA and ridicules Egypt's submissiveness.

Idwar al-Kharrat's is another leading author from the group known as *jīl al-sittīnat* (Sixties Generation). In his novel *Rama wa-l-tinnin*, 1980 (*Rama and the Dragon*, 2002), the main character, Mikhaʾil, like al-Kharrat himself a male Copt, falls in love with Rama, a young Muslim woman who is free-spirited and urban. Through Mikhaʾil's and Rama's reminiscences and musings, the novel invokes a multiplicity of Egyptian pasts and presents: the Pharaonic, the Nubian, the Coptic, the Islamic, the folkloric, and the modern. It conjures up the Pharaonic myths and figures of Egypt, yet deflects them in the similarly timeless religious mysticism of Coptic and Islamic Egypt. In this regard, *Rama and the Dragon* not only derives from the artistic project of territorial nationalism that earlier novelists like al-Hakim espouse, but also expands it by conflating many timeless elements of Egypt's historical and religious characters in the novel. As much as that conflation disrupts monolithic configurations of Egypt's historical character, it also diffuses the identity of its main characters, Mikhaʾil and Rama, who do not seem to be solely influenced by one particular heritage or the other.

Jacquemond observes that writers from the Christian minority in Egypt, Idwar al-Kharrat included, espouse, like their Lebanese and Syrian counterparts, non-realism in their literary expression, a trend that has not been popular in mainstream novelistic styles. Jacquemond relates this artistic choice to the "difficulty [they encounter] in acquiring the status of major intellectuals, having to renounce all expressions of minority identity in order to do so" (Jacquemond 2008: 97). He marks al-Kharrat as "the only writer to have escaped the curse that has lain over any deliberately non-realist project" (ibid.

p. 97) thanks to al-Kharrat's personal efforts in explaining his artistic choices to the literary establishment (ibid. p. 97). While *Rama wa-l-tinnin* celebrates a plethora of Egyptian heritages, Fabio Caiani contends that the religious character of Egypt is emphasized in the hero's "sort of ecumenical message" for both Copts and Muslims. He writes: "This ecumenism seems to function especially, if not only, on a national level. Hence, the Egyptian form of Islam occupies a privileged place in Mīkhāʾīl's rhetoric and he often appears to be instinctively led to stress that in the land of Egypt, the Coptic and Muslim creeds share the same roots" (Caiani 2005: 38).[40] In that sense, while *Rama and the Dragon* appears to underscore the multiplicity of heritages that Egypt possesses, it idealizes two, distinct religious characters of Egypt, the Coptic and the Islamic, and in so doing conflates them in a new nationalist imaginary that differs from its agrarian-founded counterpart in being grounded in Egypt's spiritual and mystical heritage.

In addition, one could argue that the feminist novel constitutes another salient genre in contemporary Egyptian novelistic production that both presaged and also necessitated the rise of the new-consciousness novel. In the 1970s and '80s, women writers like Latifa al-Zayyat (1923–96), Nawal al-Saʿdawi (b. 1931), and the late Alifa Rifʿat (1930–96) relentlessly exposed women's subservient status and unapologetically critiqued Egyptian cultural conservatism perpetuating women's subordination. In novels such as al-Zayyat's *al-Bab al-maftuh*, 1960 (*The Open Door*, 2000), al-Saʿdawi's *Imraʾa ʿind muqtat al-sifr*, 1975 (*Woman at Point Zero*, 1983), and Rifʿat's *Jawharat Firʿawn*, 1991 ("The Pharaoh's Jewel"), as well as al-Saʿdawi's memoirs *Muthakkirati fi sijn al-nisaʾ*, 1986 (*Memoirs from the Women's Prison*, 1994), cultural norms are questioned by highlighting sensitive and taboo social issues like female circumcision, sexuality, and women's limited role in the social and political spheres. However, in its continuous effort to write women's overlooked history and to combat male-dominated views of nationalism, social mores and political functions, the feminist novel has often been critiqued for its counter-essentialism. For example, al-Saʿdawi's novelistic style was scrutinized by literary critics such as Nadje Sadig al-Ali and Sabry Hafez for constructing a "reverse discourse" that is informed by the "paradigm of binary oppositions" that falls into essentializing the self (woman) and the other (man) in an attempt to resist the oppressive patriarchal order (Jacquemond 2008: 189). Interestingly, the critique of feminist endeavors in Egyptian women's novelistic production that exposes the unsettling problems created by male domination in Egyptian society did not arise from "legitimate criticism"—which Jacquemond uses to refer to the establishment of literary criticism in Egypt—alone, but also from tensions and disagreements among women writers themselves about literary style and their activist preoccupations. For example, al-Zayyat criticized al-Saʿdawi's works for prioritizing women's psychological and "internal world" issues over those of "reality" (al-Zayyat, quoted in Jacquemond 2008: 187).

Seeing al-Saʿdawi's novelistic endeavors as counter-essentialist or neglectful of reality controverts what, in postcolonial theory and particularly in Frantz Fanon's work, is referred to as the intellectual's "efforts" to "rehabilitate" themselves from the colonial assimilationist enterprise (Fanon [1963] 2007: 253–4).[41] Since colonialism persists in denying the existence of a native culture for the colonized in order to suppress their articulation of difference, Fanon explains how the native intellectual's efforts aim to counter this colonial indifferentiation by demonstrating and affirming the existence of a counter native culture. The native intellectual's efforts thus become "logically inscribed from the same point of view of colonialism" (ibid. p. 254). Gayatri Spivak applies Fanon's insight concerning rehabilitation by means of counter-essentialism to feminist resistance efforts. She observes how the subaltern, and particularly women, reinforce their existence against the grain of masculinist and nationalist conventional histories—which are the handmaidens of colonialism itself—which deny women's contributions to social, political, and cultural spheres, by subscribing to "a strategic use of positivist essentialism in a scrupulously visible political interest" (Spivak 1996: 214).[42]

Before I review examples of feminist novels, it is crucial to note how women's writings suffered from marginalization by the Egyptian literary and social establishment for the greater part of the twentieth century. Jacquemond observes how the contributions of women like ʿAʾisha Taymur (1840–1902), Zaynab Fawwaz (c.1850–1914), Labiba Hashim (1880–1947), and Mayy Ziyada (1886–1941) to the cultural *nahda* movement had been disregarded by the literary establishment (Jacquemond 2008: 36). Additionally, Marilyn Booth describes how, at the turn of the twentieth century, these women writers adopted a "surreptitious" mode in writing about the self in fragmentary narratives that underlined "family relationships, friendship networks, and collective concerns" that engaged with notions of femininity in society (Booth 2013: 36–7).[43] Nonetheless, women's literary writings were by and large overlooked by the male-dominated institution of "legitimate criticism," not only throughout the first half of the twentieth century, but also in the post-independence era, a long period of subordination that was interspersed with brief acknowledgments of certain creative endeavors by women writers, especially in the genre of the short story.[44] In the 1990s, "legitimate criticism" continued to categorize contemporary women's fictional narratives with pejorative reference to "female writing" (*al-kitaba al-niswiyya*) (Jacquemond 2008: 184–7), which led to women writers stridently voicing their discontent with this gender-based and separatist categorization of their works. Al-Zayyat, for example, notes in her critical introduction to an anthology of short stories written by women that "literary criticism continues to misunderstand the work of the Arab woman writer and to marginalize it and place it outside its proper context" (quoted in Jacquemond 2008: 184).[45]

Al-Zayyat's *The Open Door* is considered the first novel to depict women's struggles to create a space for themselves in the political sphere between 1946 and 1956; however, her literary endeavor was ironically concluded by the state's closing of the Egyptian Feminist Union in 1956 (Jacquemond 2008: 185). Al-Saʿdawi similarly engages with the marginalization of women, both in the familial institution and in the public sphere, in her works, as is the case with her fictional memoir *Mudhakkirat tabiba*, 1960 (*Memoirs of a Woman Doctor*, 1988) and *Woman at Point Zero*, 1973.

In *Woman at Point Zero*, al-Saʿdawi fictionalizes the true-life story of a woman named Firdaws, who was on death row for murdering her procurer. Al-Saʿdawi met Firdaws while conducting a psychological study of neurotic conditions among Egyptian women in the women's Barrages prison. The novel gives full agency to Firdaws as the subject and narrator of her own story. She recalls her extreme poverty and deprivation as a child living in the countryside, and recounts abuse at the hands of a violent father, genital mutilation, and sexual abuse by her uncle, her husband from an arranged marriage, and later her procurers. Although Firdaws successfully completes her high school education with honors, she joins the lines of unemployed youth and is forced into prostitution as a means of living. Insisting on reclaiming her dignity, she finds a job, but is soon let down by an opportunistic co-worker, who falsely promises her stability and marriage, yet abandons her to marry their manager's daughter and become a Socialist workers representative. Disillusioned, Firdaws returns to prostitution and later stabs her exploitative procurer to death. The novel exposes women's dispossession of their bodies and subjection to violence and ruthless male domination for materialistic and political gain. It also allegorizes colonial violence and territorial dispossession and how they obstinately continue to afflict Egyptian bodies, especially those of women, and to inform the practices of the postcolonial state.

Jacquemond makes reference to the gender equality achieved by women writers in the 1990s, at least in matching their numbers with those of their male counterparts. Examples of women writers who emerged at that time include Mayy al-Tilmisani, Sumayya Ramadan, and Miral al-Tahawi (ibid. pp. 190–1). Nonetheless, Jacquemond makes a fundamental observation regarding the geographies from which these women writers emerge: they mostly come from or live in the large Egyptian metropolises of Cairo and Alexandria, but those who live in the peripheries, particularly in Upper Egypt, are still underrepresented. This is by and large true; however, Miral al-Tahawi's Bedouin background and her upbringing in al-Sharqiyya Governorate clearly situate her in a minority position, ethnically and regionally. Her aesthetic choices in her novels illustrate the extensive influence of traditional Bedouin and peasant conditions, values, poeticism, and art forms.

In his 2010 article "The New Egyptian Novel: Urban Transformation and the Narrative Form," Sabry Hafez identifies a plethora of recent novels written by a group of young Egyptian novelists, whom he calls the "1990s generation."[46] Hafez describes the antagonism with which these novels were met both by the state and by the literary establishment, even though they demonstrate shared and distinct formal features that separate them from realist and modernist works.[47] Hafez observes how these "young writers were accused of poor education, nihilism, loss of direction, lack of interest in public issues and obsessive concentration on the body; of stylistic poverty, weak grammar, inadequate narrative skills and sheer incomprehensibility" (Hafez 2010: 49). Hafez disapproves of this institutional position regarding this "new wave" of novels and instead draws critics' attention to the correlation between these works' formal features and the urban transformations Cairo has undergone since the 1970s. As sketched by Hafez, the Egyptian poor respond to the neglect of the state and its insufficient housing provisions by taking "the matter into their own hands" (ibid. p. 47) and developing what is known as *al-mudun al-ʿashwāʾiyya*, or the "sprawling slums of Cairo" (ibid. p. 50), just as the "1990s generation" adopts common narrative features that reflect its existential crisis within an "irrational, duplicitous reality."

The new-consciousness novel exhibits similarly unrecognized tendencies among contemporary Egyptian novelists; however, it distinguishes itself from previous novelistic production as exemplified by the nationalist, anti-colonial novel, novels of the post-1967 war period, the feminist novel, and the "1990s-generation" movement. The extrinsic reality from which it draws its content and form is not merely the marginality of its protagonists across the class or gender spectrum, for it testifies to the more complex reality of the intersections of class with race, ethnicity, religion, gender, sexuality, culture, and language by bringing these intricacies to the forefront of its literary undertakings.

In surveying Egyptian novelistic production up through the work of the 1990s generation, one notes that, during colonial times and the *ancien régime*, the Egyptian novel demonstrated the culminating imagination of an independent Egyptian nation and a sensibility regarding the socio-economic inequality created by the concurrence of colonial and feudal systems. After independence, novels of the 1960s, '70s, and '80s demonstrate simultaneously their cognizance of and protest against the Egyptian state's false promises of social, political, and economic equality and prosperity. But more importantly, committedly feminist writers like al-Saʿdawi shift the focus to socio-economic inequalities by intersecting them with the problem of being a woman in a patriarchal, morally decaying society.

Such anti-colonial/nationalist and postcolonial/post-independence efforts in Egyptian novelistic production of the twentieth century can be described as circumscribed, at least insofar as their creative scope mostly overlooks the cultural and historical multidimensionality of Egyptian society.[48] In that respect, the novels in question can be said to fall short of presenting a "decentered" consciousness that renounces racial, ethno-religious, and gender-centered (with the exception of the feminist novel) imaginings and discourses. In these novels, individuals who are subjected to social inequalities pertaining to their embodiment of more than one marginal status, particularly class or gender with race, religion, or language, barely exist, and if they do exist, their appearance is decorative and static/one-dimensional, suggesting a lack of agency, an inability to generate change or even to draw attention to their particularly complex, minoritarian status. In other words, these marginal figures, though important as characters, tend to be incidental to the various political and cultural concerns of a given novel's thematic substance.

The new-consciousness novel of the twenty-first century creatively expands these various circumscribed models of representation by unsettling the boundaries of a singularly imagined nation-state, without ignoring the pressing social and economic issues associated with the groups it represents. By responding to the urgent problems raised by complex identities across the spectrum of difference, it addresses topics like national and cultural belonging, rights, social justice, and immigration. Thus, traditionally overlooked marginal characters are moved to the forefront of the new-consciousness novel, a primary position that allows readers to experience the world through their eyes and to envisage their alternative ways of life as being as viable and functional as their own. These portrayals are not necessarily heroic or celebratory, but they are probing, sensitive, and eye-opening.

The New-consciousness Novel and the Aesthetics of Difference

As demonstrated above, the new-consciousness novel is a nascent novelistic genre that constitutes a distinct body of work and that coheres as a new and clearly linked grouping; however, it does not develop as a complete break from its predecessors, since it carries on the preoccupation with responding to inequalities and asymmetries of power. What distinguishes it thematically from its predecessors, however, is its focus on the neglected host of complex differences and practices of differentiation resulting from resurgent essentialist conceptualizations, power structuring, and identities in contemporary Egypt. In recent years, the assertion of singularized identities (national, ethnic, or religious) has been on the rise as a means of resisting similarly essentialist neocolonial aggressions in national and regional affairs, which have been intensified by the American invasion of Iraq in 2003, the Israeli state's increasing oppression of Palestinians and annexation of their land,

and the foreign military interventions of global powers in Libya, Syria, and Yemen.

The new-consciousness novel responds to the resurgent, distinctive imaginings of what Egypt is, and who its inhabitants are, by foregrounding their racial, ethno-religious, gender, cultural, linguistic, and class differences, and at the same time postulating a creative vision for resistance against discourses and practices of differentiation. That nascent semantic preoccupation necessitates adoption of aesthetic features that I propose as "aesthetics of difference." The new-consciousness novel is particularly dynamic because its authors are quite creative in their literary choices and persuasive in their varied presentation of a different Egypt. They employ narrative techniques that accommodate a multiplicity of voices, and their characterization is highly diverse in order to invite the reader to impartially know, understand, and identify with this diverse pool of characters. Their representation of morality is not restricted to characters who adhere to one particular religion or belong to a certain race, culture, gender, or sexual orientation.

The events within new-consciousness novels unfold in multiple narrative times and spaces, allowing for different experiences to develop and mature without temporal or spatial prescriptions, often through the use of subplots. Their spatial sites, ranging from urban centers to marginal geographies, sometimes even connect these two for the purpose of questioning the concepts of cultural purity and geographical seclusion in a global age. If the setting of the novel is urban, the characters' spaces usually intersect or overlap, and if marginal, the setting shifts the reader's attention to a new, untested territory. Their themes and attention to realistic details exhibit their expansive research in the histories and cultures of the groups with which their works are concerned.

Additionally, their innovative and subversive language creates new relations between signifier and signified, relations that obscure the traditional tropes of racial, ethnic, and belief-system difference, as well as the imbalance in power relations that these tropes allude to. They appropriate Standard Arabic to decenter it by inserting words from other languages (like Kenzi[49] and Siwi[50] in *al-Nubi* and *Sunset Oasis*), Christian theological terminology (in *Azazeel*), Egyptian Colloquial Arabic, or unconventional and less commonly used cultural expressions and gestures (as in shared expressions among the homosexual community in ʿ*Imarat*). In other words, the novels recreate these groups' images and voices in Egyptian national discourse by revising traditional metaphors and formulas that marked them as different and, therefore, subordinate.

Before I embark on the detailed analysis of eight new-consciousness novels in the following chapters, I will present a few examples of the aesthetics of difference their authors employ. As will be explored in Chapter 3, "The Irrecuperable Heterogeneity of the Present in ʿAlaʾ al-Aswani's *The Yacoubian Building* and *Chicago*," these two recent works by al-Aswani take place in the heart of cities, Cairo and Chicago, in order to vividly demonstrate the aesthetics of difference. With considerable attentiveness to the spectrum of diversity in contemporary Egypt, ʿ*Imarat* depicts a variety of life experiences in the characterization of the many and diverse inhabitants of a multi-story apartment building in Cairo's downtown, a building that has witnessed the rise and fall of the city over the ages. Thus, we have Kamal al-Fuli (Kamal el Fuli) as the corrupt member of the ruling National Democratic Party; former aristocrats Zaki Pasha and his sister Dawlat; Hajj ʿAzzam (Hagg Azzam), the business tycoon with a questionable past; the two Coptic brothers, Abaskharun (Abaskharon) and Malak; the working-class woman, Buthayna (Busayna); and Taha, the ambitious hardworking son of a doorman. Al-Aswani accommodates their particular lives by making each character's experience unfold in its own subplot and narrative time, which are in turn divided into subsections. These subsections do not follow any orderly sequence, so that attempts to hierarchize them are disrupted, but they also intersect and connect with each other at unexpected moments. With the novel set in downtown Cairo, these characters share the space of the urban Yaʿqubiyan Building, which is vertically layered in a way that makes their private spaces at once separated and horizontally shared. This spatial device performs an essential function in subverting and ridiculing the contemporary social hierarchy: it places capitalistic conglomerates at the bottom of the building and the destitute on the top. Occupying the tin rooms on the roof of the ʿ*Imara* (building) are the Nubian soldier ʿAbd Rabbuh (Abd Rabbuh), the Coptic tailor Malak, the factory worker Busayna, and Taha, the doorman's son turned fundamentalist. These individuals seem disjoined from one another and from the rest of the building's occupants, yet the structure of the Yaʿqubiyan Building allows their paths to intersect and their differences to be negotiated. Such interactions are demonstrated in the relationships between rich Hatim and his poor partner, Abd Rabbuh; Zaki the former aristocrat and Busayna the working woman; Zaki as an employer and Abaskharon, a Coptic employee; the rich residents and Taha, the doorman's son. In the novel's configured space, the multiple fragments of the Egyptian population are brought together to voice their concerns and ailments, albeit dissonantly. They come together to form a critique of the state system, with its oppressive policies of differentiation and identity, omission and commission, exclusion and inclusion.

Chicago is set in Chicago after the events of 9/11. The multiplicity of individuals, Egyptian and American, represented in the novel are connected through their common workplace in the Department of Histology at the University of Illinois. The novel discloses the long-standing differences and disjunctions between East and West (spatially and ideologically), tradition and modernity, and, finally, Arab poetics on the one hand and religion, the state, and science on the other. The novel attempts to tear down those divides through the interaction and dialogue of its characters. Al-Aswani's thematic and spatial devices exhibit literary and political impulses of change and revolution against the authoritarianism of political and poetical systems in Egypt. Despite their different backgrounds and creeds, Naji (Nagi), the Muslim immigrant and student, Graham, the American political activist and professor, and Karam, the Coptic equality advocate and physician, bond over their shared resentment of despotic and discriminatory establishments in their respective countries. Each voluntarily shares his personal experience of resistance against such organizations: Nagi's against conservative academics at Cairo University and the Egyptian police force because of his political activism, Graham's against the US government during the Vietnamese War in the late 1960s and early '70s, and Karam's against the Dean of the School of Medicine in Cairo, who denied him a specialization in surgery because of his creed. Merging their separate stories into a single narrative of dissent, they create a plan to oust the epitome of despotism, the anonymous Egyptian president. Their shared defiance of the cultural and political establishments in their respective nations is an embodiment of a consciousness that attests to transnational negotiations and dialogues, but also to equivalent and comparable injustices across various groups and communities.

Thus, al-Aswani's two works, as key examples of the new-consciousness novel, jointly present an inclusive account of Egyptian society from local and global perspectives. However, the revolution proposed in *Chicago* expands the transformation presented in *The Yacoubian Building*. While *Chicago* proposes a more radical change when multiple characters from different backgrounds collaborate to write a manifesto of dissent and oust the Egyptian president from office, change in ʿ*Imarat* seems conservative and limited to the reconciliation of two different classes and subcultures, namely through the intermarriage between Zaki's former aristocracy and Busayna's working class.

If al-Aswani's work represents contemporary Egypt as cosmopolitan and diverse, other new-consciousness novels examine Egyptian society from more rural and insular community perspectives, as will be examined in Chapter 1, "History and Representation of Otherness in Idris ʿAli's *al-Nubi* and Bahaʾ Tahir's *Sunset Oasis*." Set at the end of the nineteenth century, *Sunset Oasis* portrays the reaction of the Amazigh population at the Siwa oasis to events befalling their community after an Egyptian colonial officer and his Irish wife arrive. *Al-Nubi* details the compulsory evacuation of Nubians from their indigenous villages located south of Aswan Dam in the 1960s and the newly independent state's blatant disregard for their heritage. The author reveals the divides and differing opinions among Nubians with regard to these imposed changes, on the one hand, and the largely unkept promises of the Egyptian state and their inadequate actualization, on the other.

These novels are, so to speak, bathed in historic light, and their authors, Tahir and ʿAli, make use of similar spatial and temporal devices. Not only are the settings in Siwa and Nubia respectively pertinent to the particular experiences of the Amazigh and Nubians, but the shared marginality of those settings helps shift the reader's perspective from the dominant concerns of the center to the equally significant and interrelated counterparts in the margins. Moreover, the choice of Siwa and Nubia as spatial devices juxtaposes their historic centrality with their present marginality. In antiquity, Siwa was the home of the Oracle of Amun and renowned as the destination of Alexander the Great in the third century BCE, whereas Nubia witnessed the establishment of the New Kingdom of Pharaohs in 1500 BCE, and revived under the Nubian Pharaohs of Meroë and Napata in the sixth and seventh centuries BCE.

The invocation of the historical grandeur of the two locations and their peoples when contrasted with their present geographical and cultural marginality creates aesthetic effects of loss, appreciation, and a desire to reclaim the past. Second, the temporal setting in colonial and early postcolonial times emphasizes the continuum of these groups' participation in Egypt's history, whether in antiquity or in the present. Regardless of the remoteness of Siwa and Nubia from the current Egyptian capital, the Amazigh in *Sunset Oasis* have not been saved from the policies of differentiation exercised by the colonial state, and neither were the Nubians from the policies of eradication of difference practiced by the postcolonial state.

Each of these novels' fictionally created worlds emanates from a distinct, yet interdependent authorial perspective. In *Sunset Oasis*, Tahir's articulation of the Amazigh experiences stems primarily from the consciousness of individuals who are well-educated. The prevalent narrative mode is lengthy introspection in the minds of characters insulated by their literacy, whether those are indigenous to the oasis, like Yahia and Ṣabir, the two Amazigh *ajwad*, or visitors, like Mahmud, the middle-class Cairene officer, his Irish wife, Catherine, and the resurrected spirit of al-Iskandar al-Akbar. This mode enables Tahir, the intellectual, to discuss complex views and practices of critical issues like race, religion, and imperialism without the interruption of much direct speech.

ᶜAli, on the other hand, articulates the Nubian experience from the perspective of a "*kātib shaᶜbī*" (public/popular writer), whose marginal position in the social, political, and literary spheres does not deter him from expressing opposition. The narrative devices he employs range from singing traditional Nubian songs to ample direct speech, infused with vernacular Arabic and Kenzi, the local Nubians' language. The agent narrator is a young observant inquirer who does not claim knowledge but is eager to attain it. He is confounded by the contrast between the promising rhetoric of the Egyptian state and the shocking realities his grieving community has to endure after their displacement.

Chapter 2, "Reading Cosmopolitanism in Yusuf Zaydan's *Azazeel* and Muᶜtazz Futayha's *Akhir yahud al-iskandariyya*," explores how Futayha's novel of 2008 and Zaydan's of the same year demonstrate a critical literary practice that resists the current surge in religious fundamentalist discourses in Egypt in the last few decades. The novels conjure up the practices and attitudes of individuals from the Jewish and Coptic populations in different periods of Egyptian history, with the goal of what Kwame Appiah calls "perspectival shift" (Appiah 2006: 77).[51] In the writers' subversion of the predominant bodies of knowledge in the Egyptian culture—be they the exclusive ethno-religious nationalist formations presented in *Akhir yahud al-iskadariyya* or the oppressive religious identity of the recently Christianized Roman empire in the fifth century CE—they portray defiant individuals who question their immediate surroundings and restlessly search for new stances that enable them to reflect on their positions in relation to others.

Yusuf, the main character in *Akhir yahud al-iskandariyya*, is a Jewish man who challenges the cultural norms of his society and his father's conservative expectations when he pursues his dream of writing and directing films—a disdained profession at the time—and when he also falls in love with a Muslim girl named Sara. In *Azazeel*, Hiba (henceforth Hypa), the Coptic monk, transcends the boundaries of monastic tradition through the liberating acts of learning pagan philosophy and optimally utilizing the act of writing to record what he sees and knows. Hypa embarks on a journey from Akhmim, his hometown in south Egypt, to Alexandria, Jerusalem, and, lastly, Antioch. During his travels, Hypa falls in love and has sexual relations with two women, a Roman and an Assyrian. He also interacts with Nestorius, the Bishop of Constantinople (428–31 CE), who contested the conventional reference in Byzantine Christianity to Virgin Mary as *theotokos*, namely Bearer of God, because in Nestorius' view it did not emphasize the human nature of Christ. Hypa's account of Nestorius challenges the traditional image of him as merely a heretic.

While Yusuf and Hypa are considered radicals from the point of view of their respective traditions, they both maintain what Rebecca Walkowitz calls "a posture of resistance" (Walkowitz 2006: 2)[52] against attempts at casting them out on account of their nonconformist practices. I argue that the two novels thus subvert fixed categories and positions and encourage the pursuit of a new consciousness and a critical stance through cultivation of vagrant positions and the spirit of developing, testing, and refining one's ideas through constant movement and conversation with the other.

Chapter 4, "Heart Deserts: Memory and Myth between Life and Death in Asharaf al-Khumaysi's *Manafi al-rabb* and Miral al-Tahawi's *The Tent*," demonstrates the aesthetic principality of the desert in these two novels of 2013 and 1996 respectively. Both novels turn to the Egyptian desert, in an uncommon spatial shift from the Egyptian city or countryside to the uninhabitable, yet extraordinary, realm of the desert, with the goal of proposing new meanings of existence. In this chapter, I examine how the desert planet—as Ibrahim al-Kuni describes it[53]—is depicted not merely as a spatial setting, but as a mythical center, a symbolic labyrinth, and a path and a destination for the two novels' plethora of characters. *Manafi al-rabb* represents perceptions and rituals of life and death among the religiously diverse inhabitants of Egypt's western desert, and more specifically those of al-Waʿira, a fictional isolated oasis there, where the novel's main character and elderly Bedouin, Hujayzi, goes on a quest for bodily incorruptibility after death. After Hujayzi's dialogues and negotiations with Sheikh Mazid at the village's mosque and with Monk Yuʾannis at the neighboring Coptic monastic community, Hujayzi reckons that his pursuit of postmortem bodily imperishability is not fulfilled in either Muslim or Christian burial practice, but rather by eating from a mythical distant orange tree in the desert. *The Tent* transfers its readers into a young Bedouin girl's world, in which the boundaries between myth and reality are blurred. Fatima's incessant attempts to alleviate the anguish resulting from her domestic confinement and lack of autonomy are halted by a physical disability that allegorically signifies her powerlessness in altering her melancholic condition. The two novels immerse the reader in the desert as a mythical center, in which the figure of the Bedouin is deeply rooted both in body and spirit and in which alternative meanings of life and existence, and, thereby, human relations, are configured.

To conclude, many contemporary Egyptian writers depart from the underlying historical ground through the innovative structure of their narratives in which new forms of collective social life are envisioned. I argue that the new critical vision embodied in their novelistic creation calls to mind how Walkowitz describes cosmopolitan style, which "tends to imply double consciousness, comparison, negation, and persistent self-reflection: 'an unwillingness to rest,' the attempt to operate 'in the world . . . [while] preserving a posture of resistance,' the entanglement of 'domestic and international perspectives,' and the 'self-reflexive repositioning of the self in the global sphere'" (ibid. pp. 2–3). The novels not only disclose the inadequacies of a social order—local or global—based on differentiation by religion, ethnicity, culture, or gender, but also postulate an alternative based on the interior morality of its members irrespective of their skin color, belief system, language, or gender, as we shall see in the chapters that follow.

Notes

1. Women writers and intellectuals have contributed to Egypt's cultural and literary movements since *nahda*, as will be discussed in more detail later in this chapter. However, it is from the 1970s onward that there has been a surge in feminist novelistic production by Egyptian women writers, who situate gender inequalities in a prominent position within the Egyptian literary field.
2. Marilyn Booth, in the critical introduction to an anthology of short stories by Egyptian women writers in English translation, observes that, in Egyptian women's fiction writing, "[w]hile oppressive and marginalizing social relations are at the center of works by certain men writers of the same 'generation,' it is in these women's writings that the combined effects of class and gender in marginalizing large numbers of Egyptians becomes central." See Marilyn Booth (ed.), *My Grandmother's Cactus: Stories by Egyptian Women* (London: Quartet Books, 1991), pp. 9–14.
3. I would like to acknowledge my doctoral dissertation advisor, Professor Tejumola Olaniyan, for his invaluable and authentic suggestion to describe the subject of my research into contemporary novelistic production in Egypt as "the new-consciousness novel." The quotation marks are used only on first mention to acknowledge his input, and will be omitted subsequently throughout the book.
4. Said, Edward W., "Orientalism Reconsidered," *Cultural Critique*, No. 1, Autumn 1985, pp. 89–107.
5. Gilles Deleuze and Felix Guattari present three key characteristics that define minor literature: (1) "A minor literature doesn't come from a minor language; it is rather that which a minority constructs within a major language" (Deleuze and Guattari 1986: 16); (2) minor literatures are all political; and (3) minor literatures "take on a collective value" (ibid. p. 17).
6. Deleuze, G. and Guattari, F., *Kafka, Toward a Minor Literature*, trans. Dana Polan, foreword by Reda Bensmaia (Minneapolis. Minnesota University Press, 1986).
7. Appiah, Kwame Anthony, *Cosmopolitanism: Ethics in a World of Strangers* (New York: Norton, 2006).

8. Hasan, Sayyid Mahmud, "Baʿd haya ʿasiba: Wafat al-katib al-nubi Idris ʿAli [The Death of Nubian Writer Idris ʿAli after a Difficult Life]," *Al-Ahram Online*, 1 December 2010, <http://www.ahram.org.eg/archive/Books/News/50974.aspx> (last accessed 24 August 2012).

9. In his book *Conscience of the Nation: Writers, State, and Society in Modern Egypt*, originally published in French in 2003 as *Entre scribes et écrivains, le champ littéraire dans l'Egypte Contemporaire* and in English translation in 2008, Richard Jacquemond sheds light on "the case of 'Nubian literature'" in Egypt. He observes the emergence of literature on Nubia in the 1960s at the hands of Muhammad Khalil Qasim (1912–68), whose *al-Shamandura* ('The Buoy,' 1968) was the first Egyptian novel to express a sense of Nubian homeland loss. Nubians, who, according to Jacquemond, are the largest non-Arabic-speaking group in Egypt, were subjected to forced evacuation from their historic villages by the Egyptian state, after it began dam-building projects on the River Nile between 1902 and 1968. These state projects led to the inundation of Nubian villages by the Nile's waters and to the state forcibly relocating Nubians in the Egyptian north, a displacement experience that has led to the near-extinction of their indigenous languages, Kenzi and Faddica. However, an awakening and invocation of a collective Nubian identity started to occur in the 1980s in novels written by Nubian immigrants, whose education in the Egyptian north led to their writing in Arabic, the major language of their education. Among these novelists are Hasan Nur (b. 1940), Idris ʿAli (1940–2010), and Haggag Hassan Oddoul (b. 1944).

10. Along the lines of Jacquemond's discussion of the status of literature on Nubia in Egypt, the Egyptian poet and literary critic Mahmud Khayrullah, in a 2016 article for the *Al-Hayat* newspaper, draws attention to the gap between the critical acclaim Muhammad Khalil Qasim's *al-Shamandura* (1968) is currently starting to receive, albeit belatedly, and the continuous disinclination of state publishing venues to publish a second edition of that significant novel in Egyptian novelistic history, it being the founding novel on Nubian experience. Khayrullah refers to the precedence of a private publisher, Dar al-Karma, in printing a second edition of the novel, given the fact that the original first edition was also by a private publisher, Dar al-thaqafa al-jadida. The article is available at <http://www.alhayat.com/Articles/18639313/---رواية---الشمندورة-متجاهلة--أسَّست-الأدب-النوبي> (last accessed 24 August 2012).

11. The International Dublin Literary Award website, <http://www.dublinliteraryaward.ie/2006-longlist/> (last accessed 24 August 2012).

12. American University Press website, <http://www.aucpress.com/p-2793-the-yacoubian-building.aspx> (last accessed 24 August 2012).
13. Jameson, Frederic, *The Political Unconscious: Narrative as a Socially Symbolic Act* (Ithaca: Cornell University Press, 1982).
14. McKeon identifies the generic instability that preceded the rise of the novel and links it to changes in modes of telling the truth in narrative. Similarly, he explains the vacillation within the social structure at the time that led to the rise of the middle class, and links it to changes in people's perceptions and signification of virtue—or in his words, "attitudes toward how the external social order is related to the internal, moral state of its [society's] members" (McKeon 2000b: q.v. for further readings).
15. This statement by Husni Hasan appears in Richard Jacquemond's *Conscience of the Nation* and is from an unpublished presentation at a colloquium on the short story and the novel which took place in Egypt in June 1997. It is entitled "Hudud al tagrib: Mashahid min sahat al-riwaya al-misriyya fi-l-tisʿinat" (translated by Jacquemond as "The Limits of Experimentation: Aspects of the Egyptian Novel in the 1990s" (Jacquemond 2008: 220–327).
16. Jacquemond, Richard, trans. David Tresilian, *Conscience of the Nation: Writers, State, and Society in Modern Egypt* (Cairo: AUC Press, 2008).
17. Young, Robert J. C., *Postcolonialism: An Historical Introduction* (Malden: Blackwell, 2001).
18. Tucker, Judith, "While Sadat Shuffles: Economic Decay, Political Ferment in Egypt," *MERIP Reports*, No. 65, March 1978, pp. 3–9, 26.
19. The historian Judith Tucker summarizes the failure of *siyāsat al-infitaḥ al-iqtiṣadi* (policy of economic openness), that led to the 1977 popular protests, as follows: "dependence on foreign investment, commitment to an internal 'free market,' and the gradual dismantling of the planning apparatus have left the Egyptian government incapable of dealing with the shortages of food, housing, transport, and employment that inform the daily life of its people" (ibid. p. 7).
20. See Tucker, 3–8. Due to Sadat's acquiescent foreign policy and conciliatory endeavors with Israel, levels of popular dissent from the right and the left soared. Sadat's regime handled all vocal dissidents in the political and cultural realms with violent repression, detention, and trials in high military courts. In 1978, the Egyptian colloquial poet Ahmad Fuʾad Najm called upon "democratic forces, artists, and intellectuals" (Tucker 8–9) to globally denounce the Sadat regime's repressive policies against political activists, poets, and artists, such as he himself. Najm recounted how they were arrested on the accusation of "*sing[ing] for the*

hungry, exploited, oppressed and poor, and not for thieves and bloodsuckers . . . for liberation and solidarity, not for surrender and national humiliation" (Najm, quoted in Tucker 1978: 8).

21. Richard Jacquemond's book *Conscience of the Nation* was originally published in French in 2003 and in English translation in 2008.
22. Talahite, Anissa, "North African Writing," in *African Literature: An Anthology of Criticism and Theory*, ed. Tejumola Olaniyan and Ato Quayson (Malden: Blackwell, 2007), pp. 38–45.
23. Amin, Galal, *Egypt in the Era of Hosni Mubarak, 1981–2011* (Cairo: AUC Press, 2011).
24. Amin, Galal, *Madha hadatha lil thawra al-misriyya* (Cairo: Dar al-Shuruq, 2013).
25. Even though the members of the Muslim Brotherhood were permitted into the political sphere under Mubarak, it was not until Mubarak's ouster and the 2011 revolution that the election of the first Muslim Brotherhood president, Muhammad Mursi, took place. In 2013, after only one year in power, Mursi was also toppled and the movement was quickly outlawed, ushering in yet another period of military rule.
26. Ajami, Fouad, "The Sorrows of Egypt," *Foreign Affairs*, Vol. 74, No. 5, 1995, pp. 72–88.
27. On the regional level, Jacquemond distinguishes between allegiances with the "'progressive' Arab regimes (Iraq, Libya, and the PLO . . . [and] with the conservative petroleum monarchies" (Jacquemond 2008: 25).
28. McKeon (2000b) describes the gradual demise of hereditary nobility due to changes in perceiving and signifying virtue in the behavior of society members.
29. Menna Khalil presents an extensive "translation" of the unity and complex relationship between Egyptian people and army, in which she explains how the army "is historically defined as liberator or savior of Egypt from corrupt rule, hegemonic dominance, and foreign invasion." See Menna Khalil, "The People and the Army Are One Hand: Myths and Their Translations," in Samia Mehrez (ed.), *Translating Egypt's Revolution: The Language of Tahrir* (Cairo: AUC Press, 2012), pp. 249–75.
30. For example, see the Egyptian newspaper *Al-Masry al-Youm*'s coverage of the popular celebration of the Egyptian Army after it pledged to fulfill people's demands for a democratic state. Al-Jallad, "Shabab al-Tahrir wa-l-nasr" (Al-Tahrir's Youth and Victory)," *Al-Masry al-Youm*, 11 February 2011.
31. Mehrez, Samia, *Egypt's Culture Wars: Politics and Practice* (Cairo: AUC Press, 2008).

32. In the *IDS Bulletin* published by the Institute of Development Studies approximately one year after the January revolution, Mariz Tadros also refers to the numerous protests that took place in the decade before the revolution to counter speculation as to "why Egyptians do not rise" (Tadros 2012: 7). Highlighting Khalid Ali's remarks, published in the same *IDS Bulletin*, on the strong presence of public dissent that was largely overlooked by public figures and intellectuals alike due to its emergence among "workers, labourers, farmers and Copts," whose organized protests were deemed "too narrow in their representation and demands, especially since they were not calling for the overthrow of the regime" (ibid. p. 7). Tadros draws attention to how such instances of dissidence by these diverse groups of citizens, and their subversion of state power, especially that of the April 6 youth group, are all significant actors in the "unruly politics" that can be seen as "incubators" for the collective revolt. Tadros defines unruly politics as "the marginal space through which citizens engage politically outside the conventional realms of state and civil society" (ibid. p. 7). For more details see Mariz Tadros, "Introduction: The Pulse of Arab Revolt," *IDS Bulletin*, Vol 43, No. 1, 2012, pp. 1–15.

33. Multiple studies discuss the generational categorization of Egypt's novelistic production by defining either their common features—see Sabry Hafez's 1976 article "The Egyptian Novel in the Sixties" (*Journal of Arabic Literature*, Vol. 7, 1 January 1976, pp. 68–84), for example—or the "anxiety" that surrounds their categorization in relation to preceding generations, as in Yasmine Ramadan's article "The Emergence of the Sixties Generation in Egypt and the Anxiety over Categorization," *Journal of Arabic Literature*, Vol. 43, Nos 2–3, 2012, pp. 409–30.

34. Jacquemond expounds that "the young prose writers of the generation of the 1990s hardly convince when they claim that theirs is an aesthetic project radically different from that of the generation of the 1960s. They are more accurate when they present themselves as continuing the project of the earlier generation, returning to its sources, and criticizing the way in which it has either gone astray or has become a matter of routine in the hands of those who initiated it" (Jacquemond 2008: 219–20).

35. Bakhtin, Mikhail, "Discourse in the Novel," in Michael Holquist (ed.), Caryl Emerson and Michael Holquist (trans), *The Dialogic Imagination* (Austin: University of Texas Press, 1981), pp. 259–422.

36. Acclaimed Arabic literature scholars like Miriam Cook, Jeff Shalan, and Samah Selim discuss extensively in their works the close affinity between the

rise of cultural nationalism in the consciousness of Egyptian writers and their novels.
37. Literary scholars such as Hoda al-Sadda, Samia Mehrez, Sabry Hafez, and Jacque Jacquemond problematize the idea of national construction by engaging with issues of gender, class, and the literary establishment in their readings of modern and contemporary Egyptian novels.
38. *Nahda* is the Arab literary and intellectual renaissance movement that, as Laila Lalami observes in her critical introduction to Denis Johnson-Davies' English translation of Tayyib Salih's seminal novel *Season of Migration to the North* (New York: *New York Review of Books*, 2009), centers around espousing "European material modernity (scientific, technological, and artistic) within the moral framework of Islamic traditions" (Lalami 2009: xv).
39. Shalan, Jeff, "Writing the Nation: Emergence of Egypt in the Modern Arabic Novel," *Journal of Arabic Literature*, Vol. 33, No. 3, 2002, pp. 211–47.
40. Caiani, Fabio, "Representations of Egypt in some Works by Idwār al-Kharrāṭ," *Journal of Middle Eastern Literatures*, Vol. 8, No. 1, January 2005, pp. 35–52.
41. Fanon, Frantz [1963], "On National Culture," in Tejumola Olaniyan and Ato Quayson (eds), *African Literature: An Anthology of Criticism and Theory*" (Malden: Blackwell, 2007), pp. 251–61.
42. Spivak, Gayatri, *The Spivak Reader: Selected Works of Gayatri Spivak* (New York: Routledge, 1996).
43. Booth, Marilyn, "Locating Women's Autobiographical Writing in Colonial Egypt," *Journal of Women's History*, Vol. 25, No. 2, Summer 2013, pp. 36–60.
44. In contrast to the marginalization Egyptian women writers' novelistic production underwent on the national level in the 1970s and 1980s, there was a more substantial regional and international acknowledgment of their fundamental contributions to Arab feminist novelistic production.
45. Al-Zayyat's remark is from her preface to a collection of short stories published in 1994.
46. Hafez, Sabry, "The New Egyptian Novel: Urban Transformation and Narrative Form," *New Left Review*, 64, July–August 2010, pp. 46–62.
47. Hafez notes that the mutual formal characteristics of these recent works include "narrative and linguistic fragmentation," shortness of the works, "focus on isolated individuals," and the entrapment of protagonists in a humiliating reality (Hafez 2010: 49).
48. This is with the exception of Idwar al-Kharrat's novels, especially *Rama wal-tinnin*, in which the heterogeneous historical and religious character of Egypt is

portrayed, but only in an idealized, harmonious manner, without any tension. Correspondingly, the two main characters representing the two spiritual heritages of Egypt, Mikhaʾil and Rama, do not seem to be influenced or conflicted by one spiritual heritage over the other. Neither seems to undergo a change of consciousness, and they can therefore be read as distant from reality where experiences and change interrupt ideas.

49. Kenzi is a Nilo-Saharan language spoken by the Nubian population of Egypt, and is believed to be a hybrid of Dongolawi and Old Nobiin. See Aleksandra Aikhenvald and Robert Dixon, *Aerial Diffusion and Genetic Inheritance: Problems in Comparative Linguistics* (New York: Oxford University Press, 2001), p. 400.
50. Siwi is an Afro-Asiatic language spoken by the Amazigh population in the Oasis of Siwa in Egypt. See the website for African Studies Center at Michigan State University, "Berber Language Page," <http://africa.isp.msu.edu/afrlang/Berber-root.html> (last accessed 24 August 2015).
51. Appiah, Kwame Anthony, *Cosmopolitanism: Ethics in a World of Strangers* (New York: Norton, 2006).
52. Walkowitz, Rebecca, *Cosmopolitan Style: Modernism Beyond the Nation* (New York: Columbia University Press, 2006).
53. Al-Kuni, Ibrahim, "In the Desert We Visit Death," interview by Anders Hastrup, Louisiana Channel, Louisiana Museum of Modern Art, 2015, <http://channel.louisiana.dk/video/ibrahim-al-koni-desert-we-visit-death> (last accessed 5 March 2016).

1

History and Representations of Otherness in Idris ᶜAli's *al-Nubi* and Bahaʾ Tahir's *Sunset Oasis*

In this chapter,¹ I examine *al-Nubi* and *Sunset Oasis* as exemplary works of the new-consciousness novel in contemporary Egypt. Idris ᶜAli's *al-Nubi*, 2001 (The Nubian) represents Egyptian Nubians' experience in the 1960s of forced evacuation from their indigenous villages located south of Aswan Dam, whose waters inundated several Nubian historic villages and obliterated their valuable heritage. The novel underscores the atrocious conditions Nubians were subjected to after their displacement by the newly independent state, and the divides that this displacement created between the Nubian youth and seniors. Whereas Nubian seniors revoked the imposed change and did not wish to leave their homes, the youth pressured them to evacuate, expecting the state to compensate them with a better future. Bahaʾ Tahir's *Wahat al-ghurub*, 2006 (*Sunset Oasis*, 2009) portrays the experience of an Egyptian district commissioner in the Siwa Oasis under British colonial rule at the end of the nineteenth century. It sheds light on the reaction of the Amazigh population at the oasis to a current of events that strike their community after that colonial officer and his Irish wife arrive.

Although both of these novels take up historical conditions, it is useful to discuss the current situation of the Nubian and Amazigh communities in Egypt. Scholarship on this topic is sparse, and even more so after the January revolution that toppled Hosni Mubarak's regime in 2011. It is no secret that these communities have been marginalized socially by mainstream Egyptian culture and politically by the state system and exclusive nationalist discourses. The peripheral geographic location of Siwa, far west of the Nile Valley, and historic Lower Nubia in relation to the larger metropolises of Cairo and Alexandria have given the state the excuse to exclude their inhabitants and throw their concerns into national oblivion. In an interview held by Gamal Nkrumah in February 2014 for *Al-Ahram Weekly* with representatives of different Nubian communities throughout Egypt—Manal al-Teiby, a Nubian political and cultural activist, Haggag Oddoul, the Nubian novelist, and Mohamed Saleh Adlan, the head of the Nubian community in Cairo—the interviewees raised collective concerns about the recognition of their rights despite their different community roles (Nkrumah 2014).[2] Firstly, they all agreed that the 2014 constitution does not recognize the ethnic diversity of Egyptians, Nubians, or any other ethnic minority for that matter. It does not identify the historical affinities of Egypt at large, and Nubian and Amazigh communities in particular, with the African continent. Secondly, although Nubians are now granted the right to return to their villages, the state will only restore three of—at least—43 villages that have been in need of rebuilding since the dam's inundation, deeming the return a dream. Thirdly, the state reacts dismissively, if not with suspicion of secession, to Nubians' demands to return to their original land on the fertile shores of Lake Nasser and to their attempts to revive their cultural heritage and language.

Similarly, the Amazigh population of the Siwa Oasis struggles to carve out its place in the Egyptian national space, especially with its long-standing and strong transnational identity with other Amazigh communities across North Africa, namely in Libya, Tunisia, Algeria, Morocco, Mauritania, Mali, and Niger. The majority of the Imazighen[3] population live in Morocco, where a strong activist movement has resurged to reclaim their indigenous heritage. That movement has been successful in reforming the Moroccan constitution; the Tamazight language is now officially recognized and taught in Moroccan schools, revived from its long-held place "behind Arabic (both modern standard and colloquial *darija*)" (Cornwell and Atia 2012: 255–71).[4] Similarly, the heritage revival efforts of the considerable Imazighen population in Algeria—around 13 million people—have recently (2016) led to the official recognition of their indigenous language by the Algerian Parliament.[5] Egypt's indigenous Amazigh communities, including the Issiwan,[6] have not been as successful in claiming their cultural rights from their respective state systems.

The creativity of *al-Nubi* and *Sunset Oasis* lies in their authors' mutual dedication to rewriting the past experiences of the Nubian and Amazigh communities within postcolonial and colonial institutions respectively, an act that reveals the unjust policies of "differentiation" (Mamdani 1996: 7)[7] and/or eradication of difference that these institutions adopt. In this way, both novels are deeply historical and suggest that we can only understand the implicit inequalities of contemporary Egyptian society by looking to the past. As Georg Lukács explains in his discussion of the historical novel, in particular Walpole's *Castle of Otranto*, history is "treated as mere costumery: it is only the curiosities and oddities of the *milieu* that matter, not an artistically faithful image of a concrete historical epoch" (Lukács 1963: 19).[8] It is the authors' "clear understanding of history as a process, of history as the concrete precondition of the present" (ibid. p. 21) that imbues their creative depiction of the Nubian and Amazigh communities' historical conditions in order to highlight their present plight.

Moreover, the two novels are equally committed to the portrayal of other critical and dynamic areas of interaction and tension among the racially and culturally diverse characters, on one level, and within the allegedly homogeneous Nubian and Amazigh communities, on the other, in order to disrupt essentialist perceptions of these significant ethno-cultural minority groups. In this respect, I argue that ᶜAli and Tahir are stirred by a common belief that difference is both a reality and a value in modern Egypt, and by a mutual desire to represent the historical and cultural experiences of the Nubian and Amazigh communities as integral parts of the larger whole of Egypt's complex culture and historical narrative. However, what gives each novel its distinct character lies in the particular "gift" of its author, his "craftsmanship" and ability—to borrow the words of Walter Benjamin—to "fashion the raw material of experience, his own and that of others, in a solid, useful, and unique way" (Benjamin [1968] 2000: 93).[9] Benjamin writes:

> [Storytelling] is . . . an artisan form of communication . . . It does not aim to convey the pure essence of the thing, like information or a report. It sinks the thing into the life of the storyteller, in order to bring it out of him again. Thus traces of the storyteller cling to the story the way the handprints of

the potter cling to the clay vessel. Storytellers tend to begin their story with a presentation of the circumstances in which they themselves have learned what is to follow, unless they simply pass it off as their own experience. (ibid. p. 82)

I examine "traces" of ʿAli and Tahir in their individual works and explore the differences in their innovative communication of the Nubian and Amazigh experiences after they left their "handprints" on them. ʿAli is the type of storyteller who "pass[es] it off as . . . [his] own experience," whereas Tahir is among the storytellers who "tend to begin [or end] their story with a presentation of the circumstances in which they themselves have learned what is to follow." So, rather than focusing on the shared goals of these two novelists to bring light to the particularities of minority communities in Egypt, I explore the very different voices that each author assumes in order to delve into these microcosms, highlighting the unique texture of the narratives, which rely upon different strategies to speak for and about Egypt's others.

The novels of the Nubian writer ʿAli (1940–2010), written in Arabic, draw their content from his personal experience as a member of this marginalized group. In an interview with the journalist ʿAbd al-Nabi Faraj for *al-Sharq al-Awsat* in 2003, ʿAli recalled his experience of immigration to the north—specifically Cairo—in 1950 and being sent by his father to the alley to interact with the local kids and learn Arabic (Faraj 2003).[10] ʿAli, who received no formal education because of his poverty (Hasan 2010),[11] was forced to take small jobs and endure many "insults and psychological wounds" (Faraj 2003). ʿAli reminisces about reading, during this difficult time, novels from all traditions—especially Russian—and about how the act of writing saved him from despair. ʿAli described himself as a "*kātib shaʿbī*" (public/popular writer) who opposed the ideal of "*naqāʾ al-ʿirq al-nubī*" (the purity of the Nubian vein), which his people believe in, and espoused a realist literary style to write about Nubia and the daily experiences of its marginalized individuals, who struggle to secure their basic needs. In 1997, ʿAli's novel *Dongola* was the first Nubian novel to be translated into English (Hasan 2010). Even though the novel received national and international acclaim, ʿAli opposed its categorization by literary critics under "*tayyār al-adab al-nubī*" (stream of Nubian literature). For him, this critical perspective constitutes a kind of critical laziness which isolates Nubian writers who write about Nubia from the mainstream of Egyptian literature (ibid.). At the same time, ᶜAli rejected "*al-naᵓarāt al-ᶜirqiyya*" (racial pride), a concept that many Nubians and Bedouins in Egypt identified with (Faraj 2003). In other words, ᶜAli simultaneously positions himself somewhere between those who seek a homogeneous narrative of Egypt by excluding other racial populations and those in marginal groups who embrace the essentialist position of identity pride to resist hegemonic and exclusive discourses and enactments.

Tahir was born in Cairo in 1935. After his graduation from Cairo University with a degree in history in 1956, he worked for the state radio as a broadcaster and drama director until 1975. During Sadat's presidency, he used his public position to criticize Egypt's poor social and political conditions and the inefficiency of state policies in improving them. Consequently, Tahir was sacked from his state job and his literary works were banned. In protest, he sent himself into exile in Geneva, where he worked as a translator for the United Nations from 1981 to 1995. Since his return to his homeland, Tahir has published many novels and short-story collections, many of which exhibit an uncommon, but conscious choice of delineating a heterogeneous picture of the Egyptian population inspired by its religious, ethnic, and cultural diversity. For example, his novel *Khalti Safiyya wa-l-dayr*, written in 1991 and translated as *Aunt Safiya and the Monastery* in 1996 by Barbara Romaine, captures the intersecting lives of Coptic monks and their Muslim neighbors in a small town in the countryside around Luxor. The novel simultaneously reveals their differences and shared destiny as a community. In 2008, he was awarded the International Prize for Arabic Fiction (unofficially known as the Arabic Booker Prize) for *Wahat al-ghurub*, in which he delves into the life conditions of individuals from another marginal group, the Issiwan, during the tumultuous time of British colonization. In *Wahat al-ghurub*'s postscript, "ᶜala Hamish al-Riwaya" ("On the margins of the novel"), Tahir reveals the sources that informed his account of the oasis in ancient and modern history, the Amazigh "internecine" wars and their customs in treating widows. He mentions resorting to archaeological, fictional, and historical works by multiple scholars, but credits archaeologist Ahmad Fakhri's account of the district commissioner, Mahmud ᶜAzmi, and his attempt to blast Umm ᶜUbayda's

Temple in Siwa in 1897 for his inspiration for the main character in *Sunset Oasis* (Tahir 2009: 303).[12]

In light of these short biographies, we understand that both ᶜAli and Tahir experienced alienation, either through compulsory evacuation to the Egyptian north, in ᶜAli's case, or through self-imposed exile to Europe, in Tahir's. In addition, both authors' works were, in a sense, set apart from, and segregated by, dominant literary and political institutions: ᶜAli's work was separated from mainstream Arabic literature by critics with exclusive special titles and categorizations, whereas Tahir's was banned by the state after he openly criticized its unjust practices. I argue that ᶜAli's and Tahir's experiences with alienation and estrangement lead to a sense of ambivalence towards the nation-state that permeates the aesthetic choices in their works. Both their novels demonstrate the formal and thematic presence of a critical perspective on *other* communities in Egypt, which are depicted as neither heroic nor virtue-exclusive, neither utterly self-enclosed nor *other*-embracing, neither homogeneous nor harmonious. Although there is a sense of despair and conflict in the image ᶜAli and Tahir conjure up—perhaps to remain faithful to the contemporary tensions among the different Egyptian groups' established bodies of knowledge and cultures—they at the same time postulate hope and conflict resolution in their comprehensive form. I argue that no matter how similar ᶜAli's and Tahir's social and political considerations are, their distinct personal experiences are reflected in their individual aesthetic choices and unique artistic imprints. In the sections that follow, I examine the two novels individually to show how their writers' commonalities of goal and critical perspective, yet differences in personal experience, is aesthetically rendered. I focus on spatial and temporal devices, prevailing themes, and functions of characterization and narrative technique.

Idris ᶜAli's *al-Nubi*

Having witnessed the Nubian community's displacement at a young age, ᶜAli draws on his personal experience to convey the conflict between his generation and that of his parents and grandparents.[13] The younger generation are depicted as nationalist enthusiasts who desire to belong to the promising force of the newly independent Egyptian nation-state and its glamorous metropolis in the north. At the same time, the older generation do not share the same aspirations as the youth. They anticipate loss and despair for having been removed from everything they know.

Both temporally and spatially, ʿAli synthesizes elements of character, action, and thought in order to transmit and explain the experience of the indigenous Nubian ethnic minority of displacement from their historic villages in Lower Nubia before its inundation by the Aswan Dam reserve water in the early 1960s. The novel is set in/between two spaces connected by the Nile River: the region south of the Aswan Dam, where the Nubian population settled in their historic villages such as Kishshi, Dabud, and Mariyya; and that north of the Aswan Dam in Mudiriyyat al-Tahrir (Liberation Directorate), where evacuated Nubians are placed, or rather displaced, by the Egyptian government. Life conditions in the new place are far worse than in the original villages. The narrator comments:

> On the day of our arrival, we hung Gamal Abdel Nasser's picture on the doors of the houses, but every time a child died from scorpion bites, his family would remove the president's picture until almost all the pictures were removed given the number of dead children.[14] (ʿAli 2001: 98)[15]

This type of setting immediately draws the reader into this time and place in Egypt, and, in the same way, into the fictional world that ʿAli weaves to create his message. The events of the novel proceed chronologically as a flashback from the perspective of the narrator, a young Nubian man from the village of Kishshi named ʿAbdullah. He belongs to the zealous aspiring youth group who are called to a national youth camp. There, they are promised future success and power as a reward for their positive answer to the national call to evacuate their villages in Lower Nubia and for persuading their parents and grandparents to do likewise. ʿAbdullah describes his initial enthusiasm for joining "the youth organization" (ibid. p. 8) as follows:

> We, students of general and technical secondary education, were very enthusiastic. When they advertised volunteering opportunities in the youth organization, we rushed to register our names . . . That was a few months before the displacement. We regularly attended the sessions of the Leaders to Victory and were instructed intensively on the nation, nationalism, and the great national projects. We knew what our next mission was: to help

our families accept the new reality and establish revolutionary thoughts in their minds. (ibid. p. 8)

In ᶜAli's portrayal, we can clearly see the divisive policies that the newly independent state implemented with regard to the Nubian ethno-cultural minority group, which were based on the principle of eradication of difference. While the Nubians value their land and distinct heritage, the government indoctrinates their youth about the majestic and unequal value of the nation. In other words, the government promises the Nubian youth state-sponsored higher education and better public services if they persuade the elderly to give up their historic villages and submit to the state's mandates, thus rendering these young new citizens the linchpin in undermining the solidity of their own cultural heritage.

The Myth of Fixed Identity and Historical Awakenings

Mahmood Mamdani proposes the "doctrine of identity," that is used by state systems in both their colonial and postcolonial forms, as a strategy of difference eradication in the interest of establishing national identity. He argues: "in organizing the relationship between Europeans and Africans: '[t]he doctrine of identity conceives the future social and political institutions of Africans to be basically similar to those of Europeans'" (Mamdani 1996: 7). In a similar manner, the Egyptian postcolonial state aims at securing its dominance over the land and people of Nubia by "conceiving" of their "future social and political institutions," cultural values, and knowledge forms as identical with those of the Egyptian nation, and also making them so. In order to achieve this goal, the state attempts to eradicate Nubian difference through indoctrinating the youth in nationalist education and forcing them to impose these views on the older members of their community.

In *al-Nubi*, ᶜAbdullah is an agent/participant narrator who is positioned on the front edge of these policies. He plays the role of an observer who struggles with uncertainty and ambivalence at a young age. ᶜAbdullah's inexperience is demonstrated in his inability to answer challenging questions such as where his ancestral roots are, how he as a Nubian relates to Arabs, why his people are marginalized in the newly independent state, and why they are unable to determine their own future. In this sense, ᶜAbdullah's position as an inquisitive, and perennially unresolved, narrator invites the reader to find the answers to these questions. ᶜAbdullah, like the reader, gradually gains knowledge through his unlimited access to his grandfather's inner conflicts regarding the promises of relocation. He becomes aware of his grandfather's suffering and attachment to his home village; nevertheless, he is in thrall to the nationalist propaganda he has absorbed in school, and replicates the rhetoric the government officials use with the Nubian youth, pressuring his grandfather and the rest of his family to pack their valuables and leave their homes.

The grandfather's life experiences make the idea of fixed and pure identity seem obscure. At the beginning, the narrator presents his grandfather's historical account of their roots as his own. They built the temples in Lower Nubia and are descendants of the noble Arab ᶜAmir Najm al-Din (ᶜAli 2001: 37–9). The narrator efficiently sums up this conflated history by saying, "my grandfather, the Nile, and the Qurʾan are one thing" (ibid. p. 43). Yet, in the midst of the Kishshi evacuation, questions on the origin of Kenuz Nubians—the ethnic Nubian group the narrator and his grandfather belong to—and how they became part of contemporary Egypt arise. A visitor, named Katba Tima Kwadi, arrives in the village to debunk all the allegedly historical myths of this group's origin. He explains to ᶜAbdullah that Kenuz Nubians are not as purely Arab as they believe and did not build the Pharaonic temples in Lower Nubia. Kwadi also claims that his people—who currently live in Western Sudan—are the origin of all Nubian communities scattered in Sudan and Egypt. He says: "We are the origin and you are the imitation . . . My son, we are the owners of Meroë, Napata, and Kush . . . It is us who stood against the pharaohs, the Arabs, and the Mamluks" (ibid. pp. 30–2). ᶜAbdullah, shaken by these claims, wonders about the stranger's alternative historical narrative of Nubians that uproots him violently from every fixed ground on which he constructs his identity:

> I imagined there was a black cloud coming from the far south that fell down on "our Nubia" until our features, sites, monuments, Nile, perch, and crocodiles were distorted. This is Doomsday. My father is no longer my father and my mother is not "Asha Hammad." After all these years of pride and fixity, I have become only a grandson of a concubine whom an Arab was enjoying. (ibid. p. 36)

In the above passage, the narrator articulates, consciously or unconsciously, his mother's Arabic name with an accent that marks his own distance from the Arabic language. While her name in proper Arabic is footnoted by the author as ʿAʾisha Muhammad, it is articulated by the narrator as "Asha Hammad." The narrator's pronunciation reflects the difficulty of producing the pharyngeal Arabic sounds of ʿayn and ḥāʾ for a person who does not speak Arabic as a first language. This articulation signifies the linguistic difference between Arabs and Nubians. Moreover, Kwadi's narrative of ʿAbdullah's roots not only obscures his grandfather's, but also precludes Kenuz Nubians from preserving their founding narrative as perennial holders of Arab-Muslim identity.

Despite the forcible move to Mudiriyyat al-Tahrir, the grandfather still tries to help his community adjust to the new setting by establishing relations with neighboring villages. He realizes that their new neighbors are mostly Arab, but still believes he shares many traditions with them: "The folk in al-Fatira village are exactly like us, people. Their religion is Islam. Our traditions and customs are the same. The only difference between us is language" (ibid. p. 100). Although his initial encounter with the neighboring village seniors reveals a common understanding and a celebration of their similarities, the children of the new village show fear of "*al-barābira*" ("berbers," a derogatory term usually used to refer to black people from the south or Black Africa). When the grandfather asks one of the village children why they all run away when they see him, the child answers: "Children say that *al-barābira* have tails . . . They were afraid you were going to eat them. Please, don't eat me" (ibid. p. 100).

The grandfather is made conscious of the racial difference between the Nubians and the neighboring village people through the children's gaze. However, he also realizes that such a "pure" Nubian community does not exist when he finds out that some Nubian families immigrated to the north at the turn of the twentieth century during the first phase of the construction of the dam. Sadly for him, these Nubian families fused with the northern population until they forgot their indigenous languages. In the same way, Hajj Muhammad (the grandfather) reconciles with the son he has previously disowned because of his marriage to an Egyptian woman from Cairo. On his deathbed, the Cairene daughter-in-law feeds Muhammad like a child and kisses him on the mouth, an erotic act that can be read metaphorically: the Egyptian woman represents the Egyptian state and her erotic kiss symbolizes the seductiveness of its rhetoric. Even though the Egyptian woman's relation to Muhammad is not genealogical, they merge through marriage. The food she offers him stands for the materialistic benefits that the Egyptian government promises Nubians, and Muhammad's immediate death after eating from her hands indicates that, in the process of homogenizing Nubians for the purpose of including them in the uniform nationalist narrative, they become stripped of livelihood, and by extension their cultural identity. With the death of Muhammad's character and its symbolic implications, the novelist demarcates the end of Nubian traditional existence and concludes his novel. This finale corresponds with Benjamin's comments on how the figurative death of a character marks "the end of the novel" to the reader: "The nature of the character . . . cannot be presented any better than is done in this statement, which says that the meaning of his 'life' is revealed only in his death" (Benjamin [1968] 2000: 88).

Death by History

Even beyond Muhammad's passing, the novelist makes use of the theme of death as a defamiliarizing device that unfolds the events of his story. Although death is a natural phenomenon in reality, it surprisingly occurs to two other characters prior to Muhammad to mark two other ends in Nubian history. ᶜAli links these deaths to the upheaval of knowledge and understanding of one's identity, and posits identity construction at the center of Nubian community life. The figurative deaths of characters bring their eclipsed histories to light and destabilize the construction of monolithic Nubian identity narratives. The first is that of Kunnud, an outcast senior in the village of Kishshi. His death disrupts the narrative of harmonious Nubian existence across Egyptian and Sudanese borders and also sheds light on the history of Ottoman rule and slave trading from the provinces of Dongola and Kordofan to the north during the nineteenth century (Spaulding 1982: 3).[16] Kunnud's family is believed to have immigrated from either Dongola or Kordofan in Sudan and not to have mixed with either Arabs or Kenuz Nubians. Kunnud dies after Kwadi, the visiting anthropologist, records his account of his ethnic group's unraveled history and the reason for his distance from the village community and Muhammad: Kunnud used to shelter and hide black African and Nubian slaves who were brought from Western Sudan to Lower Nubia by the narrator's "noble" great-grandfather (ʿAli 2001: 58–9). Once Kunnud's life acquires its full meaning and purpose by his delivering his story to others, it comes to an end.

The second death is Kwadi's own. Kwadi visits the Nubian villages to collect the concealed histories of Nubians in Egypt and Sudan and their relation to the Kush Kingdom in black Africa. Kwadi's unearthing of this *other* Nubian history was strongly rejected by the Kishshi community since it unsettles its past, established identity, and ancestral morality. The narrator expresses his desire to kill Kwadi, saying: "I will silence him with force. There is no escape from killing him" (ibid. p. 43). Although the narrator does not commit the murder himself, he relays the incident in which another Nubian young man named Hasan al-Kashif executes it. Thus, Kwadi's character plays an integral role in moving the plot forward through the unfolding of one hidden historical narrative after another.

Linguistic Defamiliarization

In mirroring the linguistic particularity of the Kenuz-Nubian minority, the novelist incorporates either the Kenzi language or an accented Arabic language in their direct speech. For example, when a female character starts to bewail her dead, she says in Kenzi: "*waguri . . . waguri.*" The author footnotes the Arabic meaning as "*yā khusāra*" (what a loss) (ibid. p. 94). The grandfather on his deathbed articulates indistinctly his wish "*ʾāwiz . . . ʾāwiz Kishshi*" (I want . . . I want Kishshi) (ibid. pp. 112–13). The transcription of the *alif* in which the words are written instead of *ʿayn* with which the Arabic would typically be written conveys the grandfather's accented Arabic, influenced by his mother tongue. The novelist, in this way, uses a true "dramatic representation" and the mimetic mode in the characters' direct speech. At the same time, he utilizes the diegetic mode for authorial narration, his commentary, and action summary, which are all rendered in Modern Standard Arabic. David Lodge describes mimesis as the subjective showing of characters' direct feelings and thoughts and diegesis as the objective telling or reporting of the events (Lodge 1996: 355).[17] He argues that critics should abandon prioritizing either of the narrative modes over the other since both modes create certain aesthetic effects that are as different as they are valuable for the author in strategizing his plot. ᶜAli's fusion of mimesis and diegesis in different degrees aims at representing the disparate positions that each character maintains in regard to the Nubian tradition and its Kenzi language vis-à-vis the Egyptian state and the myth of wholeness and linguistic singularity that it offers.

Although the narrator alternates between telling the story in the narrative past and dramatically showing what the other characters say directly in the present tense, ᶜAli often makes use of singing as a creative means of communicating characters' emotions rather than the familiar, flowing narrative discourse and direct speech. For example, Zaynab, the narrator's sister, expresses her excitement about moving to the north, especially after anticipating an end to the infinite labor of bread baking and water filling from the river in the burning sun. She sings, "O twelve o'clock train that is approaching Upper Egypt" (ᶜAli 2001: 74), a popular song celebrating the reception of a train that carries a beloved. The grandfather, on the other hand, sings in mourning over the loss of his home, Kishshi: "Nile! O our Nile. Kishshi, O our country!" (ibid. p. 95). In response, the youth sing: "My country! O My Country! My Country!/O Kishshi, mother of all countries!/Egypt is my desire and hope" (ibid. p. 95). Even though the lyrics sung by the youth are improvised to alleviate the situation, they replicate the Egyptian national anthem, making one change: replacing "Egypt" in the original anthem with "Kishshi." Their substitution renders the national anthem unfamiliar, thus creating an aesthetic impression on the reader that reinforces the hybrid position the youth adopt with regard to their tradition (represented in Kishshi) and their future (represented in Egypt).

In using these sets of thematic, spatio-temporal, narrative, and linguistic devices, ᶜAli fully engages the reader in deciphering the logic behind the story; through them, he is either "showing" or "telling" the racial, linguistic, and social differences between Nubians and people from the north. Benjamin proposes that the reader of the novel is left to make the psychological connections between the events he is presented with (Benjamin [1968] 2000: 81–2). J. Arthur Honeywell proposes a similar idea when analyzing fictional plots:

> the reader is involved in the plot to an unusual degree . . . It is the job of the reader to actively contribute to the plot by seeking for the significant

relations between the facts and by grasping the resulting patterns of reality as they emerge from the facts. In particular, he must, on the basis of the evidence he has, work out for himself the moral standards, the sources of happiness and suffering, and the operative causes in the world of each novel. (Honeywell 1996: 157)[18]

Both Benjamin and Honeywell agree that it is essential for the reader to make the proper connections between spatial, temporal, and ideological aspects within any novel. This active involvement of the reader adds to the realistic dimension: experiences that characters undergo, in the course of the novel, feel completely real and identifiable to the reader.

An analysis of *al-Nubi* demonstrates how ʿAli artfully and innovatively presents the displacement experience of the Nubian ethnic minority in the 1960s during and after their separation from their linguistic and cultural heritage in Lower Nubia. His juxtaposition of incongruent spatial, temporal, ideological, and linguistic elements depicts the changes that came upon the Nubian community before and after the Aswan Dam project. The two spatial poles of the north and the south are paralleled by the two ideological contrasts of tradition and modernity, the two temporalities of past and present, the two Nubian generations of elders and youth, and finally the indigenous Kenzi language and Arabic. The novel's projection of these spatial, temporal, social, and linguistic differences in constant interaction blurs the conventional borders that separate them into fixed and unchanging categories. In addition, the novel definitely evidences the richness of novelistic production in Egypt and helps expand the available critical tools used to evaluate and understand it.

The novel's spatial and temporal aesthetic principles cogently underline its commitment to include other perspectives and broaden the spectrum of its concerns and representations. Although the events seem to take place in a spatially limited geography in the Egyptian south, the characters' backgrounds and the ideas they embody carry the reader beyond such limited space. The two recurrent references to the poles of north and south entail more space than the new village north of the dam and its ancient counterparts south of it. The north refers to various locations, Mudiriyyat al-Tahrir, Aswan, Cairo, and also Europe—where political modernity and the nationalist imagination of homogeneity were first heralded and gradually disseminated to other spaces.

The south, on the other hand, refers to the original Nubian villages, their Sudanese counterparts, and Africa, where traditional bounded communities are celebrated ways of life. Thus, the two spatial poles represent not only geographic spaces, but also ideological spheres that become further complicated by ʿAli's depiction of other types of tension. He illustrates the disparate perspectives on relocation, Muhammad's and ʿAbdullah's, in the temporal tension between their generations, namely the generation of the grandfather's communal past and that of ʿAbdullah's modern aspirations in the present. A pattern of spatial movement is taken back and forth, with the youth on board a ship, transporting their people from their respective historic villages to Mudiriyyat al-Tahrir. The narrator's grandfather responds to the forcible evacuation by calling northerners in general, and government officials in particular, "*āl firʿawn*" (Pharaoh's clan) (ibid. p. 43), a label that connotes their deception and oppression of believers as is written in Al-Qurʾan 3: 11.[19] The destination signifies the travelers' mood; if the journey is southward, it is marked with singing and the traditional Nubian dancing of *al-arājīd*, but if it is northward, it is marked with wailing and weeping.

Bahaʾ Tahir's *Sunset Oasis*

Sunset Oasis (*Wahat al-ghurub*) takes place primarily at the oasis of Siwa in the western desert, far outside of Egypt's major cities, although some incidents occur in the metropolitan centers of Cairo and Alexandria, where Mahmud, the commissioner and main character, worked before his transfer to the oasis. The events are set at the end of the nineteenth century, during the height of British colonial presence in Egypt. The reader gains access to Mahmud's life prior to his transfer to Siwa by weaving back and forth the elements of his past life that unravel through intermittent flashbacks to the time when he was a hopeful young police officer and son of an affluent merchant in Cairo. Eventually, Mahmud falls into existential despair and commits suicide at the oasis, a fate that resonates with the experience of the Amazigh community, marginalized under dual colonial rule by the Egyptian government and the British administration.

Destabilizing the Spatial Center/Margin Binary

The choice of Siwa as the primary place—where the interactions between the Issiwan and the Egyptian government officials unfold—and Cairo and

Alexandria as secondary places—where the interactions between the colonial administration and Mahmud take place—encourages the reader to pay more attention to the otherwise overlooked peripheral geography than to the prevalent metropolises. Yet the legacy of colonial political economy in the cities of Cairo and Alexandria infiltrates the peripheries, as is evident in the exploitation and heavy taxation of the locals. However, the Amazigh in Siwa, like the local Alexandrians, fight against colonial oppression despite their inadequate, outdated armory. This spatial interconnection enables readers to understand the correlation between the center and the margin and how they jointly, rather than separately, influence the destinies of Egyptians, urban and rural.

Furthermore, in the consciousness of the main characters, Mahmud, Catherine, and al-Iskandar al-Akbar (Alexander the Great), the oasis acquires a somewhat mythical significance that is lacking from its metropolitan counterparts. Tahir depicts it as a desirable destination that lures each of the characters with the promise of self-realization and fulfillment. Their feelings during their journeys towards and inside the oasis reflect their excitement and rapture at the prospect of discovering the unknown, as a mode of identifying themselves in relation to others. Mahmud's primary wish is to escape his conflicted position as a colonial officer in the metropolis and retreat to the potential peace and quiet at the oasis for self-discovery. Catherine is Mahmud's Irish wife. She is infatuated with Egypt and has an obsession with the historical figure of Alexander the Great, whom she believes was buried at the oasis, thinking that finding his burial place will give her life purpose and meaning. In her pursuit, Catherine invokes al-Iskandar's dormant spirit for direction, but to her dismay, the spirit awakens only to reveal its troubled imperial past. The fictional spirit provides an account of al-Iskandar's historical quest at the oasis, seeking guidance from his mythical, divine father, Amun, and his oracle. In this sense, the oasis constitutes a spatial emblem of self-quest, in which characters embark on journeys that, as we will see in the following sections, may or may not change their perspective on themselves and others.

Tahir's rewriting of the turbulent history of colonialism in Egypt re-enacts the predicament of the colonial subject after his/her entrapment in the colonizer's preconceived image and prescribed role. Even though Mahmud does not object to his Commander's orders, he is internally ruptured and alienated by the colonialist appropriations of the conditions of his social, political, and material existence. Frantz Fanon explains the colonial regime in these terms: "Because it is a systematic negation of the other person and a furious determination to deny the other person all attributes of humanity, colonialism forces the people it dominates to ask themselves the question constantly: 'In reality, who am I?'" (Fanon 1996: 250).[20]

Mahmud's account of his meeting with Mr Harvey, the Italian émigré and Advisor to the Ministry of the Interior, sheds more light on the policies colonial administrators apply to rule the locals. Harvey instructs Mahmud on how to control the Issiwan at the oasis, where he has been recently appointed as a district commissioner. In Harvey's view, the administration should not intervene in the relationship between the Amazigh and *al-zajjāla*, peasants whom the Amazigh recruit to work in their fields and orchards, but do not allow to live in the same city. Harvey regards this work model as being like that of Sparta, the ancient Greek city, that produced the finest soldiers of Greece. He also forewarns Mahmud to ignore "their primitive customs" (Tahir 2009: 6), such as the separation of men and women. The one important aspect about the community that Mahmud is asked to pay attention to is the animosity and division between the Amazigh into *al-sharqiyyīn* and *al-gharbiyyīn* (Easterners and Westerners, respectively). Harvey asserts that they should not be concerned with the feud itself, but rather with how this feud can serve the colonial administration:

> it should be possible, through specific alliances with one clan or another, to turn this into a means to assure our domination. It is a tried and true method, so long as the alliance with one party does not go on too long. The alliance has to be with one group this time and with their opponents the next. Do you understand? (ibid. p. 7)

The colonial state, thus, exacerbates existing rifts among the locals by allying with one group against the other, precisely in terms of Mamdani's "doctrine of differentiation" (Mamdani 1996: 7).

Historically, both the oasis and its Amazigh population were politically independent until Muhammad ᶜAli annexed Siwa to the Egyptian territory in 1819. Its forced annexation, exploitation of its natural resources, and its remoteness from the Egyptian capital echo what Mamdani describes as a form of indirect colonial rule of a non-settler colony: the colonized are differentiated from the colonizer on the basis of their race and culture. They are deemed not eligible to utilize the colonizer's "social and political institutions," and are thus ruled by their own local or "ethnic" institutions (ibid. p. 7). Mamdani's analysis of indirect rule also explains Mr Harvey's attitude towards the Amazigh community and the colonial government's plan to rule them indirectly. The local Issiwan are permitted to use their conventional, local methods of government, their council known as *al-ajwād* ("heads of families" (Tahir 2009: 5)), because they are perceived as being racially, culturally, and politically inferior to the colonizer and hence as being ineligible to use his advanced ways of governance. At the same time, Harvey and Wasfi Niyazi, the Circassian colonial officer appointed later at the oasis, are keen on exploiting the rift between the Easterners and Westerners in application of the colonial strategy of divide and rule. Niyazi allies with Sheikh Sabir, a member of western Issiwan and chief of *al-ajwād* council with a thirst for power over his people.

The (Re)configuration of Imperial History

Tahir evokes an imperial history much longer and deeper than that of the British Empire through the long introspection of the awakened spirit of the fictional al-Iskandar (Alexander the Great) in order to: first, embody the ideology and practice behind imperial expansion in the ancient world; second, urge the reader to draw connections between imperialism and modern colonialism; and third, contest the validity of both imperial and colonial projects. Using interior monologue as a narrative mode, Tahir employs al-Iskandar's spirit to shed light on two contradictory facets of the past life of the fictional Iskandar, borrowing heavily from historical accounts of Alexander the Great. However, rather than celebrating his military prowess, the spirit is conjured to reveal al-Iskandar's hidden insecurities and mistrust of people in his close circles in juxtaposition with his self-perception as a privileged person in relation to others. On his quest for grandeur, he visits Amun's Oracle at the oasis to become both one supreme world emperor and a divinity. In his conceit, he draws a picture of the world he desires to create:

I was going to fashion a new world without peer. A world in which the races of man would become one and speak one language, which would be Greek, the most sublime of languages, the language of the Iliad, and whose peoples would marry one another, so that there would be only one race throughout the world ... I dreamt of filling the world with a new strain, from the loins of the Europeans and the Asians, after which there could be no ill will among them or wars. Alexander wanted to bring about what the other gods have failed to do—to create a world in which there was neither blond nor brown and in which there was no difference between those who worshipped Zeus and those who worshipped the fire of the Persians or the gods of the Indians ... "Must I, for the sake of this dream, wade through a sea of blood—the blood of the defeated and the blood of my soldiers?" (Tahir 2009: 121–2)

As portrayed by Tahir, al-Iskandar's imperial project is not based on unity; rather, it emanates from a sharp hierarchical perception of conquered others as inferior in power, race, or cultural beliefs. Yet, it aims at abolishing these differences and establishing one identity across the empire, by which all imperial subjects would become one race, speak one language, and worship one supreme god and emperor: al-Iskandar himself. The fancy that al-Iskandar pursues in his colonies seems to ensue from "the racist usurpation of the colonizers" (Sartre 1991: xxii).[21] Tahir's depiction of al-Iskandar's anguish over his excessive use of violence and bloodshed to realize his project, which in turn leads to his own death, illustrates Albert Memmi's description of the colonizer's disease: "Colonization can only disfigure the colonizer. It places him before an alternative having equally disastrous results; daily injustice accepted for his benefit on the one hand and necessary, but never consummated self-sacrifice on the other" (Memmi 1991: 147).[22]

Knowing the Self through the Other

Mahmud, al-Iskandar, and Catherine seek the oasis in search of truth, virtue, peace, and fulfillment inside their own selves and in the other people they meet. They carve their own paths using their bodies of knowledge as tools. Mahmud sympathizes with the Amazigh people, but, at the same time, is obliged to enforce the oppressive and differentiating colonial administrative methods. His inability to save an Amazigh boy from a falling rock at the temple suggests his impotence and incapability to change the unbalanced power relations in the oasis. Moreover, al-Iskandar's self-love obscures his perception of others and fuels his desire to rule a world empire where everyone is loyal to him and identical with his image. In realizing his project, he becomes overwhelmed with others' difference and disagreements. He discovers he is unable to differentiate who is loyal from who is a traitor, who is Greek from who is Persian, until he falls prey to death. On the other hand, Catherine's endeavors to find truth are marred by her selfishness and narrow infatuation with different others. When she first meets Mahmud, she imagines him as an ancient Egyptian king with a "pharaonic crown" (Tahir 2009: 14), an image that shows her irrational idolization of Mahmud's figure and background. Initially, relating to Mahmud and the Amazigh people seems to be her goal; however, this goal turns gradually into a means of self-realization, and in her frantic pursuit of a purposeful life in the ancient oasis she ignores the customs and traditions of the Amazigh people and invades their privacies—a conduct that prompts their resentment and later her husband's.

While Mahmud, al-Iskandar, and Catherine constitute a set of characters that embody themes of quest, desire, and lack of fulfillment, Malika, Fiona, and Niʿma, on the other hand, represent the object of desire and its unattainability or loss. Malika is a young Amazigh widow who is forbidden from communicating with foreign women like Catherine, although she defiantly breaks the rules and initiates contact with her. Their forbidden desire to know one another turns sexual and deadly. Fiona, also referred to as "the saint" (ibid. p. 23), is Catherine's chronically ill and subservient sister who is perceived by their family members as the more beautiful and virtuous one. Niʿma, Mahmud's concubine, is his first and only true love, who runs away from him when she realizes her irredeemable status of servitude.

All three characters represent women and their marginalized status irrespective of their racial, cultural, and linguistic difference in male-dominated societies. Tahir reflects their social reality aesthetically by denying them individual voices and providing them with existence only in the consciousness of the other characters: Mahmud, Catherine, and Yahya. Yahya is a revered Easterner and member of *al-ajwād* council, who is depicted by Tahir in a positive light. Yahya sympathizes with his beloved niece, Malika, whose curiosity to know others and neglect of strict Amazigh traditions lead to her death. Yahya also agrees to treat Fiona by giving her his rare medicinal herbs despite her sister's role in Malika's death. The reader's inability to have direct access to these women's thoughts and emotions parallels their isolation from public life. Malika presents the dilemma of women suffering from multiple oppressive institutions simultaneously, the colonial and the patriarchal. Her openness and desire to learn about others—whether foreigners like Catherine or idolaters like the ancient Egyptians (as perceived by the women in her community)—are reciprocated with distrust and violence.

Fiona captures Mahmud's heart because she reminds him of Niᶜma. Both women are captivating storytellers, who are able to transfer Mahmud to the magical world of the possible. Their stories compensate Mahmud's helplessness and inability to fully resist the powerful colonial institution by introducing him to a world of heroes and loving heroines whose romances empower them to overcome obstacles. Nevertheless, Mahmud's inability to realize a love relationship with his sister-in-law Fiona or with Niᶜma because of her lower social status as a concubine is symbolic of his existential crisis as an officer in the colonial state and an occupant of the higher classes of the social structure. His failure to materialize his love signifies his impotence in resolving the predicament of colonial alienation and functions as a precursor to his end as a colonial subject. Mahmud's anguish and sense of defeat lead to his suicide at the temple of Amun, a site that symbolized foreign infatuation with Egypt, its treasures, and its history.

Sunset Oasis not only presents a profound criticism of imperial doctrines and practices of differentiation at the end of the nineteenth century in Egypt, but also revokes the invasive and unethical forms of knowledge that heedlessly disregard others' values and customs in the selfish pursuit of one's own desires. In Mahmud's and Yahya's attempts to change themselves through forgiveness and reconciliation of their conflicts with others, Tahir suggests alternative ways of approaching others with consideration of the impact of one's actions on surrounding persons. However, the symbolic death of Malika and loss of Niᶜma indicate the despair and powerlessness that surround the attempts at reconciliation.

In light of Tahir's aesthetic depiction of difference(s) and disjunctions through the versatility of his characters across both racial and gender lines, and movement in space between the metropolitan centers of Alexandria and Cairo and the marginal Siwa oasis, as well as the triadic collapse of history in the amalgamation of ancient and modern historical moments in *Sunset Oasis*'s narrative time (Alexander the Great's ancient imperial reflections from the fourth century BCE and the Assiwans' subjection to modern dual colonial rule by Britain and Ottoman Egypt in narrative time), it is obvious that Tahir blurs the falsely established divides between all the above categories to propose a new perspective on human unity. In his critical study of the representations of constructed binaries such as that of self and other and East and West in Arabic fiction, Rasheed El-Enany contends that Tahir's works provide "a vision that transcends both the violent clashes of the past and the political differences of the present in order to concentrate on the ultimate concord of human beings on the individual level, their ultimate unity in suffering, in fragility before the cruelty of the human condition, be they from East or West" (135).[23] El-Enany's observation is echoed in Tahir's statement about his other novel, *al-Hubb fi-l-manfa*, 1995 (*Love in Exile*, 2001), in which he confirms that his work aims at conveying that "individual salvation is an impossible notion; we shall always need human solidarity, no matter how different our nationalities and inclinations, to deliver our civilization from its dilemma" (Tahir, quoted in El-Enany 2006: 141).

Conclusion

In conclusion, *al-Nubi* and *Sunset Oasis* are both earnestly committed to exploring the worlds of marginalized groups in Egypt. Both ʿAli and Tahir make use of spatial and temporal devices. Not only is the geographical setting of each of the novels pertinent to the individual and unique experience of each of the groups they portray, but their common marginality helps shift the reader's perspective from the Egyptian metropolis, commonly the setting for contemporary literature, to its equally significant and interrelated counterparts in the margins, which possess historic importance but have now fallen into irrevocable marginality. Nubia witnessed the establishment of the New Kingdom of Pharaohs that ruled Egypt from its capital, Napata, from the eighth to the seventh century BCE. The Kingdom was revived by the Nubian Pharaohs of Meroë between the late sixth and the fifth century BCE. Siwa, however, was the home of the Oracle of Amun and the desirable destination of Alexander the Great in the fourth century BCE. The invocation of the historic grandeur of these two locations and the significance of their peoples when juxtaposed with their present geographical and cultural marginality creates aesthetic effects of loss, appreciation, and a desire to reclaim the past relationships with Nubia and Siwa.

Furthermore, the imperial, colonial, and early postcolonial temporal settings bring into relief the shifting fortunes of these groups in Egypt's history, whether in antiquity or in the present. Regardless of the remoteness of Nubia and Siwa from the current Egyptian capital, the Nubians in *al-Nubi* have not been saved from the policies of eradication of difference by the postcolonial state regime, and the Amazigh in *Sunset Oasis* have not escaped the policies of differentiation exercised by the colonial state.

Although the two works present cogent accounts of the conditions of the Nubian and Amazigh minorities and express strong critiques of state policies, each writer articulates the experiences from a different, though complementary, perspective. ʿAli articulates the Nubian experience from the perspective of a "public/popular writer," whose marginal position in the social, cultural, political, and literary world does not deter him from expressing his oppositional views. Yet, unlike Tahir, he articulates his views through divergent modes of address that range from traditional Nubian songs to the use of direct speech more than narration. This mode allows him to use more spoken Arabic, filtered through the accents of Nubians and the Kenzi language, in the characters' exchanges. These devices reflect the "popular" stance he adopts as a writer: His agent narrator is a young observant inquirer who does not claim knowledge but is eager to attain it.

Tahir's articulation of Amazigh cultural and historical experiences, on the other hand, emanates primarily from the consciousness of individuals who are well-educated. The main character and generator of the plot, Mahmud, is a middle-class officer. Catherine's European background and education provide her with the powerful status that women like Malika are unable to enjoy. Yahya and Sabir are two Amazigh *ajwād* who received their education at, respectively, al-Azhar in Cairo and al-Zaytuna Mosque in Tunis, the two most reputable Islamic universities at the time. In this sense, Tahir's sources/agents of the Amazigh experience are informed by the knowledge and power they attained through their education. Along these lines, the prevalent narrative mode is characterized by long introspection in the minds of these educated, powerful individuals. This enables Tahir, the intellectual, to discuss complex views around critical issues like race, religion, and imperialism without the interruption of much direct speech.

Whether the articulation of marginal experiences stems from popular or intellectual/well-educated positions, they are not necessarily prescribed to succeed or fail. In fact, the various deaths as well as the prevalence of uncertainty and despair in both novels demonstrate the limits of both stances in going beyond the contemporary conflicts between the Egyptian state and Egypt's different groups, on one level, and in bridging the existing sociopolitical and cultural gaps between these different groups, on the other.

Notes

1. A version of this chapter has appeared as an article in *Alif: Journal of Comparative Poetics*.
2. The full article is available on the *al-Ahram Weekly* website, <http://weekly.ahram.org.eg/News/5313/32/Knocking-on-Nubia's-door.aspx> (last accessed 20 July 2012).
3. *Imazighen* is the plural of *Amazigh* (Cornwell and Atia 2012: 271).
4. Cornwell, Graham H., and Atia, Mona, "Imaginative Geographies of Amazigh Activism in Morocco," *Social & Cultural Geography*, Vol. 13, No. 3, 2012, pp. 255–74.
5. For more information on Algeria's recent reform with regard to the Amazigh heritage, see the BBC online article "Algeria reinstates term limit and recognises Berber language," <http://www.bbc.com/news/world-africa-35515769> (last accessed 19 September 2016).
6. I refer to the inhabitants of Siwa as "*Issiwan*," which is the local term they use in their Siwi language to refer to themselves. For more information see Alain Blottière, *Siwa: The Oasis* (Cairo: Harpocrates, 2000).
7. Mamdani, Mahmoud, *Citizen and Subject: Contemporary Africa and the Legacy of Late Colonialism* (Princeton: Princeton University Press, 1996).
8. Lukács, Georg, *The Historical Novel*, trans. Hannah and Stanley Mitchell, preface by Irving Howe (Boston: Beacon Press, 1963).
9. Benjamin, Walter ([1968] 2000) "The Storyteller," in Michael McKeon (ed.), *Theory of the Novel: A Historical Approach* (Baltimore: Johns Hopkins University Press, 2000), pp. 77–93.

10. Faraj, ᶜAbd al-Nabi, "Idris ᶜAli: Jil al-sittinat inkasaru b-inkisar batalihim alladhi habasahum fi maᶜmaᶜat al-siyasa," *Al-Sharq al-Awsat*, 29 September 2003, <http://www.aawsat.com/details.asp?section=19&article=195200&issue no=9071#.U2EqfV5GqDo> (last accessed 30 April 2014).
11. Hasan, Sayyid Mahmud, "Baᶜd haya ᶜasiba: Wafat al-katib Idris ᶜAli" *Al-Ahram Online* (1 December 2010), <http://www.ahram.org.eg/Books/News/50974.aspx> (last accessed 20 July 2012).
12. Tahir, Baha⁾, *Sunset Oasis*, trans. Humphrey Davies (London: Sceptre, 2009).
13. ᶜAli's *al-Nubi* is not the first novel on the Nubians' displacement. Muhammad Khalil Qasim's *al-Shamandura* ('The Buoy') was first published in 1968.
14. Translations of all the Arabic excerpts from *al-Nubi* are my own.
15. ᶜAli, Idris (2001), *al-Nubi* (Cairo: al-ᶜAlamiyya Press, 2008).
16. Spaulding, Jay, "Slavery, Land Tenure and Social Class in the Northern Turkish Sudan," *The International Journal of African Historical Studies*, Vol. 15, No. 1, 1982, pp. 1–20.
17. Lodge, David, "Mimesis and Diegesis in Modern Fiction," in Michael J. Hoffman and Patrick D. Murphy (eds), *Essentials of the Theory of Fiction* (Durham, NC: Duke University Press, 1996), 2nd edn, pp. 348–72.
18. Honeywell, Arthur J., "Plot in the Modern Novel," in Michael J. Hoffman and Patrick D. Murphy (eds), *Essentials of the Theory of Fiction* (Durham, NC: Duke University Press, 1996), 2nd edn, pp. 147–57.
19. *Al-Qur⁾an al-Karim* (Misr: ᶜAbd al-Hamid Ahmad Hanafi, 1935).
20. Fanon, Frantz ([1963] 1996) *The Wretched of the Earth*, trans. Constance Farrington, preface by Jean-Paul Sartre (New York: Grove Press, 1966).
21. Sartre, Paul, Introduction to Albert Memmi, *The Colonizer and the Colonized*, trans. Howard Greenfeld (Boston: Beacon Press, 1991), pp. xxi–xxix.
22. Memmi, Albert, *The Colonizer and the Colonized*, trans. Howard Greenfeld, introd. Jean Paul Sartre (Boston: Beacon Press, 1991).
23. El-Enany, Rasheed, *Arab Representations of the Occident: East–West Encounters in Arabic Fiction* (London: Routledge, 2006).

2

Reading Cosmopolitanism in Yusuf Zaydan's *Azazeel* and Muᶜtazz Futayha's *Akhir yahud al-iskandariyya*

The novels *ᶜAzazil*, 2008 (*Azazeel*, 2012) by Yusuf Zaydan (b. 1958) and *Akhir yahud al-iskandariyya*, 2008 (translated as The Last Jews of Alexandria) by Muᶜtazz Futayha (b. 1987) underline Coptic and Jewish experiences, respectively, in different historical periods in Egypt. *Azazeel* is set in the fifth century, when Coptic Christianity was a new, yet prevailing, religion among the masses, whereas the events of *Akhir yahud al-iskandariyya* take place in the first half of the twentieth century, particularly the 1940s, when Egypt was home to a considerable number of Jews—estimated at between 70,000 and 80,000 people (Beinin 1996).[1] Written by the writer and established scholar of Egyptian antiquity Yusuf Zaydan, *Azazeel* received critical acclaim and was awarded the prestigious International Prize for Arabic Fiction in 2009.[2] *Akhir yahud al-iskandariyya*, on the other hand, is the first published work by the budding young novelist and screenwriter Muᶜtazz Futayaha, and has not drawn equal attention from the literary critical establishment, though it was popular enough among a general readership to have been reprinted six times.[3] Despite the career-stage differences between the two authors, their works have given rise to controversies[4] (albeit to a much greater extent in the case of *Azazeel*) because of their unconventional depiction of sectarian and social tensions between ethno-religious groups in Egypt. On the one hand, *Azazeel* highlights the fifth-century schism that pertained to the nature of Christ and divided the Coptic Orthodox Church from the majority of Orthodox Churches in the East. However, its in-depth engagement with the Coptic theological understanding of Christ from the perspective of the novel's main character Hypa, a fictional Coptic monk on a quest for truth, was vehemently denounced by several members of the Coptic population in general, and by Coptic clergymen in particular. One Coptic Bishop likened Zaydan's work to *The Da Vinci Code* in its contempt for and distortion of traditional Christian beliefs and history (Bayyumi 2008).[5] Similarly, Futayha's representation of the Egyptian Jewish minority in the first half of the twentieth century from a sympathetic perspective was considered radical, given the heightened national and regional sectarian tensions currently being experienced in Egypt. However, in an interview, Futayha revealed that it was that sectarian atmosphere—which has persisted in Egypt and across the Middle East region for decades now—that inspired him to embody "*al-ʾākhar*" (the other) in the image of the Egyptian Jew, for the purpose of unsettling the stereotypical perception (ʿAbd al-ʿAlim 2009).[6]

The marginalization of Coptic and Jewish ethno-religious groups (before the latter's exodus during World War II and post-independence) in contemporary Egypt is not a secret. However, it is important to attend to the historical conditions that surround that marginalization in order to understand what *Azazeel* and *Akhir yahud al-iskandriyya* are trying to accomplish on the cultural plane: after all, "novels might function as effects and symptoms of a national culture" (Walkowitz 2006: 20).[7] In this connection, I will provide a brief overview of the political tensions that led to the evacuation of Jews from Egypt in the 1940s and 1950s, and then shed light on the growing sectarian discourses against Copts in the present time.

Gudrun Krämer writes that between 1945 and 1952—the time of political tensions culminating in the 1952 revolution—the Egyptian government of Fahmi al-Nuqrashi engaged in a "bitter power struggle" (Krämer 1989: 210)[8] with multiple opposition groups. These mainly included the Muslim Brotherhood, Communist political activists (who were mostly Jews), and Zionists. The first two groups rejected the British colonial presence, capitalist economic practices, and monarchical rule, whereas the third group, the Zionists, actively disagreed with the popular sentiment that stood for the preservation of the Muslim-Arab character of Palestine. In what is referred to as "the Palestine campaign," in May 1948, al-Nuqrashi issued the currently familiar "state of emergency . . . followed by [the enforcement of] martial law," and "'for reasons of public security related to the present situation,' hundreds of Zionists and communists, mainly Jews, were arrested, as well as numerous Muslim Brothers, who were then interned in separate camps" (ibid. p. 211):

> The Palestine campaign offered the perfect opportunity to eliminate the most dangerous oppositional elements, regardless of their attitudes on the Palestine issue itself. The Muslim Brotherhood, which in the postwar period had become the strongest challenger to the regime in power, was banned in early December 1948. The arrested Zionists and communists presented a simple case from Prime Minister al-Nuqrāshī's point of view: both groups were represented by Jews so they must be identical. (ibid. p. 211)

Krämer's account explicates the strategies the Egyptian state implemented before the 1952 revolution to stay in power under the guise of defending a political cause.

The Egyptian state in the 1990s and 2000s ironically continued to apply the same notorious tool that al-Nuqrashi used in 1948, namely, effectuating emergency and martial laws against opposition for "security purposes." The Egyptian political analyst ʿAmr al-Shubaki (Amr el-Shobaki) perceives this as the regime's "grave political failure," commenting: "For the first time since the revolution of 1919, Egypt is being ruled by a regime that relies solely on security measures to stay in power" (el-Shobaki 2011).[9] In the aftermath of the bombing of the Coptic Church in Alexandria in January 2011 and only a few days before the eruption of the revolution that ousted Mubarak, el-Shobaki wrote that "Egypt's ruling regime is the main reason behind the mounting sectarianism" (ibid.). Despite Mubarak's regime's boastful remarks about the unprecedented approvals Copts were granted to build churches under his rule, and, also, the occasional appointment of a Coptic governor here or a Coptic minister there, the regime failed to pay attention to the growing socio-political divides between Muslims and Copts. Instead, the regime was content to run the state's affairs on a "day-to-day" basis, and, with its die-hard strategy to remain in power, it focused its energy on suppressing political opposition voices, especially Islamists'. In doing so, it neglected the growing separatist discourse on the basis of religion against the Coptic minority, and overlooked Copts' rights to freedom, security, and equality. In their turn, Egyptian Copts demonstrated, in el-Shobaki's words, signs of

"Coptic anger," and developed a counter-discourse of Coptic self-assertion to resist this antagonistic cultural and political environment. This, in addition to the lack of a "viable" multi-party system that represents all sects and interests within the Egyptian population, has contributed to a fertile environment for sectarianism:

> The Coptic problem in Egypt is not just about legal discrimination or restrictions on the building of churches. Instead, it's rooted in Copts' daily interactions in a sectarian environment, which has turned the moderates among them into victims of two fundamentalist discourses. The first, an Islamist discourse, has marginalized Copts politically and culturally from the public sphere and has offended their faith. The second, a Christian discourse, has isolated the Coptic community from the rest of Egyptian society and has entrenched its hatred for the "other". It is closely connected with post 9/11 anti-Islam discourse that has taken hold globally. (ibid.)

After the ouster of Mubarak, sectarian rifts continued to develop with the rise of fundamentalist discourses, exacerbated by essentialist resistance movements to neo-colonial interventions in the region as well as polarizing media outlets streaming from overseas. The interim state under military control, meanwhile, sought to oppress dissidents, even if that required the arbitrary killing of demonstrators, whether Copts or Muslims.

In anticipation of the results of Egypt's presidential elections in 2012, in which the two final presidential nominees, Ahmad Shafiq, the former commander in the Egyptian Air Force, and Mohammad Musri (Morsi), the Muslim Brotherhood political leader, epitomized the perennial oscillation of power between military officers and Islamists, Zaydan drew similarities between the military and Islamists. In his article "al-Asʾila al-Taʾsisiyya: Hal Taqum bi-Misr Dawla Diniyya?" (Foundational Questions: Will a Religious State Be Held in Egypt?), Zaydan argues that no matter how military officers and Islamists seem in conflict over the monopolization of power, their systems operate under similar principles, which situate them far from any civil state they allege to have established or promise to establish. He writes:

> Is it not obvious to all the perpetual harmony between military officers and Islamists since the eruption of the Egyptian revolution—that was aborted

and became an "outburst"? Is it not obvious to all how religious symbols were raised in preparation for the winning of Islamists in the parliamentary elections and might likewise transpire in a few hours in the presidential elections? Harmony is present because the military order is permanently similar to authorial and religious order. They share the pyramidal hierarchy of authority, the disdainful look upon women, the unquestionable obedience to higher commands, the sanctification of who is above, and the contempt for others. "Now military leaders will be angry with me."[10] (Zaydan 2012b)[11]

At the same time, while Copts are doubtless left out of this political power struggle, Zaydan illustrates what he sees—on both the Islamist (albeit with a much more influential political configuration and heavy supporters) and the Coptic side—as parallel political visions and attitudes that hold to theocratic principles in the presumably modern state of Egypt. He explains that, during the power vacuum in the wake of Mubarak's ouster, the leaders of "*al-Islam al-Siyāsī*" (political Islam), particularly the Muslim Brotherhood, proposed to the public the establishment of "*dawla dīniyya*" (a religious state), which he describes as an inventive idiom used by Islamists in Egypt to replace the well-known political entity of the theocratic state (ibid.). The proposition is defined as "*dawla madaniyya bi-marjiʿiyya dīniyya*" (a civil state with a religious reference), which, Zaydan argues, is paradoxical considering that the civil state separates itself from religion and grounds its values and system solely in modern, secular law; whereas, if the proposed religious (Islamic) reference is taken into account, the state will resort to sharia, *fiqh* (Islamic jurisprudence), and religious texts as definitive sources of legislation, turning hence into a theocracy. Zaydan, by the same token, questioned a comparable approach by the late Coptic Pope, Shenouda, when he refused to have the Church abide by a judicial ruling that granted divorce to Coptic couples, expressing the view that he took orders only from God.

In light of the above discussion on existing religious and political tensions and inconsistencies, one can perceive the significant role that the state, colonial and postcolonial, has played in inflaming sectarianism to guarantee its monopoly of power. As creative reflections of that charged national atmosphere, *Azazeel* and *Akhir yahud al-iskandariyya* highlight all forms of political and religious intolerance towards the "other." Although *Azazeel* is imbued with history in its depiction of the fifth-century schism in the early Christian church, it bespeaks persistent sectarian strife in different parts of the world in different times. Yes, sectarianism in contemporary Egypt appears to be the most perceptible of *Azazeel*'s treatments, but it inevitably invokes other incidents of sectarianism across history, such as that between Catholics and Protestants and that between Muslim Sunnis and Shiites in Iraq in medieval times. These historical reflections and recollections function as reminders of the conflicts humanity has suffered in the course of history. In like manner, *Akhir yahud al-iskandariyya* is concerned with the rise in cultural and political contention with the Jewish population in Egypt in the late 1940s, but juxtaposes that period of strife with the prewar time in which Egyptian Jews, Muslims, and Christians are portrayed as coexisting irrespective of religious difference. It does so by focusing on the deep human connections and mutual understanding Jewish characters build with their ethno-religiously diverse neighbors in Alexandria. At the same time, the novel transcends the local encounters of Jews in Egypt by delving into the lives and values migrant Jews from other parts of the globe (especially Europe)[12] bring to the Jewish community in Alexandria and Egypt at large.[13]

Both novels conjure up unconventional attitudes and practices by individuals from the Coptic and Jewish populations in different periods of Egyptian history, with the goal of what Kwame Appiah calls "perspectival shift" (Appiah 2006: 77).[14] In the writers' subversion of established bodies of knowledge in Egyptian culture—be they the oppressive religious identity of the recently Christianized Roman empire in the fifth century CE, or the exclusionary ethno-religious nationalist formations in the first half of the twentieth century presented in *Akhir yahud al-iskandariyya*—they portray defiant individuals who critically question the established forms of knowledge in their immediate surroundings and restlessly search for new, unconventional stances that would enable them to reflect on their positions in relation to others in both domestic and global spheres.

In *Azazeel*, Hypa, the Coptic monk, transcends the boundaries of the Coptic monastic tradition through the liberating acts of learning philosophy, interacting with other humans outside his tradition and homeland, and writing to vigilantly record what he sees and knows. Yusuf, the main character in

Akhir yahud al-iskandariyya, is a Jewish Egyptian who challenges the cultural norms of his society by falling in love with a Muslim woman named Sara, and by pursuing his dream of screenwriting and directing against his father's conservative career expectations from him. While Hypa and Yusuf are considered radicals from the point of view of their respective traditions, they both maintain "a posture of resistance" (Walkowitz 2006: 2) against attempts to ostracize them from their communities. Hypa remains a monastic despite being a dissident and a vagrant, and so does Yusuf when he insists on returning to his homeland, Alexandria, despite his Jewishness. I argue that the portrayal of Hypa and Yusuf as incessantly comparing, criticizing, and repositioning themselves, while attempting to "operate in the world [by] preserving a [cultural] posture of resistance" (ibid. p. 2), demonstrates the contrastive processes of self-preservation and restless self-criticism present in critical stances.

In her explanation of the notion of "critical cosmopolitanism," Rebecca Walkowitz distinguishes it from the cosmopolitan project of "planetary humanism" that tends to reinforce "heroic tones of appropriation and progress, and a suspicion of epistemological privilege, views from above or from the center that assume a consistent distinction between who is seeing and what is seen" (ibid. p. 2). Instead, she describes a *dynamic* aspect of cosmopolitanism in its "critical" form, which can be adopted by writers in their narrative style and by literary critics in their analytical reading. It involves what she calls "a new reflection about reflection" and "critique of critique" that prompts thinkers, writers, and scholars to continue efforts to reevaluate "categories that seem to be neutral to the affective conditions (rationality, purpose, coherence, detachment)" (ibid. p. 3). In her theory of critical cosmopolitanism, Walkowitz incorporates the critical theory developed by Max Horkheimer which "rejects the idea of 'neutral' categories and 'the insistence that thinking is a fixed vocation, a self-enclosed realm within society as a whole'" (quoted in Walkowitz 2006: 3). Considering dynamism as a key feature of critical thinking, Walkowitz argues that developing critical cosmopolitanism as a style and an attitude means not only "thinking beyond the nation [or immediate community] but also comparing, distinguishing, and judging among different versions of transnational thought; testing moral and political norms, including the norms of critical thinking; and valuing informal as well as transient models of community" (ibid. p. 2).

In the following section, I demonstrate how *Azazeel* and *Akhir yahud al-iskandariyya* engage the strand of "critical cosmopolitanism" in their literary styles, and how they revoke narrow and exclusive programs of religious communities and nationhood that seek purification from difference, whether those programs were fifth-century ones or at work in present-day Egypt. I will also illustrate how their thematic and structural devices correspond with their display of human creativity in the attitudes of their characters: As both novels seek to disrupt authorized thought and established bodies of knowledge through inventive form and content, so do their characters when they creatively venture into unknown terrains as a means of self-liberation and exploration of new values.

Azazeel—Yusuf Zaydan

The sensitivity of the historical content of the novel pertains to its depiction of episodes of religious violence during the patriarchal leadership of Cyril I of Alexandria in the fifth century, causing grievances on the part of some members of the Coptic Church (East 2012).[15] Zaydan addressed these Coptic concerns by explaining that the historical content of his work "wasn't a historical manuscript I'd found, but a novel . . . [It] wasn't a work of theology—but still it seemed to frighten some people" (Zaydan, quoted in East 2012). Zaydan asserted how he yielded historical facts to his imagination in order to create a fictional world that is all too human. He described his main character, the Coptic monk Hypa, as "a human being who has dreams and temptations," and added that his choice of the religious historical content was intended to shed light on coercive systems within established religion in general. He says: "Judaism, Christianity, Islam—you can't understand one without the other, and I wanted to try to explore how the past still works in the present. And what I came to believe is that religious violence isn't only wrong, it's ugly and dangerous. You just haven't the right to kill someone else because he doesn't believe the same thing as you" (Zaydan, quoted in East 2012).

Azazeel is formulated as the autobiographical narrative of Hypa, who narrates his journey from his hometown in Upper Egypt, *Akhmim* (ancient Panopolis), to Alexandria, Jerusalem, and Antioch, where he settles at a nearby monastery and writes about what he witnessed during these journeys. The day Hypa begins writing, September 27, 431 CE, is fictionally set two months after the ecumenical council of Ephesus convened to renounce Nestorius' controversial Christological doctrine. Having known Nestorius—the fictional character sketched in the image of Nestorius, Bishop of Constantinople (428–31 CE)—while in Jerusalem, Hypa, with a heavy heart, decides to narrate his personal experience of Nestorius, not as a theologian, but as another man of God, thus not taking sides in the church debate Nestorius' doctrine aroused.

It is worth noting at this juncture that Nestorius, Bishop of Constantinople, contested the conventional reference in Christianity to Virgin Mary as *theotokos*, namely Birth Bearer of God, because, in his view, it does not emphasize the human nature of Christ. Nestorius' doctrine was strongly opposed by his contemporary, Cyril I, Bishop of Alexandria, who sent twelve anathemas to Nestorius, asserting the preservation of tradition handed out to orthodox churches universally from the apostles. Theologians have examined the embittered battle that broke out between the two influential theologians, Nestorius and Cyril I, who oversaw the two most influential Church sees in the Roman Empire at the time, Alexandria and Constantinople. Were the Church teachings so homogeneous across the Roman Empire? Or, to put it too simply, was this a battle between tradition and innovation? Robert L. Wilken's articulately poses this important question: "Does this . . . mean that Cyril was right and Nestorius a dangerous innovator?" (Wilken 1965: 123).[16] While some scholars examine the conflict from a political perspective—"the pope of Alexandria was seeking to crush the see of Constantinople, a young upstart challenging Alexandria's primacy in the East" (ibid. p. 124)—Wilken warns of isolating "theological factors at the expense of political and ecclesiastical factors" and attempts to find an answer to what he calls the fifth-century "explosion" by examining "the conflict" from "the perspective of the exegetical tradition preceding Cyril and Nestorius" (ibid. p. 124). Without delving into the Christological debate, but adopting a critical point of view, we can observe that that historical battle seems to emanate from the very familiar struggle over—to borrow Wilken's concise words—who "alone possessed the truth" (ibid. p. 124). While Cyril I is still revered in both Eastern Orthodox and Coptic Churches, Nestorius was excommunicated and sent into exile after the Council of Ephesus in 431 CE deemed his Christological doctrine heretical. However, despite the widespread perception at the time of Nestorius' teachings as heretical, they found their way "among [Christian] minorities scattered across Asia from Mesopotamia into India and to the China Sea" from 950 to 1350 CE (Latourette 1975: 564).[17]

Hypa's narrative does not center upon Nestorius or the Christological debate that swept the early Christian Church during his fictional lifetime. Neither is it about Hypa's personal attestation to the Church disagreements, the death of the Greek philosopher and mathematician Hibatia (henceforth Hypatia) at the hands of religious zealots in Alexandria, the excommunication of Nestorius from the Church, or the beginning of the demise of the Græco-Roman Empire itself, under whose influence the early Church held its organic unity. Rather, Hypa's autobiographical narrative encapsulates the existential "drama of sin and salvation" (Wills 2011: 27)—to borrow Garry Wills' phrase[18]—that humans undergo when spiritually conflicted.

Unearthing the Scrolls

The novel's prologue is imbued with symbolic devices that demonstrate the author's intricate and creative approach to history, and therefore command analytical attention. In the prologue, readers learn about the circumstances that led the anonymous character of *al-mutarjim* (the translator) to Hypa's life narrative. The translator explains that the "*Riwāya*" (narrative) is his Arabic translation of Hypa's autobiography, which was excavated in good condition from the ruins of an ancient town, located north-west of present-day Halab (Aleppo), in 1997. The translator/narrator notes that the autobiography was originally written in Syriac[19] over thirty scrolls, and that the narrative's thirty chapters deliberately correspond to the number of the scrolls to stay true to the original narrative form. He finally adds that his translation was completed in Alexandria on April 4, 2004, and acknowledges the help of an abbot at a Syriac monastery in Cyprus, whose insights and recommendations concerning ancient theological terminology improved the translation. This diligent account of the time and place of the discovery of the scrolls, their language, number and condition as well as the timeframe of their translation process, may seem to present obscure, if not irrelevant, details in relation to the autobiographical content; however, it is a device that establishes the translator's credibility, vigilance, and accuracy.

The translator attributes concealing his identity to the gravity of the revealed affairs and the potential sensitivities Hypa's autobiography might aggravate. His request to readers for discretion and postponement of the translation publication until after his death attests symbolically to a context of mounting sectarianism and religious intolerance, which seems to suggest the existence of sectarianism in contemporary times as well as centuries ago in the past. The translator alludes to a similar request made by an anonymous Arab monk from al-Ruha[20] Nestorian Church after his discovery of the same scrolls in the fifth-century Hijri. The Arab monk wrote in Arabic on the margins of the scrolls "*taʿlīqātahu al-khaṭīra*" ("his dangerous commentaries")—the nature of which the translator declines to reveal—and buried the scrolls back because the time for their revelation had not arrived then.[21] The symbolic fear of those who handled these scrolls ironically presages the real societal clamor *Azazeel* generated after its publication, while the fact that it has already been published indicates that the time for the thought behind it to come to light must have arrived.

Zaydan's inventive introduction to Hypa's story permeates it with mystery and prepares readers for incidents that lie somewhere in between history and fiction, theology and philosophy, and for ample conflict of thought. On one level, Zaydan draws freely from the intricate historical realities of the early institutionalized religion in Egypt and across the Græco-Roman Empire, but, on the other, he liberally reconstructs them in a novelistic order to convey his message. For example, Syriac and Arabic, two languages known to express two different religious traditions, ancient Christianity and Islam, are creatively merged together on Hypa's autobiographical scrolls, in order to symbolically gesture the strong influence Nestorian Christians in Mesopotamia[22]—who combined knowledge in Syriac, Greek, and Arabic—had on Arab thought. In his historical study of the beginnings of Christianity, Kenneth Scott Latourette writes:

> The Nestorians in Mesopotamia had tutored their Arab conquerors in Hellenistic culture, and in the process had put some of the Greek philosophers into Arabic, but the Arabs had proved apt pupils of the Nestorians and other subject peoples and were producing a culture which appeared to be fully as "high" as that of Constantinople" and "higher" than that of

the Franks or others in the Germanic peoples who had been converted to Christianity. (Latourette 1975: 276)

In this respect, *Azazeel* pays tribute to Nestorians and their introduction of Hellenistic philosophy to Arabs and the Arabic language, positioning itself favorably with regard to avid Nestorian cultural exchange. However, this position exasperated the Coptic Church as it contends with the Coptic perception of Nestorian doctrine as heretical.

The translator's prologue, thus, subtly arouses readers' curiosity about the church divisions Nestorian thought causes. Before the appearance of the character of Nestorius, readers are beguiled by the "dangerous" commentaries that an Arab Nestorian monk had to write on Hypa's account of Nestorius, and, at the same time, are denied access to them because the translator abstained from publishing them. This complex narrative device impels readers to carefully examine themselves the upcoming narrative and its historical background in order to conjecture what those commentaries could contain.

Azazeel, Hypa's Diabolical Muse

The first scroll opens with Hypa engaging in a long prayer to God, a style that invokes the unique style of "direct address" to God used by Saint Augustine (354–430 CE) in his *Confessions*. Scholar Garry Wills notes that *Confessions* is St. Augustine's only work that contains the "prayer framework," and is, therefore, perceived as his "retreat" into the self in "the presence of the silence (and darkness) of God" (O'Donnell, quoted in Wills 2011: 27).Similarly, Hypa's opening prayer suggests that his autobiography writing is primarily a retreat into his anguished self and a cry for God's mercy: "My Lord, do You hear me? I am Your faithful servant, the perplexed, Hypa the monk, Hypa the physician, Hypa the stranger as people call me in my land of exile" (Zaydan 2012a: 5). The prayer tone, and the several ways Hypa defines himself ("the monk," "the physician," and/or "the stranger") indicate his uncertainty about who he is and his feeling of estrangement. But, as much as doubt permeates Hypa's being and self-articulation, his narrative does not appear to seek support or approval from any entity, since it does not address anyone in particular. Rather, it functions as an act of self-criticism, of contemplation, and of repositioning the self in relation to others, away from influential perceptions and attitudes. As will be explained below, Hypa's state of bewilderment and spiritual anxiety are skillfully embodied in the ever-present mythical character of Azazeel.

Azazeel's character is drawn from the ancient mythical figure of Azazel, mentioned in the Jewish tradition "four times in the prescriptions for the Day of Atonement (Lev 16: 8, 10, 26) . . . Although many scholars have identified Azazel with a demonic figure to whom the sin-laden scapegoat was dispatched, the term remains undefined in the biblical text" (Helm 1994: 217).[23] Scholar Robert Helm adds that the "two noncanonical Jewish works, *1 Enoch* and the *Apocalypse of Abraham*, reveal a tradition in which Azazel was regarded as a demon, and in which the scapegoat rite was utilized as a symbol of demonic expulsion" (ibid.). Moreover, "Azazel was the personification of uncleanness and in later rabbinic writings was sometimes described as a fallen angel" (*Encyclopedia Britannica*, "Azazel" 2012).[24]

Azazel's demonic attributes in the ancient Jewish tradition are invoked here in the character of Azazeel, who appears to Hypa as a diabolical muse, an imaginary supernatural figure that incessantly urges him to overcome his inhibitions and reveal his hidden knowledge. Azazeel addresses Hypa in an authoritative tone. For example, he dictates that Hypa give an account of Hypatia, the mathematician and philosopher he met in Alexandria, and her gruesome murder by a fundamentalist mob in Alexandria: "'Write, Hypa, write in the name of truth, the truth preserved in you'" (Zaydan 2012a: 125). Azazeel thus constitutes the impetuous force behind Hypa's storytelling, or, rather, telling of the untold truth. His duplicity is rendered, contrary to common reason, essential for truth revelation and, thereby, Hypa's self-redemption.

Azazeel's fluid depiction as between diabolism and spiritual impetuousness regarding truth-telling blurs preconceived boundaries between sin and virtue and right and wrong. Nonetheless, Hypa resists Azazeel, the muse of truth revelation, and sees his urging of writing about conflict, Hypa's and others', as an external diabolical force that cannot exist within himself. Azazeel disputes Hypa's perception by saying: "'I am not around you, Hypa. I'm inside you'" (ibid. p. 287), and gives an account of who he is, not whom people perceive him to be. Here is the insightful exchange between Hypa and Azazeel:

> I whispered to him, "But Azazeel, you are the cause of evil in the world."
> "Hypa, be sensible. I am the one who justifies evil. So evil causes me."
> "Have you not sown strife between the bishops? Confess!"
> "I perpetuate, I don't confess, which is what they want from me."
> "And you, don't you want anything?" I asked.
> "I am you, Hypa, and I am them. You see me at hand whenever you want or whenever they want. I'm always available to bear burdens, ward off sins and exonerate every convict. I am the will, the willer, and the willed. I am the servant of mankind, the one who incites believers to pursue the threads of their fancies." (ibid. p. 292)

Azazeel refutes man's conception of the supernatural fiend by presenting himself to Hypa, not as the guilty-as-accused who is behind all human atrocities and Church divisions, but as an invention that is skillfully woven in man's imagination and is as old as culture itself. As much as man desires to locate evil in a diabolical force that exists outside his natural world—as Hypa does outside Azazeel—modern scholars and intellectuals explain that evil and "the fallen angels, with all their faults and foibles, are of our kin," whereas the "fair angels—perfect in their virtues—are beyond our ken" (Rudwin 1931: 56).[25] In this way, Azazeel's account of himself reconfigures human definition of evil and invites Hypa, as well as the book's readers, to rethink what really constitutes evil, and so immanently disjoins it from good; perhaps then, man will understand what surrounds the eternal conflict between the established categories of evil and good and thereby understand what causes his own perennial suffering from their warring forces. Could evil be any rebellion against established truth or disturbance of held tradition? Could good then be the exact opposite?

Searching for Truth

Hypa's restless quest for truth is prompted by and infused with suffering, his as well as others'. As a child, Hypa witnesses his father's murder at the hands of Christian zealots who did not tolerate seeing the pagan fisherman provide fish for the besieged priests of Khnum, the ancient Egyptian deity. Agonized by the inexplicable atrocity and its corollary of religious prejudice, from a young age Hypa dedicates himself to knowledge acquisition in an attempt to resolve his bewilderment and spiritual agony. He learns Greek, Syriac, Hebrew, and Coptic: a diverse linguistic background that enables him to study pagan, Judaic, and Christian philosophies, logic traditions, and sciences. For example, Hypa speaks of his education in the neo-Platonic philosophy of Plotinus, which is believed to have influenced Christian thought, especially in the aspect of divine trinity. Hypa also studies medicine to alleviate other people's suffering, from a physical standpoint.

Armed with the knowledge he has acquired and the curiosity for more, Hypa leaves his hometown, Akhmim, to go to Alexandria as a young Christian ascetic aiming to improve his primitive education in medicine and physiology, but, more notably, quench his thirst for other types of human knowledge, especially that of the self through the encounter with the other.

Throughout his travels, Hypa demonstrates a cosmopolitan attitude towards the people he meets irrespective of their gender, language, lifestyle, or faith. There is a pattern that can be detected, in which Hypa creates human connections by means of sharing experiences of suffering. For example, while travelling up the course of the Nile to Alexandria, Egypt's central metropolis at that time, Hypa meets many other men, with whom he exchanges personal testimonies of persecution of early Coptic Christians. He relays a Coptic man's account of Alexandria, which, according to the man, used to banish poor Egyptians who professed the new faith, but has now opened its gates for them (Zaydan 2012a: 64). This functions as a historical reference to the decades in which Christianity was outlawed across the Roman Empire until Emperor Constantine Augustus I himself embraced the new monotheistic religion and declared tolerance of it across the empire under the Edict of Milan in 313 CE.[26] At the time of Hypa's visit, approximately one century later, the historic city was still home to a multitude of religious beliefs, pagan, Jewish, and Christian. The diversity opened Hypa's eyes to new ways of life and bodies of knowledge, as well as more human suffering. At the moment when Hypa enjoys feeling the winds of the vast Mediterranean Sea on his face, he meets Octavia, a Greek widow, whose husband was killed under the rubble of a Serapis temple. The Græco-Egyptian deity's temple was destroyed by a group of fundamentalist Christians while Octavia's husband was offering incense. Octavia and Hypa connect over sharing similarly painful experiences of losing loved ones due to religious intolerance. In like manner, when Hypa arrives at the monastery near Antioch and Aleppo, he connects with Marta, an Antiochian woman who lost her father after a group of Kurdish bandits murdered him. The emotional connection between Hypa and Octavia grows sexual, and so does that between him and Marta. The relations Hypa establishes with these women can be read as a means of his and their pursuit of healing through fulfilling a new-born love that may compensate for the ones lost. Furthermore, being a physician, Hypa reaches out to suffering others and medicates them indiscriminately. He treats Bishop Theodore of al-Missisa (Mopsuestia) during his visit to Jerusalem, the Arab merchant, and the poor people living nearby the monastery he settles in.

Between Alexandria and Antioch, Hypa stops in Jerusalem to visit Christian holy sites. There, he meets Nestorius, Bishop of Constantinople, and enjoys the sermons of Bishop Theodore of Mopsuestia. In their conversations, Hypa and Nestorius show that their yearning for knowledge is commensurate: they exchange opinions on major philosophical works, Plotinus's *The Enneads*, Arius's *The Thalia*, Ciceronian texts, Saint Augustine's *The City of God*, Bishop Theophilus of Alexandria's work on the Holy Family's trip to the land of Egypt, and other ancient Egyptian and Coptic Christian texts (Zaydan 2012a: 34–41). Their wide and versatile education in these different philosophical traditions, Christian and non-Christian, canonical and denounced, demonstrates their "critical" stance towards authoritative texts. Hypa, for example, reveals to Nestorius his possession of "*al-anājīl al-muḥarrama wa-l-kutub al-mamnūʿa*" (forbidden gospels and prohibited books, also known as Apocrypha) (ibid. p. 36), whereas Nestorius admires his ability to collect copies of such influential texts while living in the Egyptian South.

Hypa's retelling of the incident of his father's murder at the hands of Christian fanatics reveals Nestorius' compassionate character, but, more importantly, his understanding of the vicious cycle of religious intolerance. Nestorius explains to Hypa how early Christians' previous persecution by pagan Roman rulers had unfortunately created a legacy of oppression towards religiously different others. As soon as Christianity achieved validity and popularity across the empire, the few remaining adherents of pagan religions were correspondingly persecuted. Hypa writes:

I began to sob and Nestorius stood up and put his arm around me. I was cowering just as I did the first time, the time when he sat next to me, patted me on the head and made the sign of the cross several times on my brow. He kept repeating, "Calm down, my child." Then he said, "My child, our life is full of pain and sin. Those ignorant people wanted salvation on the old basis of oppression for oppression, and persecution for persecution, and you were the victim. I know your pain was great and I feel it. May the merciful Lord bestow on us His compassion. Arise, my child, and let us pray together the prayer of mercy." (ibid. p. 29)

Nestorius' words summarize the cumulative effect of religious intolerance and fanaticism, as he himself, ironically, becomes subjected to persecution from his contemporaries because of his different Christological thought.

Although Hypa and Nestorius come from two different places and backgrounds—Hypa is from Panopolis in South Egypt and Nestorius from Germanicia, Syria Euperatensis in Asia Minor—their shared intellectual and spiritual curiosity and nomadic lifestyle (evident in their departure from their birthplaces), as well as a mutual experience of suffering, connect them deeply on a human level. More notably, they share a "critical" stance towards religious tradition and canon in the way that their thorough education in Græco-Roman literature, known to have influenced Christian theologians (like Plotinus' works on Augustine of Hippo), allows them to go beyond prescribed religious texts and bodies of knowledge and question fixity of thought. Yet the conclusion of Nestorius' and Hypa's meeting with prayer suggests that they maintain principles of communion with their divinity, while holding a "posture of resistance" to human institutionalization of perception of the divinity.

Despite Hypa's thirst for knowledge and freedom from established religious authority, shown in his critical stance towards what is right and what is wrong, his writing demonstrates what Walkowitz describes as "ethos of uncertainty" (Walkowitz 2006: 5). Hypa admits to the "limits of self-knowledge" after what he has done and witnessed throughout his life. He wonders what really describes him: "I no longer know how exactly to describe myself? Am I a physician or a monk, consecrated or impenitent, Christian or Pagan?" (Zaydan 2012a: 279). Hypa's self-doubt and vulnerability are amalgamated when he refrains from fulfilling a request by Nestorius, in which Hypa was asked to deliver to Cyril I a letter written by Nestorius in defense of his perception of the nature of Christ. His decision not to be the messenger who delivers Nestorius' self-defense not only indicates his perennial hesitation, but is also a novelistic gesture that Hypa is not the typical hero who would turn around the course of history; Cyril's contestation of Nestorius' doctrine climaxed in the First Council of Ephesus, in 431 CE, in which Nestorius was ruled a heretic and sent into exile.

The Cosmopolitan Style of "Hesitation"

The style Zaydan uses to deliver the philosophy-, theology-, and humanity-laden content of the novel takes the shape of Hypa's self-articulation, which combines his being a doubtful thinker, a philosopher, a theologian, a physician, a poet, a monk, a traveler, and a human being. His style reflects this array of human knowledge and the many experiences Hypa underwent, but, at the same time, it demonstrates "the limits of self-knowledge," conflicts, and uncertainties. In a prayer to God, he discloses:

> You know that I obtained these scrolls many years ago, on the shores of the Dead Sea, to write on them my poems and my orations to You in my times of seclusion, that Your name may be glorified among those on earth, as it is in heaven. I had intended to record on them my supplications, which bring me nearer to You and which may after me become prayers recited by monks and godly hermits in all times and all places. Yet when the time came to make this record, I was about to write such things which had never before come to my mind and which could have led me to the ways of woe and evil. My Lord, do you hear me? (ibid. p. 5)

Hypa's original intention was to write poetry, prayers, reflections, and supplications, which are notably present in his writing, as a means of retreating into the self and becoming closer to the divine. For example, he composes church hymns such as the following:

> *This is where the light of Heaven appeared,*
> *Banished the dark from the face of the Earth and*
> *gave souls comfort against affliction.*

> *This is where the Sun of Hearts rose,*
> *With the radiance of the Saviour, shining with*
> *compassion on the Cross of Redemption.* (ibid. p. 15)[27]

Hypa also writes about the spiritual teaching he has received from notable theologians, like the sermon by Bishop Theodore of Mopsuestia, which he listened to at the Church of the Holy Sepulcher in Jerusalem. The sermon addresses the topics of original sin, salvation, and Christ's teachings in the Beatitudes.

In this respect, religious and spiritual content pervades Hypa's writing in his hymn compositions and spiritual edification content, but the diabolical muse, Azazeel, dismantles Hypa's goals and re-forms his self-expression into unconventional configurations of spiritual struggles and human relations. Thus, Hypa's style ranges from long descriptions of his encounters to reporting the exchanges between himself and other characters like Nestorius, Marta, and Azazeel in direct speech. He, on many occasions, reveals his suffering and his confusion in the form of long introspections, prayers, and supplications. Yet he does not eschew cursing Azazeel and his diabolical mission to expose his human vulnerabilities. In this sense, Hypa is not only the novel's main character, but also its writer and the first-person narrator of his autobiography. At the same time, the intervention of other voices like Azazeel's, Nestorius', Bishop Theodore's, Marta's, and Octavia's emphasizes Hypa's distance from any claim to authority, superiority, or god-like knowledge.

Akhir yahud al-iskandariyya—Muʿtazz Futayha

The events of *Akhir yahud al-iskandariyya* (2008) begin in 1999, when the main character, Yusuf Haddad, returns to Alexandria, his hometown, at the age of seventy, after nearly five decades of emigration. In a flashback style, the reader is transported in time to 1941, when Yusuf was a twelve-year-old, living in his affluent Jewish family's home in Alexandria. Centering upon Yusuf's life before emigration, the novel highlights the changes Yusuf's family undergoes during the socially and politically unstable time of World War II and after Egypt gained its independence from foreign colonial rule in 1952. The events are mainly set in Alexandria in the 1940s, to underline the remnants of a golden time of coexistence for the multitudes of Alexandrian inhabitants, who were characterized by racial, linguistic, and religious diversity. The novel, thus, is a throwback to the cosmopolitanism that used to set Alexandria apart from other living places around the Mediterranean basin and typify its image as indiscriminately embracing all who seek it as home. Romanticized though that time in the city sounds, historically, there is a justification for that idealized perception: the Egyptian government during the late nineteenth and early twentieth centuries (during the rule of Muhammad ᶜAli's Circassian dynasty) provided ample social, political, and economic facilities for foreigners to encourage them to live in and invest their wealth in Egypt. These favorable conditions for foreigners are also known as Capitulations. That, certainly, does not hide the fact that foreign pressure from Western imperial powers such as Britain also ensured that these favorable conditions were unfailingly enforced (Krämer 1989: 8).

What *Akhir yahud al-iskandriyya* does is, in a way, to invoke that idealized picture of Alexandria in order to distort or, rather, repaint it with the brush of reality. In other words, the novel aesthetically exhibits the disintegration of Alexandria's cosmopolitan image by reflecting that shattered image on two other levels of instability. The first is the transformations in Yusuf's life and the dispersal of his Jewish family, and the other is the socio-political transformations Alexandria undergoes during the anti-colonial, nationalist upheavals of the mid-twentieth century. The question that the coming analysis attempts to answer is whether *Akhir yahud al-iskandriyya*, by disintegrating the idealized image of cosmopolitan Alexandria and reflecting that fracture on socio-political levels, conjures up forms of "critical cosmopolitanism," which constitute, as demonstrated earlier in Walkowitz's view, "a new reflection about reflection" and "critique of critique" (Walkowitz 2006: 3). Situated at the peak of the social and political marginalization of Egyptian Jews and their consequent mass departure to different parts of the globe, Yusuf develops what W. E. B. Du Bois (2007: 8) calls "double consciousness,"[28] according to which he feels that he is both Egyptian and Jewish and that his being cannot be constrained by one identity or the other; however, exclusionary, nationalist discourses would not allow the combination of this "two-ness . . . two thoughts, two unreconciled strivings" (ibid.). At the same time, Yusuf's socio-political "powerlessness" inspires him to pursue alternative ways of understanding and articulating himself as well as the others he relates to, away from predominant systems of knowledge. Yusuf resorts to the art of filmmaking.

The Task of the Narrator

The story is told in the third-person narrative style by a god-like, omniscient narrator, who is able to enter the minds of all the characters, reveal their inner thoughts, and interpret their different languages and behaviors. Since the characters come from different linguistic and racial backgrounds, the narrator fulfills the task of translating these characters' voices and expressions into Arabic. Their tongues range from Egyptian Arabic, Hebrew, Yiddish, Czech, and Polish to Italian, Spanish, English, and French. At other times, the narrator delves into lengthy philosophical explanations of ideas or characters' activities that might be seen as peculiar or unconventional according to Egyptian cultural norms. For example, when Yusuf engages in gambling on race horses, the narrator digresses with a long explanation of the history of horse racing, its association with traditional Arab culture, and how its losses and gains parallel those of life (Futayha 2008: 276). In another event, the narrator comments on how millions of people in World War II sacrificed, or were forced to sacrifice, their lives in the name of an idea. He contests the idea of conflicts and wars erupting in pursuit of power or due to a difference woven in the imagination of each warring side (ibid. p. 233). Understanding the sensitivities of introducing culturally unacceptable activities or contesting popular ideas about nationalism, the narrator often resorts to using the addressee-pronoun ʾ*anta* (you) in order to establish familiarity with readers, and, thus, appeal to their perceptiveness in viewing other ways of life.

More importantly, given the novel's preoccupation with disrupting the stereotyped image of Jews—propagated by the establishment of the Israeli state, the Arab–Israeli wars, and the oppressive practices of the Israeli state against marginalized Palestinians—the narrator takes responsibility for elucidating the overlooked history of Jews in Egypt. Starting with biblical times, the narrator invokes the story of the Prophet Moses receiving the Ten Commandments in the desert of Sinai, but, at the same time, alludes to the legendary Jewish exoduses from and returns to Egypt after the Pharaohs sought their eradication for fear of their growing power (Exodus 12). Since then, the narrator observes, "the relationship [between Jews and Egypt] has undergone intermittent periods of mutual enmity and peace" (Futayah 2008: 50),[29] as demonstrated in the series of Jewish exoduses from and returns to Egypt from the Ptolemaic era to modern times. However, the narrator remarks that, during Arab-Muslim rule, Jews enjoyed freedom in practicing their faith and were "an original part of the fabric of Egyptian Society" (ibid. p. 51), pointing out the intersections of Jewish and Muslim histories. For example, the narrator recalls their mutual subjection to expulsion in the Middle Ages, when both populations were forced to flee from Muslim Andalusia during the Reconquista. The narrator recalls how, even during the French Campaign in Egypt (1798–1801), Napoleon Bonaparte's troops heedlessly raided the holy, historical sites of al-Azhar and Eliyahu Hanavi Synagogue (constructed in Alexandria in the fourteenth century) (ibid. p. 52). He concludes the historical introduction by discerning two communities of Jews in Alexandria, those who were Arabic-speaking and those who were not, leveraging historical facts concerning which Jewish groups settled in Alexandria, and at what time:[30] "The Jews of Alexandria were divided into two halves; a homegrown Egyptian half and a foreign one" (ibid. p. 51).

This historical account aims to acknowledge the place of Jews in Egyptian history and culture. At the same time, the narrator ventures into other histories of Jewish communities elsewhere in order to place Jews in a larger global context. The events, thus, do not unfold in one space or in linear time. They launch themselves in Alexandria in 1999, but the reader travels in time and space to Prague in 1938, for example, to return to 1999 in Alexandria and then, once more, go back in time to 1941 in Alexandria. In one of the narrative segments in 1938 Prague, the background of one of the characters, Barbora Samkova, who flees to Alexandria because of the Nazi persecution of Jews in Prague, is revealed. The narrator seizes the opportunity to shed light on Jewish communal history in Prague. Although the Jews there enjoyed stability in the seventeenth century, they were expelled in the 1740s by the Austrian Empress, Maria Theresa, and were later permitted return to only one spot, Josefov, the ancient Jewish quarter in the heart of the city. Meanwhile, the narrator vividly portrays the streets of Prague in 1938, the exquisite architecture of its buildings, the Rudolfinum Orchestra Hall, and the Vltava River and its multiple bridges. The accurate historical accounts of Jewish communities in Egypt and East Europe (besides Prague, the narrator draws attention to other Jewish experiences in Lublin, Poland, Germany, and the regions of Bohemia, Silesia, and Moravia) (ibid. pp. 76–8), as well as the narrator's meticulous spatial descriptions of Alexandria and Prague, are narrative devices that aim to solidify his credibility and all-knowingness. They invite readers to reflect on the experiences of the Egyptian Jewish community, not through the lens of current domestic and regional sectarian tension alone, but also as part of a larger whole of human experience of suffering due to religious persecution. Moreover, the restless movement of narrative time and space, with no expected pattern, functions as an aesthetic reflection of the unsettled movement of different Jewish populations in Europe and the Mediterranean world to places of safety.

Growing Tensions: Alexandria Then, Alexandria Now

Characters belonging to a variety of backgrounds from across the spectrum of difference—in religion, race, language, socio-economic status, and gender—are depicted in interaction with one another to affirm their shared humanity, but at the same time highlight conflicts arising among them because of changes in their socio-political atmosphere, especially after the break-out of World War II. For example, Hakim's close friends of over forty years—ʿAbd al-Jawwad Muhsin, a Muslim, ʿAdli Ghattas, a Christian, and Inzo, an Italian émigré who has lived in Egypt for over forty years—discuss freely their positions with regard to colonial resistance and the state's economic policy. ʿAbd al-Jawwad and Inzo disagree as to whether the extensive financial privileges, known as Capitulations, granted to foreign businessmen in Egypt should continue or cease. ʿAbd al-Jawwad wants them to cease, whereas Inzo thinks keeping them is essential for the success of foreign investment and Egypt's economy at large:

> [ʿAbd al-Jawwad]: You are right, *Khawāga*![31]
> [Inzo]: I am not a *Khawāga*; as I am a better Egyptian than you are.
> [ʿAbd al-Jawwad]: No, you are self-Egyptianized. Your country is trying to colonize Egypt so that it changes from being under British rule to Italian. (ibid. p. 97)

The debate indicates ʿAbd al-Jawwad's nationalist zeal and desire for complete Egyptian sovereignty and economic autonomy, whereas Inzo feels he is as Egyptian as ʿAbd al-Jawwad is and refuses to be called *khawāga*. The narrator's following comment shows sympathy towards Inzo's position: "If you spend more than forty years in a place during which time you share its people's concerns, rejoice with them in good times, and prove your complete loyalty; this place will become one thing in your heart; . . . home" (ibid.). The narrator here addresses the reader directly using "you" to prompt them to assume Inzo's immigrant position and answer the challenging question with regard to the immigrant's cultural belonging in a nationalist, exclusionary atmosphere.

At the beginning of events, the city of Alexandria is presented as an embodiment of the spirit of cosmopolitanism in an idealized respect: it embraces multi-religious, multi-racial, and multi-lingual communities with equal appreciation. Barbora expresses how safe and unthreatened she feels when she reveals her Jewish faith to people in Alexandria. During her family's escape-journey from pursuit by Nazi troops, Barbora's father, Novak, decides on a safe destination:

> "We are going to a faraway place where peace prevails and all religions are accepted." Bara replied with eagerness, "Are we going to paradise?"
> Novak answered smiling, "We are going to Alexandria." (ibid. p. 216)

Along with the paradisiacal depiction of Alexandria, the history of Yusuf's family seems laden with social and economic triumphs. The father, Hakim Bey Haddad, was born into the well-known Dawud family. His anticolonial activism during his young adulthood does not frighten his beloved's similarly wealthy family, the ʿIzras, from giving their daughter's hand to him in marriage. Hakim and his wife have their daughter Irina and their son Isaac happily, but the reel of happy events ends when the mother dies giving birth to their third child, Yusuf. The death of the mother, a protectress figure, foreshadows the future disintegration of her family and signals the difficulties they will have to endure in her absence. Hakim owns an upscale jewelry store, which Isaac also runs to carry on the family business. The father expects all his children to maintain the family legacy by marrying eligible Jewish Egyptians who should come from similarly affluent and conservative families.

After the novel has gradually conjured up a harmonious picture of the past affairs of the traditional Haddad family, it begins to dismantle that picture of the people and their city. For example, the family's first-born, Irina, after having lost her virginity in her young adult years, refuses to conform to traditional marriage guidelines despite the many eligible men who pursue her. She falls in love with a poor Spaniard named Augustine, who works at a modest job in al-Jamarik District, and elopes with him for fear of her family's fury. Isaac falls in love with and, later, marries Barbora, whose perennial homelessness is allegorically implicated in the meaning of her Latin name. At one of their first meetings, Barbora explains to Isaac that her name means "*al-ʾajnabiyya*" (the foreigner) (ibid. p. 125). Isaac's espousal of Zionist thought, given his wife's dream of a stable homeland for Jews, creates a situation that leads to his political detention by Egyptian government officials. The father, Hakim, dies shortly after the family are forced to leave their home and business behind and flee to Cairo for fear of Nazi troops advancing towards Alexandria and the looming threat of Jews being banished there. In short, things are falling apart.

Although the romantic picture of the harmonious communal past of Alexandria and the Haddad family is fractured by the realities of historical change, *Akhir yahud al-Iskandriyaa* reimagines that community in a novelistic manner that gestures reconciliation between conflicting individuals or groups. However, such reconciliation seems to be attainable only by subverting cultural norms and breaking with tradition. For example, the love relationship between affluent Irina, the Jew, and poor Augustine, the Spanish Christian, allegorizes reconciliation not only between their disparate socio-economic statuses, but also between the two ethno-religious groups with which the two are historically associated.[32] Similarly, Jamal, Yusuf's best friend, belongs to an upper-class Muslim family, and yet marries the daughter of his father's personal tailor, Antonella, despite his father's threats to disown him (ibid. p. 239). While reconciliation of differences is achieved either by marriage (in Jamal and Antonella's case) or by mutual love and sexual fusion (in Irina and Augustine's relationship), it is denied to Yusuf and the love of his life, Sara, who comes from a similarly wealthy and conservative upper-class family. The denial of their love and fulfillment metaphorizes the insurmountable differences growing between Yusuf's and Sara's communities.

The moment Yusuf and Sara express their love for one another occurs at the cinema, while they are watching a movie together. Moved by the artistry of the film, Yusuf realizes how much he loves Sara, and the then untraditional art form of film. When two worlds of romance—Yusuf's and Sara's, and the one in the black-and-white movie—merge, Yusuf's world becomes a whole, sensible configuration. The narrator comments on Yusuf's fascination with the many creative aspects of the movie:

> Yusuf felt complete joy. He was taken by the image. The music was pleasant and the costumes were wonderful. The city where the film events take place, like "Alexandria," enjoys the presence of different people with multiple nationalities . . . Yusuf was surprised by the protagonist's reply to a question about his nationality. Rick [the actor] said that he was a drunkard, and was thus identified as a global citizen. (ibid. pp. 254–5)

Yusuf's emotional reaction to the movie is encapsulated in Walter Benjamin's description of the wider array of aesthetic impressions that the art of film delivers when compared to other traditional forms of art:

> For the entire spectrum of optical, and now also acoustical, perception the film has brought about a similar deepening of appreciation. It is only an obverse of this fact that behaviour items shown in a movie can be analysed much more precisely and from more points of view than those presented on paintings or on the stage. As compared with painting, filmed behaviour lends itself more readily to analysis because of its incomparably more precise statements of the situation. (Benjamin [1968] 2000: 235–6)[33]

Yusuf's appreciation of the image, the music, the costumes, and the urban setting emanates from the film's ability to capture the ordinary state of the place, its people, and their unheroic behavior. He sees not only a true reflection of the Alexandria he knows in the setting of the movie, but also a true reflection of himself in the actor's free spirit and vagrant attitude.

Eventually, Yusuf and Sara are forced to separate due to religious difference. Sara's family arranges her marriage to the more eligible suitor—at least from the cultural standpoint: her cousin ʿAsim, an established military officer. Sara's family's inclination towards marrying their daughter to a blood relative and a military officer allegorizes the national trend that placed hope for national stability in the Egyptian military. Yusuf decides to rebel against cultural norms and his father's conservative career expectations by expressing his forbidden love for Sara in the then frowned-upon art of film. Yusuf captures his restless spirit and consciousness of difference in a film he produces, *The Occupation Is Different*. However, shortly after its being shown to the public, Yusuf is forced to leave Alexandria. The narrator comments:

> His first film, entitled *The Occupation Is Different*, was acclaimed by audience and critics alike, but he had to leave Alexandria shortly after the first showing. After his artistic effort to convey his dreams to people, Yusuf becomes a mere parenthesis, dispensable . . . After all, he is not guilty of anything; he did not attempt to bomb a place or kill someone . . . The nation's political priorities do not include his dreams. Even the decision to force him to depart from the only place he knew for a crime he did not commit . . . This is life. It gets closer and closer to you until you embrace it, wrap your arms around it, feel it in your chest. Then, you close your eyes from ecstasy only to open them later and find a mirage; nothing but dreams inside you that do not mean much to others. (Futayha 2008: 329–30)

Although Yusuf's film receives public recognition and cultural appreciation, the newly independent state seems to turn a blind eye to its artistic value, as its policies force its maker to depart from Alexandria. The narrator's comment is suffused with emotion, as shown in the incomplete utterance "Even the decision of forcing him to depart the only place he knew for a crime he did not commit . . ." and the existential statement "This is life." The narrator's fragmented expressions signify his inability to explain Yusuf's departure via the logical principle of cause and effect. Nonetheless, the novel proposes hope after Yusuf returns to Alexandria in 1999 to meet with Sara and with his best friend from schooldays, Jamal. The narrator describes Sara as living alone and eager to meet Yusuf after fifty years of separation. The novel thus casts doubt on the couple's endless separation and gestures towards them resuming the human connection they established a long time ago.

By foregrounding ethno-religious minority histories and experiences, *Azazeel* and *Akhir yahud al-iskandriyya* challenge familiar and conventional approaches to Egyptian society and culture. Not only do the novels highlight these minorities' experiences in Egypt, they also shed light on them in a global context. This beyond-the-nation literary reflection evinces the decentered consciousness *Azazeel* and *Akhir yahud al-iskandriayya* conjure up, which is also clearly exhibited in the in-depth research and knowledge their authors strove for in painting Coptic and Jewish historical and cultural particularities. Moreover, what makes these works stand out among those of their contemporaries is that they manage to place Coptic and Jewish experiences within larger, whole, all-too-familiar, fallible human experience in contexts of conflict over power. The novels speak to rising exclusionary nationalisms and puritanical isolationism on the basis of religion—whether practiced in a historical imperial or a modern nationalist context. The novels' attempts to conjure up different pictures of Egyptian society are focalized in Alexandria, a city known for its cosmopolitanism. However, the novels invoke that Alexandrine idea only to disrupt it by rebuilding an Alexandria from the perspective of its inhabitants and visitors. While the city is historically perceived as a spatial entity that metaphorically had its arms wide open for all who seek it for a home, *Azazeel* and *Akhir yahud al-iskandriyya* disclose the city's social, cultural, and political instabilities. They mirror the city's tumult in its fictional inhabitants' uncertainties, conflict, and vagrancy. At the same time, the invocation of Alexandria's idealized past functions as a novelistic rehabilitating device, via which its suffering fictional inhabitants are enabled to criticize and subvert the fixed thought and the predominating bodies of knowledge that eclipse the city's past glory and undermine their all-too-human experiences.

Notes

1. Beinin, Joel, "Egyptian Jewish Identities: Communitarianisms, Nationalisms, Nostalgias," *Contested Polities: Stanford Humanities Review (SEHR)*, Vol. 5, Issue 1 (February 1996), <http://web.stanford.edu/group/SHR/5-1/text/beinin.html> (last accessed 15 September 2016).
2. The novel has also been translated into many languages, including English, Italian, Czech, German, and Croatian.
3. It is worth noting here that the scale of reprints among publishers in Egypt is modest. Reprints do not usually exceed 1000 copies whether the publisher is state-run or private. Smaller publishers may even print fewer copies per edition, usually between 200 and 500.
4. Futayaha's venture into screenwriting came in a film titled *Regatta* (2015), starring Ilham Shahin and Mahmud Humayda and directed by Muhammad Sami.

The film, which focuses on socio-political marginalization of the poor, did not succeed commercially and was attacked by conservative cultural circles for its explicit content. A court order sentenced the film's producer, Rana al-Subki, to one year's imprisonment and gave her a 10 000 LE fine. For more details see Khalid Faraj's report in the *Al-Watan* newspaper, "Muʿtazz Futayha baʿd al-hukm bi-habs Rana al-Subki: Man yarfaʿ hadhihi al-nawʿiyya min al-qadaya 'tufayliyyat,'" *Al-Watan* (20 January 2016), <http://www.elwatannews.com/news/details/927658> (last accessed 19 September 2016).

5. Bayyumi, ʿAmr, "Muʾallif Riwayat *Azazeel* yuʾakkid anna waqaʾiʿaha haqiqiyya . . . wa yutalib al-ʾnba Bishuy biʾiʿadit qiraʾtiha," *Al-Masri al-Yawm* online (26 July 2008), <http://today.almasryalyoum.com/article2.aspx?ArticleID=114789> (last accessed 15 September 2016).

6. ʿAbd al-ʿAlim, Dina, "Muʿtazz Futaya: yahud ma qabl al-thawra lisu khawana" (Muʿtazz Futayha: The Jews from the pre-revolution period are not traitors,) *Al-Yawm al-Sabiʿ* (3 August 2009), <http://www.youm7.com/story/2009/8/3/124053/معتز-فتيحة-يهود-ما-قبل-الثورة-ليسوا-خونة> (last accessed 15 September 2016).

7. Walkowitz, Rebecca L., *Cosmopolitan Style: Modernism Beyond the Nation* (New York: Columbia University Press, 2006).

8. Krämer, Gudrun, *The Jews in Modern Egypt: 1914–1952* (London: I. B. Tauris, 1989).

9. El-Shobaki, Amr, "Ending Sectarianism in Egypt," *Egypt Independent* (14 January 2011), <http://www.egyptindependent.com/opinion/ending-sectarianism-egypt> (last accessed 16 September 2016).

10. All translations from Zaydan's Arabic article are my own.

11. Zaydan, Yusuf, "al-Asʾila al-taʾsisiyya: hal taqum bi-misr dawla diniyya?" (Foundational Questions: Will a Religious State Be Held in Egypt?), *Al-Masri al-yawm* (22 May 2012), <http://www.almasryalyoum.com/news/details/220371> (last accessed 16 September 2016).

12. In an article published in *al-Masri al-Yawm* about *Akhir yahud al-iskandariyya*, Futayha explains that he resorted to 130 sources—most of which are in English and concern Jewish experiences in Europe and across the globe—to inform his story writing. Among these, Futayha says, are books written by French Jewish thinkers who lived in Egypt in the first half of the twentieth century, as well as ʿAbd al-Wahab al-Misiri's book *Man hum al-yahud? Wa ma hiya al-yahudiyya? Asʾilat al-huwiyya wa azmat al-dawla al-yahudiyya* (translated as "Who are the Jews? And what is Judaism? Questions on identity and the crisis of the

Jewish state"). For the whole article, see ᶜAlya Tamraz's "Nashir 'Akhir yahud al-Iskandariyya:' 'hasasiyyat al-mawduᶜ' awqafat tahwil al-riwaya ila film," *Al-Masri al-Yawm* (19 October 2010), <http://www.almasryalyoum.com/news/details/91436> (last accessed 6 June 2017).

13. It is worth noting here that the secondary sources that address the production or creativity of *Akhir yahud al-Iskandariyya* are sparse, if not nonexistent. While I made use of the available interviews with its author and some available reviews, I also tried to contact Mr Futayha for an interview about his novel, but without success.
14. Appiah, Kwame, *Cosmopolitanism: Ethics in a World of Strangers* (New York: Norton, 2006).
15. East, Ben, "Award-winning Book from Youssef Ziedan Gets Translated into English," *The National* (26 March 2012), <http://www.thenational.ae/arts-culture/books/award-winning-book-from-youssef-ziedan-gets-translated-into-english> (last accessed 30 July 2012).
16. Wilken, Robert L., "Tradition, Exegesis, and the Christological Controversies," *Church History*, Vol. 34, No. 2, June 1965, pp. 123–45.
17. Latourette, Kenneth Scott, *A History of Christianity Volume 1: To A.D. 1500*, rev. edn, foreword by Ralph D. Winter (New York: Harper San Francisco, 1975).
18. Wills, Garry, "The Trials of an Unquiet Heart," *New Statesman*, Vol. 140, 18 April 2011, pp. 24–7.
19. The University of Alabama website provides a description of the significance and historical background of Syriac:

> Syriac is a dialect of Aramaic that originally developed in the kingdom of Edessa (modern Urfa in Turkey), beginning approximately in the first century of the common era. A Semitic language with its own script, Syriac flourished as a literary language in both the Sassanian (Persian) and Roman Empires. Texts in Syriac comprise the third largest surviving corpus of literature (after Greek and Latin) from the period of Late Antiquity (circa fourth through seventh centuries C.E.). As one of several dialects of Aramaic, Syriac also served as a *lingua franca* enabling both commerce and religious missionary activity across political boundaries. (Excerpt from University of Alabama: Syriac Research Group. "What is Syriac?," 16 November 2011, <http://syriac.ua.edu/about.html> [last accessed 15 September 2016])

20. Al-Ruha is located north east of Syria in what is now Urfa in Turkey.

21. Zaydan, Yusuf, *Azazeel*, trans. Jonathan Wright (London: Atlantic Books, 2012).
22. Nestorian teachings found its way "among [Christian] minorities scattered across Asia from Mesopotamia into India and to the China Sea" between 950 and 1350 CE (Latourette 1975: 564).
23. Helm, Robert, "Azazel in Early Jewish Tradition," *Andrews University Seminary Studies Journal, Online Archive*, Vol. 32. No. 3, Autumn 1994, pp. 217–26.
24. "Azazel," *Encyclopædia Britannica Online* (31 July 2012), <http://www.britannica.com/EBchecked/topic/46745/Azazel> (last accessed 15 September 2016).
25. Rudwin, Maximilian, "The Devil in Literature," *The Open Court*, Vol. 45, No. 896, January 1931, pp. 56–64, University of Southern Illinois Open Library website, <http://opensiuc.lib.siu.edu/cgi/viewcontent.cgi?article=4352&context=ocj> (last accessed 21 September 2016).
26. For more details see Paul Halsall's "Galerius and Constantine: Edicts of Toleration 311/313," *Internet Medieval Sourcebook*, Fordham University Center for Medieval Studies website, <http://sourcebooks.fordham.edu/halsall/source/edict-milan.asp> (last accessed 22 September 2016).
27. The italics are in the original English translation by Jonathan Wright.
28. Du Bois, W. E. B., *The Souls of Black Folk*, ed. Brent Hayes Edwards (New York: Oxford University Press, 2005).
29. All English translations from the Arabic of *Akhir yahud al-iskandariyya* are my own.
30. Gudrun Krämer (1989) examines the communal structure of Egyptian Jewry and the socio-economic conditions that surrounded their lives in Egypt. She lists different Jewish communities that settled in Egypt in the nineteenth and the first half of the twentieth century as Sephardis from the Ottoman Empire, Greece, the Balkans, Corfu, and Italy; Orientals from North Africa; Jews from Yemen and Aden; and Ashkenazi Jews from Russia, Rumania, and Poland (11).
31. "Khawāga" is an othering term used to refer to foreigners in Egyptian Colloquial Arabic.
32. The latter group was persecuted at the hands of the former in the fifteenth century.
33. Benjamin, Walter, "The Work of Art in the Age of Mechanical Reproduction," in Hannah Arendt (ed.), *Illuminations*, trans. Harry Zohn (New York: Brace & World, 1968).

3

The Irrecuperable Heterogeneity of the Present in ᶜAlaᵓ al-Aswani's *The Yacoubian Building* and *Chicago*

The books *ᶜImarat yaᶜqubiyan*, 2002 (*The Yacoubian Building*, 2006) and *Shikagu*, 2007 (*Chicago*, 2007), by the Egyptian writer ᶜAlaᵓ al-Aswani (b. 1957), constitute two complementary parts of a whole picture of contemporary Egyptians. Set in downtown Cairo at the end of the twentieth century, *The Yacoubian Building* gradually and carefully uncovers the layers of the social, political, and cultural instabilities within Egyptian society. *Chicago* contextualizes these instabilities and rising tensions among Egyptians as well as with nonnative others in a contemporary setting of migration to the West, Chicago. The two novels search exhaustively for truth and virtue amid prevalent conditions of despair and moral corruption, by depicting a plethora of life quests undertaken by the diverse pool of their characters. Both novels illustrate how their characters' life trajectories are circumstantiated by their class, race, religious and national affiliations, sexual orientation, and gender. Although the novels divulge so openly and unrestrictedly in disclosing an array of intense conflicts among the different fictional characters, their proposals for the reconciliation of differences vary. On the one hand, one proposed change in *The Yacoubian Building* is merely reconciliation between the two different classes and subcultures from which Zaki and Busayna emerge. That is to say, the book suggests a restructuring of the social order through Zaki and Busayna's traditional marriage at its end. *Chicago*, on the other, suggests a revolutionary change in the political domain when its characters—all from different backgrounds—collaborate to oust the Egyptian president from office. The proposed political overhaul, however, is set in a migrant, non-local setting, and eventually fails.

The nuances in these two novels, when they are read together, lie primarily in their compelling, encyclopedic representation of issues of difference and asymmetries of power on two levels, the domestic and the public as well as the local (Cairo) and global (Chicago), all during a time of growing essentialist perceptions of the self and the other. While *The Yacoubian Building* captures the problems of inequalities in the Egyptian postcolonial state, *Chicago* unravels them in a Western metropolis setting, in order to evidence the ineradicable connections between global margins and centers in contemporary times. The following analysis demonstrates how al-Aswani constructs his fictional worlds aesthetically with an unrelenting commitment to reality, observable to readers who are familiar with the spatial landmarks and social particularities of either Cairo or Chicago. However, the unprecedentedly overt treatment of sensitive cultural and social issues like sex, alcohol consumption, women's subordination, and homosexuality has stirred controversy and aroused criticism in both literary and cultural circles.

It is important to note how al-Aswani's works, especially *The Yacoubian Building*, were received with considerable attention by public and literary critics alike.[1] First published in 2002, *The Yacoubian Building* accorded al-Aswani "celebrity" status after it became the "world's best selling novel in the Arabic language"[2] for five consecutive years, at the end of which time *Chicago* was published. As the novels were translated into numerous languages, they stirred controversy in different circles, most notably in Egypt and the West, where al-Aswani's lay-it-bare approach to reality (also deployed by other contemporary Egyptian authors such as Nawal al-Saʿdawi) was seen either as "courageous" in treating "pressing issues" in Egyptian society (Allen 2009: 11)[3] or as confirming and perpetuating stereotypical perceptions of socio-political problems in Egypt and the Arab-Muslim world at large (Ismail 2015: 918).[4] Roger Allen reflects on the phenomenon of best-sellers in Arabic novels and observes the evaluation challenge it constitutes for literary critics when reading them (Allen 2009: 9), whereas Sherif H. Ismail relays the marketability of these works' translations in the West to a context which seeks to validate the recent declaration of "war on terror" by Western powers (Ismail 2015: 917). It is not my concern here to examine questions of popularity, reception, and local or global marketability; however, it is highly beneficial to look into what Allen refers to as a trend in contemporary, best-seller Arabic fiction, to which *The Yacoubian Building* and, to the same extent, *Chicago* belong. The trend, Allen observes, avoids the "ambiguity, uncertainty, and stylistic and generic complexity that is characteristic of much recent novelistic production in Arabic, and at the hands of writers as varied as Ilyas Khuri, Ibrahim Nasrallah, and Ibrahim al-Kuni (to name just a few)" (Allen 2009: 10). Moreover, Allen remarks another similar view of the trend as a "return to 'traditional,' pre-(post)modernist modes of writing critical realism, simple chronologies, non-fragmentation, omniscient narrators" (Stephan Guth, quoted in Allen 2009: 10). The questions to pose here are: what does the trend of "return to 'traditional' . . . modes of writing critical realism" entail for the evaluation of realist contemporary novels like *The Yacoubian Building* and *Chicago*? Does the realistic method reduce the novels' aesthetic value when compared to the more complex and ambiguous "postmodernist" technique? These questions invite us to explore the realist aesthetic adopted by al-Aswani and what he attempts to achieve with it in his two novels.

George Levine explains first that "the word 'realism' is . . . not dead," adding that "'realism' seems to be a term from which there is no escaping in discussions of fiction" in both literary traditions and innovations (Levine 1996: 235).[5] Realism, nonetheless, is an "elusive" term because of its relationality to reality, which is, in its turn, variable and constantly changing in the view of human consciousness (ibid. p. 236):

> Writers and critics return to "realism," from generation to generation, because each culture's perception of reality changes and because literature requires ever new means to intimate the reality . . . to avoid the inevitable conventionality of language in pursuit of the unattainable mediated reality. Realism, as a literary method, can in these terms be defined as a self-conscious effort, usually in the name of some moral enterprise of truth and extending the limits of human sympathy, to make literature appear to be describing directly not some other language but reality itself (whatever that may be taken to be); in this effort, the writer must self-contradictorily dismiss previous conventions of representation while, in effect, establishing new ones. (Levine [1981] 2000: 617)[6]

In light of Levine's explanation of realism as a literary method, writers like al-Aswani, no matter at what place or time they may be, are faced with the challenge of re-structuring language, as the medium of fiction, and of creating new meanings while giving the illusion of writing about an experience that is all too familiar and realistic to their readers. Since language is laden with prescribed historical and cultural views and values, novelistic reconfigurations of language are necessary for writers in order for them to offer new possibilities and versions of experience and reality. In this respect, I argue that while al-Aswani's *The Yacoubian Building* and *Chicago* seem to represent a "return" to a realist tradition of writing, they actually draw on their immediate reality, their "here and now," and the writer's imagination, consciousness, and novelistic goals. Jamal al-Ghitani observes that the significance of *The Yacoubian Building* (and, by extension, *Chicago*) is that they "pump new blood in the arteries of realism, which is subsiding in the face of predominant [literary] currents that focus on the self" (al-Ghitani 2005: 351).[7] The novels, thus, work their "here and now" out in their innovative form, verbal structures, characterization, and spatial and temporal devices to convey new visions of what reality is or ought to be. In the analysis to follow, I will demonstrate how the reality captured in these two novels not only exposes—to criticize—the inequalities and persistent power asymmetries among Egyptians due to differences in socio-economic status, gender, sexual orientation, religion, and race, but also destabilizes these established power relations in their novelistic forms.

The Yacoubian Building—ᶜAlaᵓ al-Aswani

The events in *The Yacoubian Building* relate to the changing socio-economic and political affairs in contemporary Egypt. In order to vividly illustrate these changes, the omniscient narrator, with an exceptional ability to transcend time, juxtaposes three different periods in Egypt's recent history: the 1930s, the 1960s, and the 1990s. The 1930s mark the period Egypt was under the *ancien régime* and foreign colonial rule, whereas the 1960s highlight the power shift to the military after military leaders assumed political control of the newly independent state. The 1990s, when the majority of events unfold, mark the atrocious socio-economic conditions resulting from nearly two decades of the state's unwise application of free-market economics, by which only a privileged class of beneficiaries could enjoy these economic policies and amass the country's wealth. As the novel makes a claim to the material world, downtown Cairo—Egypt's preeminent business district and parameter of its economic strength—is selected for its spatial setting. The author's particular choice of a real downtown landmark named the Yaᶜqubiyan Building on Talᶜat Harb Street (previously Sulayman Pasha Street) stems from his familiarity with downtown, both as a resident and as a professional: besides being a writer, al-Aswani is a dentist and owns a practice in Cairo's city center. Al-Aswani's immersion in the particularities of downtown, its streets, vendors, businesses, and buildings, has provided him with a reservoir of lifetime experiences, his and those of the people he met there, with which to construct his fictional world of the Yaᶜqubiyan Building (al-Aswani, quoted in al-Hufi 2006).[8]

The narrator explains that the building is named after its original owner, Hagop Yaᶜqubiyan, the multi-millionaire investor and doyen of the Armenian community in Egypt in the 1930s. The narrator sets what seems like a quiet, orderly past of the Yaᶜqubiyan Building against its chaotic present. In the snapshot of the building's past, readers know that "[t]he cream of the society of those days took up residence in the Yacoubian Building—ministers, big land-owning bashas [pashas], foreign manufacturers, and two Jewish millionaires (one of them belonging to the famous Mosseri family)" (al-Aswani 2006a: 11).[9] That painted picture is of class harmony among the 1930s inhabitants, who, despite their multi-ethno-religious and multi-national background, shared being at the top of Egypt's socio-economic order.

The narrator presents a brief account of a subsequent period, the 1960s, during which the Yaᶜqubiyan Building remained seemingly unchanged from the outside, but its affluent residents, mentioned above, who used to occupy the center of the social, economic, and political arenas, were forced to evacuate it. This happened after military officers took political control of the country and abolished the economic privileges given to foreign business owners, also known as the Capitulation system. The military officers, who led the 1952 revolution and the whole country to independence from foreign rule, nationalized the Egyptian economy and rose up in the social order as the new powerful, ruling class. This political and class reshuffle is reflected in the high-ranking officers seizing the vacant apartments in the Yaᶜqubiyan Building. At the same time, a new class surfaced in Cairo and consisted mainly of poor peasants who migrated to Cairo from Egypt's rural areas to take small jobs, like serving in the military officers' households. Ironically, these rural migrants were also granted a space in the Yaᶜqubiyan Building, the rooftop storage rooms that are made of steel (ibid. p. 13). What was created for storage by the owner was inhumanely used by the military families to accommodate their poor household servants. This accommodation can be interpreted in two ways. First, it functions as a castigatory remark for the new state leaders who launched the 1952 revolution in the name of giving justice to and liberating the "*fallaḥ*" (peasant) from feudal exploitation (Selim 2004: 2).[10] In her study of the novelistic representations of Egyptian peasantry, Samah Selim explains how the image and name of the "*fallaḥ*" (peasant) became the catalyst for mobilizing anti-colonial, nationalist, and reform movements in the late nineteenth and twentieth centuries. Egyptian peasants, in their turn, became aware of their significance as Egypt's modern social and economic forces and thus migrated to Cairo looking for opportunities (ibid. p. 2).[11] Second, the accommodation of poor migrant peasants, who occupy the lowest position in the social hierarchy, on the building's rooftop can be read as an ironic repositioning of their class.

Vista Display of Cairo and Cairenes

In the late 1990s, which is the narrative present, readers are introduced to a third wave of residents, who have already been settled in the Yaᶜqubiyan Building. These residents represent the urban demographic of present-time Cairo, and include the new wealthy and powerful class of business owners which emerged after the state has adopted free-market economic policies for nearly two decades. Now, readers are introduced to the novel's plethora of characters, who come from diverse backgrounds: socio-economic, religious, and ethnic. Diverse characterization, therefore, constitutes a significant structural instrument that enables the author to present these characters' disparate human experiences in *The Yacoubian Building*. Given the characters' complex differences, each of their life quests unfolds in its own subplot and narrative time, which are not presented by the narrator in a single, uninterrupted storyline. Each life experience unfolds over a number of subsections, and the subsections do not follow any orderly sequence, so that attempts to hierarchize the multiple characters' life quests are disrupted. Even though the characters share the space of the urban Yaᶜqubiyan Building, it is vertically layered in a way that makes their private spaces separated and, at once, connected and overlapping. This spatial device performs an essential function in presenting these seemingly disjoined individuals as sharing a common space and thereby possibly interacting, negotiating their differences, and even transcending the boundaries of the current social order that falsely separates them. In the following part, I examine the individual experiences of the diverse residents of the Yaʿqubiyan Building and explore how their lives intersect.

There is no main character per se in *The Yacoubian Building*. Rather, each character—whether they are residents of the building apartments or its rooftop iron rooms—is sketched in adequate narrative time and space. Hagg Azzam, for example, is one of the latest residents, whose former life the narrator describes as follows:

> [He] started out thirty years ago as a mere migrant worker who left Sohag governorate for Cairo looking for work . . . then disappeared for more than twenty years, suddenly to reappear having made a lot of money. Hagg Azzam[12] says that he was working in the Gulf, but the people in the street do not believe that and whisper that he was sentenced and imprisoned for dealing in drugs, which some insist he continues to do to this day, citing as evidence his exorbitant wealth, which is out of all proportion to the volume of sales in his stores and the profits of his companies, indicating that his commercial activities are a mere front for money laundering . . . while his influence has been consolidated recently by his joining the Patriotic Party[13] and by his youngest son Hamdi subsequently joining the judiciary as a public prosecutor. (ibid. p. 50)

Azzam is a member of the new wealthy class. However, the narrator implies that his wealth may have been accumulated through drug dealing and immoral economic practices. Azzam becomes a member of the ruling Patriotic Party and bribes its corrupt secretary general to win a seat at the People's Assembly. Ironically, his son is a public prosecutor who helps his father in the bribery deal. Through Azzam's narrative, al-Aswani captures an obscure political situation in Egypt through the hypocrisy of these politician characters. Azzam undoubtedly lacks the political transparency that would allow him to faithfully represent the opinions and concerns of the people of the central Cairene district he represents. He is also portrayed as an uneducated man who conceals his polygyny because it could ruin his public image as a modern politician.

Hatim is one of the old-time rich individuals whose family was part of the pre-revolution bourgeoisie. He was born and raised in the Yaᶜqubiyan Building, and continues to live in his parents' apartment after their death. His father was an Egyptian university professor and his mother was French. Hatim's distinct education and fluency in French, Arabic, and a few other European languages earn him the position of editor-in-chief of *Le Caire*, a French-language newspaper that was first issued one hundred years ago for the considerable French-speaking population that existed at the time in Cairo. Hatim's job as a journalist should enable him to participate in the public sphere and discuss an array of concerns and opinions raised by different groups in Egypt. Nonetheless, Hatim is socially isolated, due to his sexual orientation. He is unable to publicly reveal his homosexuality due to its lack of accordance with the predominant religious norms and social conventions. The foreignness of the print language of Hatim's newspaper and the inability of the majority of the Egyptian people to understand it symbolically correspond with the strangeness of Hatim's life from the conservative cultural perspective in Egypt.

Hatim is agonized and tormented by suppression and isolation. The narrator describes the intimacy of the homosexual relationship between Hatim and Abd Rabbuh, the Nubian conscript who lives in one of the building's iron rooms, on two different occasions as his "sinful desire" (ibid. p. 76) and "deliciously selfish craving" (ibid. p. 131). The description of their relationship as "ʾāthima" (al-Aswani 2006b: 108),[14] which is translated as "sinful" (al-Aswani 2006a: 76), implies a condemnatory cultural attitude towards homosexuality. The relationship between Hatim and Abd Rabbuh is governed by their sexual attraction and, at the same time, their religious, racial, and class differences. Affluent Hatim is described as having "fine French features" (ibid. p. 38), which he probably inherited from his French mother. Abd Rabbuh is portrayed as a poor "dark-complexioned young man" (ibid. p. 37) from Upper Egypt, who migrated with his wife and infant child to Cairo to complete his military service. While Hatim is often overcome with feelings of misery and loneliness due to his inability to fulfill his love and sexual desires, Abd Rabbuh feels torn between his sexual attraction to

Hatim and his religious beliefs, which prohibit the practice of homosexuality and urge marital faithfulness. Abd Rabbuh's and Hatim's encounters are erotic and filled with temptation, power conflict, and resistance. When Abd Rabbuh's son dies, he believes his death is a punishment from God and ends his relationship with Hatim, who desperately tries to win him back by offering him money and a job. Under pressure, Abd Rabbuh violently attacks Hatim until, the narrator describes, Hatim's blood is shed (al-Aswani 2006b: 334). The failure of Hatim and Abd Rabbuh's relationship metaphorizes the irresolvable discord between their religious, racial, and class backgrounds, on the one hand, and, on the other, their suppression by the conservative cultural and religious systems under which they live.

As is demonstrated in the analysis of the subplot of Hatim and Abd Rabbuh's story, the narrator can be described as an anonymous person who closely observes and, at times, comments on the behaviors and private lives of the different characters in the novel. He demonstrates an extraordinary ability to penetrate the most intimate thoughts and activities of these characters, whether they conform to societal standards or not. However, his description of Hatim and Abd Rabbuh's sexual life as "sinful" can be read as chastising rather than sympathizing, and thereby as heeding restrictive cultural norms on homosexuality. At the same time, the powerful illustration of Hatim's and Abd Rabbuh's agony and suffering due to their cultural alienation elicits readers' empathy. This narrative attitude urges readers to evaluate and respond to the narrator's observations and, thus, participate in the negotiations between predominant, suppressive cultural norms and homosexuals' rights and personal freedoms.

Zaki comes from an aristocratic family, whose background justifies his estrangement after the revolution. His father, ʿAbd al-ʿAl Pasha (Abd el Aal Basha) was a former state minister and a leading figure in the liberal Wafd party before the revolution. According to the narrator, the father sent Zaki to France to get a degree in engineering and was grooming him to hold a leading position in the same political party. However, the father was politically detained by the revolutionary regime, and his wealth was also confiscated. Zaki uses his father's apartment in the Yaʿqubiyan Building as an obscure engineering office, which turned gradually into a place for casual meetings with his friends and for having affairs with women. As a former aristocrat,

Zaki suffers cultural and political estrangement, but is portrayed as seeking love and fulfillment in the warmth of human relationships.

The narrator juxtaposes the past and the present one more time, when he compares politicians' attitudes and self-conduct before and after the 1952 revolution. On the surface, the two groups seem different, but, as my analysis demonstrates, both groups are similarly exclusionary and not keen on the interests of the Egyptian people they represent. In a meeting at the Sheraton's "kebab restaurant" (al-Aswani 2006a: 144), postcolonial state politician Kamal el Fuli—the corrupt secretary of the ruling Patriotic Party—finalizes a bribery transaction with Azzam, who has just won a seat in the parliament thanks to al-Fuli's assistance with voting fraud. The narrator, at that moment, reminisces about the meetings of aristocratic politicians in the pre-revolution period. He describes their meetings at the downtown Automobile Club for evening socials, in which they drank whisky and played bridge and poker. Their wives accompanied them, wearing revealing evening dresses. The narrator explains that their lifestyle was influenced by their Western education and liberal ideals. After the revolution, the narrator comments:

> The great men of the present era, however, with their largely plebeian origins, their stern adherence to the outward forms of religion, and their voracious appetite for good food, find the Sheraton's kebab restaurant suits them, since they can eat the best kinds of kebab, kofta, and stuffed vegetables and then drink cups of tea and smoke molasses-soaked tobacco in the waterpipes that the restaurant's management has introduced in response to their requests. And during all the eating, drinking, and smoking, the talk of money and business never ceases. (ibid. p. 145)

The description of the current political scene explains the changing social and cultural ethics of the ruling elite. Before the revolution, politicians valued Western ideals as they envisioned themselves in a secular, modern state. Their space was exclusive and their cultural habits were neither diverse nor relevant to those of the destitute majority of Egyptian people. In the post-revolution era, the ruling elite establish a new, and also exclusive, space of their own, where women are not admitted at all, even as spouses, not to mention politicians. Unlike the pre-revolution elite, their present counterparts do not drink alcohol or play bridge. They indulge, instead, in eating the best kebabs, drinking tea, and smoking. Although these habits do not seem to disagree with an "outward" adherence to religion, their interaction is marked with moral decay and corruption: El Fuli and Azzam involve their sons in their bribery agreement, an act that suggests the persistence of the ruling elite—in both eras—in transmitting their power to their heirs/sons: Abd el Aal Basha, the Wafdist, tried to groom his son, Zaki, in a similar manner. In this respect, the two groups are similar in showing superficial signs of conforming to a certain set of values, that is, secularism (under the *ancien régime*) and religiosity (in the postcolonial state), while altogether disregarding Egyptian people's interests.

Different characters from the working class live with their families in the fifty iron rooms on the rooftop. Among them is Taha, the son of the building's doorman. Taha is described as an intelligent, hardworking, and devout young man who, in his quest for self-fulfillment, obtains a score of 98 percent in his high school diploma and aspires to become a police officer. Through his interactions, Taha exhibits a combination of dignity and patience, especially with the rich building residents who attempt to demean him because of his poverty. However, his unjustifiable disqualification by the police academy admission committee and the disregarding of his personal petition to the country's president impel Taha to renounce this unjust, discriminatory environment and search for a more meaningful existence. Joining the Faculty of Economics and Political Sciences at Cairo University, Taha again feels like an outcast because of his modest appearance and realizes that the university is a similar microcosm to the Yaʿqubiyan Building, in which the working class is subordinated by the rich and precluded from their circles. As the narrator puts it, at Cairo University Taha and "all country boys, good-hearted, pious, and poor" (ibid. p. 92) group together and separate from their rich peers like water separates from oil (al-Aswani 2006b: 128).

Taha turns to Islamism as a means of protesting against the oppressive and unjust state system and reforming the country's conditions. However, with the influence of extremist thinkers like the character of Sheikh Shakir, Taha envisions himself as being in a community, which—like the state regime it rejects—does not acknowledge the validity of other cultures and lifestyles and conjures up a glorious past of religious homogeneity and dominance. Shakir preaches: "We do not want our Islamic Nation to be either socialist or democratic. We want it Islamic-Islamic, and we will struggle and give up our lives and all we hold dear till Egypt is Islamic once more" (al-Aswani 2006a: 96). The state regime, ironfisted, responds to this power threat by using all possible deterrents, even if they violate dissidents' human rights. In political detention, Taha is subjected to sexual abuse, and upon his release, he assassinates the police officer that allowed that abuse. Taha is himself killed by the police force in the same assassination scene.

The novel, by highlighting Taha's experience, shapes a possible reality with which the Egyptian people are all too familiar,[15] namely, the vicious circle of power abuse by some regime officials and the subsequent violent resistance of armed individuals or groups. The depiction invites readers to judge the atrocious socio-economic and political conditions that lead to such extreme violence. At the same time, through novelistic attention to Taha's character and youthful dreams, and the injustices he was subjected to, readers are provided with a chance to develop an understanding for Taha's experience, a narrative strategy that is denied to the regime officers who detained and abused Taha, as they are merely sketched as stereotypes of power abusers.

Abaskharun (henceforth Abaskharon) and Malak are two Coptic brothers, who are as socially and economically disadvantaged as their neighbors in the iron rooms. Abaskharon works for Zaki as his engineering-office attendant, and Malak is a tailor. Abaskharon is disabled because of his amputated legs, but like many other Egyptians with a disability has no state benefits that would secure him a decent life. Therefore, he is forced to maintain a job, but ventures to secure his needs and empower himself with dishonest acts, like stealing unnoticeable amounts of sugar and tea from his employer's office. In like manner, knowing from his brother that Zaki has a weakness for women, Malak exploits his similarly poor neighbor, Busayna, and prompts her to financially manipulate Zaki, for Malak's own benefit. The representation of two Coptic individuals suffering from destitution and falling under the same dictates of a morally decaying society, like their neighbors in the Yaᶜqubiyan Building, subverts archetypal representations of Copts as either members of an affluent urban minority or poor peasants. It also challenges societal censorship attempts that enforce principles of "possessive exclusivism" (Said 1985: 106),[16] by which only positive representations of marginal groups gauge "good literature" (ibid. p. 106). This type of scrutiny has led contemporary writers to impose what Rasheed El-Enany calls "self-censorship" upon their writing when it comes to depicting religion and, by extension, religious groups (El-Enany, quoted in Zohny: 2009).[17]

Women in the Yaʿqubiyan Building

In addition to its innovative exposure of the material microcosm of downtown Cairo and its miniature model, the Yaʿqubiyan Building, *The Yacoubian Building* foregrounds the double subordination that working-class women endure. Busayna, one of the iron room residents, is the primary breadwinner for her big family after her father's death. With the epidemic-scale problem of unemployment, Busayna has difficulty obtaining a job. Her dilemma worsens, since when she does find a job her employers, who are usually small retail shop owners, ask her for more than what retail sale requires, that is, sexual favors, and she succumbs. Fifi, Busayna's similarly poor comrade, advises Busayna to follow the "*shaṭāra*" (al-Aswani 2006b: 63), translated as "being smart" (al-Aswani 2006a: 43), principle, which allows her to keep both her virginity and her job. Busayana's and Fifi's experiences as poor, working women are represented side by side with that of Suʿad (Souad), Azzam's secret second wife. Souad is a young single mother from Alexandria, whose poverty and inability to support her son force her to agree to secretly marry wealthy and powerful Azzam and not bear him any children, because of the sensitivity of his political status. Ironically, Azzam is represented as a sexually impotent husband in a state of denial, whereas Souad is portrayed as faking complete satisfaction in their relationship in order to sustain a place in the material world. Azzam's sexual impotence allegorizes the unproductiveness of his political representation, irregular economic practices, and immoral lifestyle. Ironically, polygyny is legally and culturally permitted in Egypt, but Azzam's hypocrisy drives him to conceal his bigamy in order to appear in public as a modern statesman.

The Yacoubian Building recreates the socio-economic and political conditions in Cairo as well as the forces that govern interactions among diverse Cairenes in the microcosm of the Yaʿqubiyan Building. Through juxtaposition of the building's past with its present, readers realize that in both eras—the colonial and the postcolonial—the beneficiaries of national wealth and power are neither Egypt's poor peasants (in the former) nor its exploited working class (in the latter). They are a few, select individuals who divorce themselves from the impoverished Egyptian majority, though they are responsible for that majority's atrocious conditions. Although *The Yacoubian Building* can be interpreted as an elegiac novel that mourns the loss of what seems like the glorious and orderly past of downtown Cairo, I argue that with its compelling attention to the heterogeneity of Cairo's present, albeit, chaotic and discordant, the novel suggests a new collectivity of the marginalized and the subordinate. *The Yacoubian Building*'s captivating narrative style, realistic characterization, familiar spatial references, and inclusion of as many of Egypt's social groups as its narrative space allows give evidence that the novel is written about contemporary Egyptians and for them. In its suggested space, the multiple fragments of the Egyptian population are brought together to, first, voice their concerns and ailments and, second, criticize their state system, with its oppressive policies of differentiation and identity, omission and commission, exclusion and inclusion.

Chicago—ᶜAlaᵓ al-Aswani

Poetical and Political Dissent

Chicago is set in the city of Chicago after the events of 9/11. The lives of the multiple individuals, Egyptian and American, represented in the novel with their different backgrounds, affiliations, experiences, and aspirations intersect when they share Chicago's urban space and, more specifically, work closely together in the Department of Histology at the University of Illinois. The novel sheds light on long-standing differences and disjunctions between East and West (spatially and ideologically), tradition and modernity, and finally poetics in relation to religion and the state. In its representation of these categorical conflicts, the novel attempts to obscure their divides through their interconnections and negotiations. Al-Aswani's choices of literary devices—thematic and spatial—exhibit poetical and political impulses of change, if not rebellion, against the contemporary poetical and political establishments in Egypt.

In *Chicago*, al-Aswani uses two alternating points of view: the omniscient, third-person narrator and the first-person narrator and participant in the novel's events. On the one hand, the omniscient narrator, with god-like knowledge and presence, allows al-Aswani uninhibited exploration of what goes on in the minds and actions of the novel's characters like John Graham, Karam Dus (Karam Doss), Shaymaʾ Muhammadi (Shaymaa Muhammadi), Tariq Hasib (Tariq Haseeb), and Ahmad Danana. It even allows him to open the novel with an inspirational overview of the history of Chicago, its native American background, the fire that ravaged it in the nineteenth century, and its miraculous reconstruction by its hardworking residents. The first-person narrator's voice, embodied in Naji ʿAbd al-Samad's (Nagi Abd al-Samad), on the other hand, carries the burden of building up his own credibility to readers through his actions and views. Upon Nagi's arrival in Chicago, his interactions with diverse others appear to be premised on caution and suspicion of their differences in race, language, and/or religion. However, Nagi's preconceived notions of what these others may be like dissipate through shared dialogue and personal connections. Despite some collisional first encounters—especially with Karam Doss, the Coptic surgeon whose permanent migration to the USA Nagi judges as unpatriotic and cowardly—Nagi gradually becomes aware of the experiences he has in common with the diverse individuals he meets, and develops better understanding of their different paths and backgrounds. The use of these two narrative voices simultaneously enables al-Aswani to convey his messages from an authorial, all-knowing perspective, while maintaining another voice—Nagi's—which readers can identify as developing and transforming over narrative time and experience in the same way as their perspectives.

The novel engages with the problematic of pre-established notions of the other, especially the perennial disparity between East and West that has considerably inflated after the 9/11 attacks and the subsequent military interventions in Iraq, Libya, and Syria by Western powers. For example, the omniscient narrator sheds light on how a few faculty members in the histology department were concerned about admitting Nagi to the graduate program on the basis of his Middle Eastern background. The narrator also relays how Shaymaa Muhammadi, who wears hijab, was subjected to scrutiny and suspicion upon her arrival in the USA. While these narrative incidents intend to draw attention to possible experiences Arab-Muslims undergo in Western migrant settings, the novel doesn't focus so much on such tensions as it does on possibilities of reconciling them. In the following, I will demonstrate how *Chicago* proposes two creative activities as symbolic instruments of self-liberation from constraining, pre-established bodies of knowledge.

Although many views deem al-Aswani's texts—and *Chicago* is no exception—to be sources of sensual pleasures because of their unprecedented depiction of illicit sex and alcohol consumption, I argue that the unconventionality of this literary expression can be seen as a means of articulating oppositional thought and dissidence regarding cultural dogmatism. The characters' sexual and drinking activities can also be interpreted as acts of self-liberation, of experimenting with what is unexplored and concealed, in order to perceive and understand new possibilities of existence. Adonis invites us to return to "the root of the Arabic word for poetry (*shiʿr*), that is to the verb *shaʿara*, [so that] we see that it means 'to know', 'to understand' and 'to perceive'. On this basis, all knowledge is poetry" (Adonis 1990: 57).[18] If so, all perception and knowledge that are based on human experiences can be rendered in creative and poetic expressions, and when characters in *Chicago* challenge prescribed cultural mores and venture into new human experiences, horizons of the unknown are open for them to explore.

It is not surprising that al-Aswani invokes the Abbasid era, the period that witnessed modernist poets diverging from the poetic and political standards of their time, through the character of Nagi Abd al-Samad, who is a poet, a scientist, and a political activist—like al-Aswani himself. Nagi likens his love of wine drinking to that of Abu Nuwas (756–814 CE), the controversial Abbasid poet whose attitude and aesthetics can be connected with those of al-Aswani and his pseudo-autobiographical character, Nagi. Adonis describes Abu Nuwas as "*shāʿiru al-khaṭīʾa liʾannahu shāʿiru al-ḥuriyya*" (the poet of sin because he is the poet of freedom) (Adonis 1979: 52),[19] because he explicitly rebels against the cultural taboos and religious moral orders of his time by celebrating wine consumption and drunkenness. Additionally, Adonis explains that sin for Abu Nuwas is a human virtue that brings man to innocence. It breaks the barrier set against the knowledge of the inner self and the other, and drinking wine is a liberating act that obliterates the gap between poetics and thought, emotion and action, desire and fulfillment (Adonis 1990: 60–1). When wine drinking is done communally, participants are "masters and mistresses of their own thoughts, actions, and conducts" (ibid. p. 61). Abu Nuwas, thus, solicits joy and bliss through the violation of cultural and religious taboos and contends that "he has no desire to commit the sins of ordinary people, but aspires to sins equal in stature to the liberation he strives for . . . 'My religion is for myself! Other people's religion is for other people!', he cries" (ibid.). Adonis further explicates Abu Nuwas's instrument of liberation, wine, as follows:

> Wine is not wine: it is a symbol and an indicator, a force which transforms, annihilates, constructs, rejects and affirms. It is the ancient creator, to which everything is related, but which itself is related to nothing. It is the beginning of life and the eternal return, and between the two it is life in one of its most splendid meanings: love. It is a life-changing power, which reconciles opposites and makes the ordinary logic of time meaningless. It is the intoxication of the encounter with the self, and of the joining of the self with the world. (ibid. pp. 60–1)

Similarly, the characters' unorthodox attitudes and activities in *Chicago* can be read as instruments for breaking their socio-cultural and political barriers in order to perceive and engage with the world from a new perspective. The world in *Chicago* is expansive and intricate because it includes the experiences and conflicts of Egyptian immigrants in their host US culture, and engages with changing socio-cultural and political world relations after 9/11. The vehicles via which readers can learn and understand about these intricate and interfacing world forces are, first, the perspective of an insider, who can closely examine the experiences of humans entangled in their midst and who has the ability to transport readers to their world. It is worth mentioning that the novelistic world of Chicago is based on al-Aswani's personal experience of living and studying dentistry in Chicago, Illinois. Second, the recurrent themes of wine drinking and sex can be read as the symbolic rituals that "transport" the individuals who partake in them—whether they are *Chicago*'s characters or readers—to another time and another place beyond the tangible, the visible, the logical, the known, and the permissible.

Nagi Abd al-Samad, Muhammad Salah, Karam Dus, and John Graham partake in wine drinking in order to break through the constraints of tradition and authoritative systems and set themselves on the threshold of freedom, knowledge, and innovation. For example, Nagi drinks red wine only in adherence to the practice of Abbasid poets, not to blindly imitate the past as it was delivered to him, but because of the yearning for knowledge its modernist poets inspired. Nagi on one occasion invokes Abu Nuwas's poetry when he suffers from a hangover: "Abu Nuwas said, 'Treat me with that which made me sick'" (al-Aswani [2007] 2009: 155).[20] Nagi is a dissident, who openly criticizes the oppressive regime in Egypt. This leads to his political detention, persecution at his home university, and exile overseas. In the same way as Abu Nuwas is accused by his critics of participating in the foreign cultural and political movement from Persia, *al-Shuʿūbiyya*, because of his radical thought (Adonis 1990: 88), Nagi is accused by Ahmad Danana, the Director of the Egyptian Students Association in the USA, of being a communist because of his dissident political attitude (al-Aswani [2007] 2009: 130).

The first time John, Nagi, and Karam drink together, they open up to each other about their personal experiences of persecution by individuals, institutions, and state systems. John tells about his participation in the anti-government riots during the American Vietnamese war in the 1960s and the violent repression he and other protestors were subjected to at the hands of their own government forces. Karam relays his personal experience of religious persecution in Egypt because of his Coptic background: when Karam was an aspiring medical student, the chairman of the surgery department at ʿAyn Shams University disapproved of his admission to surgery training because of his creed. Nagi reveals the story of his political detention and poetic aspirations. While these individuals are participating in this symbolic act of self-liberation, wine drinking, they are inspired to take a stand to end the atrocities committed in the name of this political system or that religious view. They write a manifesto which decries the corruption of the Egyptian state officials and the regime's ironfisted oppression of dissident voices. It also demands that the despotic Egyptian president leave office and affirms the Egyptian people's right to freedom of thought and expression as well as self-representation, social justice, and equality.

There is a close connection between sexual desire as a sign of searching for the inner self and its fulfillment as a sign of self-discovery and achievement. Shaymaa Muhammadi is another graduate student sent by her Egyptian university to obtain a doctorate in histology from the University of Illinois. Portrayed as a young woman from rural Egypt, whose scholarly achievements have intimidated potential suitors and delayed her chance of marriage, Shaymaa seizes the opportunity to leave her small home town and go to Chicago to discover different life possibilities. After a short time feeling estranged and homesick in the foreign metropolis, Shaymaa meets Tariq, her neighbor in the student housing and fellow graduate student from Egypt. They become attracted to one another, but the omniscient narrator reveals Tariq's and Shaymaa's inner conflicts about their potential relationship. On the one hand, Tariq, whose father is a high-ranking police officer, is torn about Shaymaa's eligibility to be his wife, because of her modest, rural background. Shaymaa, on the other, is inhibited by repressive cultural and religious beliefs that impugn her desire for Tariq. Having fallen in love, they start a sexual relationship

The narrator describes how Shaymaa and Tariq have been transformed: Shaymaa experiences a blissful joy and fulfillment of love and desire, whereas Tariq abandons his aggressive behavior and becomes more cheerful (ibid. p. 345). Nonetheless, Shaymaa's new experience leads to the collapse of the world as she had always known it: when Tariq impregnates her and refuses to marry her, Shaymaa understands how her expectations and decisions have been culturally conditioned, but understands too that she is now faced with determining her own position in the new world. As much as she, and readers, may expect Shaymaa to have complete autonomy and freedom in her new world, and thereby make a clear divide between her old and her new worlds, at the pregnancy help center in Chicago Shaymaa hears voices similar to the ones in her head, which condemn abortion: a pro-life mob demonstrating in front of the center yells at her, "'Ruthless Murderer!'" (ibid. pp. 338–9). This incident not only reflects on the similarity in the conservative cultural stance with regard to abortion between Egypt and the USA: it also captures the challenges migrants face when their home and host cultures connect and collide at one and the same time. The novel proposes another transformation on Tariq's side when he decides to visit Shaymaa at the abortion clinic. The immigrant couple's storyline ends at that instant for readers to speculate about the possibilities and directions their relationship may take.

Instances of political and religious repression go hand in hand in the novel. Ahmad Danana exercises his political domination by means of religious subjugation. As the head of the Egyptian Students Association, he declares in a meeting that the Egyptian president[21] is scheduled to visit Chicago, and takes the liberty of sending a telegram on the students' behalf to the president, in which they renew their pledge of allegiance, "*nujaddidu . . . al-bayᶜa*" (al-Aswani 2007: 129).²² Nagi objects to such a telegram, and argues that the president and his regime have left more than half of the Egyptian population destitute, and that in Cairo alone there are four million people who live in slums. Danana defends the president:

> [Danana] "Even if you think there are negative aspects in the way our revered president rules, your religious duty mandates that you obey him."
> [Nagi] "Who said that?"
> [Danana] "Islam, if you are a Muslim. Sunni jurisprudents have unanimously agreed that it is the duty of Muslims to obey their rulers if they are oppressive, so long as that ruler professes his faith and performs the prayers on time, because sedition arising from opposing the ruler is much more harmful to the Muslim nation than putting up with oppression."
> (al-Aswani [2007] 2009: 92–3)

Danana's language illustrates the infusion of political subjugation rhetoric with religious duties, but Nagi's attitude, which represents the merging of political activism with modern poetics, calls that rhetoric and the authorities behind it into question.

At this juncture, I will present a summary of Adonis's discussion of the historical interconnections between religious and state institutions and their simultaneous disjunction from poetics. Given the current conflict that many innovative artists, writers, and intellectuals have with the contemporary Egyptian state, the existing conservative religious and cultural authorities, and what is now referred to as "street censorship,"²³ Adonis's explanation should provide insight into the persistence of these politico-cultural dynamics in present-day Egypt. Historically, revolutionary thought and new intellectual movements were strongly resisted by those who held political power during Arab-Muslim rule: "The dominant view held that the state was founded on a vision or message which was Islam" (Adonis 1990: 75). Attempts to revolt against the political establishment were considered an attack on religion and innovative intellectuals were deemed heretics. The non-conformists were referred to by the system of the caliphate as "'the people of innovation'" (*ahl al-iḥdāth*). Adonis points out how the terms *iḥdāth* (innovation) and *muḥdath* (modern, new), which are now used to describe innovative poetics, came originally from religious terms: "[W]e can see that the modern in poetry appeared to the ruling establishment as a political or intellectual attack on the culture of the regime and a rejection of the idealized standards of the ancient, and how therefore in Arab life the poetic has always been mixed up with the political and the religious, and indeed continues to be so" (ibid. p. 76).

In addition to calling authoritative discourses into question, the novel condemns state systems' use of violence to silence opposition and quell revolutions. For example, John—like Nagi and Karam—has been subjected to persecution by his own government. As a young man, John participated in the 1960s uprisings against the US government, in which the revolutionaries demanded an end to the war in Vietnam and revision of the internal neo-capitalistic policies that left the majority of American people chasing an elusive American dream. The omniscient narrator provides an account of the revolution: "The police struck at the demonstrators with all possible means and with utmost cruelty: with thick nightsticks, water hoses, tear gas bombs, and rubber bullets. The students defended themselves by throwing stones and hair spray canisters that they lit and turned into small bombs" (al-Aswani [2007] 2009: 135). That violent encounter between protestors and state forces is fictional, yet bathed in historical light. It immediately calls to mind the Egyptian state's recent adoption of very similar violent measures against its own people to quell their revolution on January 25, 2011. It is stimulating to see *Chicago* conjure up revolutionary ideology and action, on one level, and states' oppressive and violent reaction to them on the other, while also watching this construct come into being in Egypt a few years after the novel's publication.

Migrant Crisis

Muhammad Salah, the Egyptian immigrant and professor of histology, joins Nagi, Karam, and John in writing the manifesto and obtaining as many Egyptian immigrants' signatures on it as possible. He also volunteers to publicly read the manifesto to the Egyptian president at the reception organized by the Egyptian community in Chicago. The narrator, nevertheless, reveals another aspect of Muhammad's life that shows his vulnerability and inner struggle. Thirty years previously, Muhammad had abandoned the love of his life in Egypt to seek a successful and stable career in the USA. Being a nationalist, his love, Zaynab, refused to leave her country owing to political turmoil, and called Muhammad's decision to immigrate cowardly. Although Muhammad succeeds in the USA and marries an American woman who loves him, he is so overcome by his longing for the past that he loses interest in the present. The narrator describes how, one night, Muhammad goes to his basement to try on his old Egyptian clothes. Ironically, "[h]is body had filled out and they no longer fit him . . . the shirt stuck to his body in a way that almost hurt . . . He was filled with wonderful serenity and felt contained in dark, moist serenity, as if he were once again at his mother's bosom" (ibid. p. 207). Muhammad's sorrowful present due to his longing for an irretrievable past, signified in the unfitting clothes, captures the immigrant's "perpetual desire, a longing that is never fulfilled in the ambiguity of existence caught between a consciousness of roots elsewhere and the realities of routes, of life shaped by movement through different locations that are never quite home" (Friedman 2007: 278).[24]

Although Muhammad desires so badly to amend his homeland loss and retrieve his past love, at the last moment he refrains from reading the manifesto. Instead, he reads a statement written in the rhetoric of empty praise to the president. The novel demonstrates that the inspiration and idea for revolution can emerge in people's consciousness (Karam, Nagi, Muhammad, and John) rather than in a specific territory such as Egypt or the USA. These individuals represent a collective of dissident intellectuals, who are also male, migrant, and scientists. Muhammad's inability to voice the collective's opposition implies the novel's dislocation of the revolutionary act from his and, by extension, their fragmented existence, but perhaps also attempts to relocate revolution, at the least textually, in its act of creative writing and in the de-centered consciousness it stems from. While *Chicago* does not provide definitive answers as to why the political revolution it contains does not succeed, it sheds light on truths that are prescribed neither by religion nor by philosophical argumentation. It treats issues of love, desire, and individual freedom that are not supported by established thought, and presents an uncharted territory of knowledge. It is true that *Chicago* does not give definitive solutions to the array of conflicts and tensions depicted in it, but it inspires change for the better.

Al-Aswani's novels, *The Yacoubian Building* and *Chicago*, jointly communicate the political, social, and cultural instabilities within contemporary Egypt. Together, they present a comprehensive account of Egyptian society from local and global perspectives by means of their spatial settings in the urban centers of Cairo and Chicago. Although *The Yacoubian Building* provides a decadent picture of a society in which socio-political and moral decay are prevalent, *Chicago* ventures to postulate revolution against the established systems and bodies of knowledge that cause the decadence. Both novels represent a multiplicity of individuals whose experiences reveal their distinctive searches for self-assertion and dignity. While they present the experiences of individuals who succumb to moral decay in their lust for power and wealth or resort to extremist ideology and violent resistance, the novels also present the experiences of other individuals who understand and value human diversity. The differences these characters exhibit in class, gender, religion, ethnicity, sexuality, and culture and, hence, in their reactions to the socio-political and cultural challenges within their society do not exempt them from confronting their societal problems as a collective.

Notes

1. It is worth noting here that, prior to the best-seller *The Yacoubian Building*, al-Aswani's attempts to publish his first two novels, *Al-lathi ʾiqtarab wa raʾa* (This Who Got Close and Saw) in 1990 and *Jamʿiyyat muntadhiri al-zaʿim* (The Organization of Leader's Expectants) in 1998, failed after they were both rejected by The Egyptian General Book Organization for their offensive political content towards the regime. For more details see the interview with al-Aswani by Nashwa al-Hufi, "ʿAlaʾ al-Aswani: I wrote *The Yacoubian Building* while I was preparing for immigrating to New Zealand," in *al-Sharq al-awsat*, 22 March 2006, <http://archive.aawsat.com/details.asp?article=354235&issueno=9976#.V_UQ_xQ5aB8> (last accessed 5 October 2016).
2. American University Press website, <http://www.aucpress.com/p-2793-the-yacoubian-building.aspx> (last accessed 24 August 2012).
3. Roger Allen comments on the "best-seller" phenomenon of contemporary Arabic novels, exemplified in al-Aswani's *The Yacoubian Building*, Saudi author Rajaʿ al-Saniʿ's *Banat al-riyad*, 2006 and the Algerian writer Ahlam Mustaghanimi's *Dhakirat al-jasad*, 1993. He relates the global marketability of their translations, especially in the West, to the eagerness of their implied readers to receive their

"apparent 'insights' into what is widely viewed as a closed world" (Allen 2009: 9). For the whole essay, see Roger Allen's "Fiction and Publics: The Emergence of the 'Arabic Best-Seller,'" *The Middle East Institute Viewpoint: The State of the Arts in the Middle East*, 2009, pp. 9–12, <www.mei.edu> (last accessed 15 September 2016).

4. Sherif H. Ismail details how Arabic literature critics, like Jennine Abboushi Dallal, took issue with the phenomenon of Arab authors who write with translation in mind, and therefore cater to what publishers, especially in the West, look for in terms of "substantiating western preconceptions of Arab Others" in works of Arabic literature (Ismail 2015: 918). For more details see Sherif H. Ismail, "Arabic Literature into English: The (Im)possibility of Understanding," *Interventions*, Vol. 16, No. 6, 2015, pp. 916–31.
5. Levine, George, "Realism Reconsidered," in Michael J. Hoffman and Patrick D. Murphy (eds), *Essentials of the Theory of Fiction* (Durham, NC: Duke University Press, 1996), 2nd edn, pp. 235–45.
6. Levine, George, "From the Realistic Imagination: English Fiction from Frankenstein to Lady Chatterley," in Michael McKeon (ed.) *The Theory of the Novel: A Historical Approach* (Baltimore: Johns Hopkins University Press [1981] 2000), pp. 613–31.
7. Al-Ghitani, Jamal, "Nuqtat ᶜubur," an essay published at the end of ᶜAlaᵓ al-Aswani, *The Yacoubian Building*, 8th edn (Cairo: Maktabat Madbuli, 2005) pp. 350–1.
8. Nashwa al-Hufi, "ᶜAlaᵓ al-Aswani: I Wrote *The Yacoubian Building* While I Was Preparing for Immigrating to New Zealand," *al-Sharq al-awsat*, 22 March 2006, <http://archive.aawsat.com/details.asp?article=354235&issueno=9976#.V_UQ_xQ5aB8> (last accessed 5 October 2016).
9. Al-Aswani, ᶜAlaᵓ, *The Yacoubian Building*, trans. Humphrey Davies (New York: Harper Perennial, 2006).
10. Selim, Samah, *The Novel and the Rural Imaginary, 1880–1985* (Albany: State University of New York Press, 2004).
11. Selim describes how the mass migration of Egyptian peasantry to Cairo was also motivated by "neo-feudalist patterns of landownership and farming practices, and the penetration of mass media and technologies in the countryside" (231).
12. Characters' names in Humphrey Davies' English translation of the novel are transliterated differently.
13. The translator, Humphrey Davies, notes at the end of the novel that "no party

by this name exists in Egypt" (al-Aswani 2006: 251). In the Arabic novel, al-Aswani uses "*al-ḥizb al-qawmi*" (al-Aswani [2002] 2006: 72) as the name of a fictional party; however, the name resonates with that of the former ruling party in Egypt at the time, *al-ḥizb al-watani* (National Party).

14. Al-Aswani, ᶜAlaʾ, *ᶜImarat yaᶜqubiyan*, 9th edn (Cairo: Maktabat Madbuli [2002] 2006).
15. Egyptian and world news agencies report such incidents on a frequent basis. Amnesty International describes, in its annual reports, the violence of armed groups targeting state officials and civilians as well as the state's excessive use of force with dissidents from all domains, intellectual, political, socio-economic. For more information, see the annual report on current conditions in Egypt by the Amnesty International Organization available on its website, <https://www.amnesty.org/en/countries/middle-east-and-north-africa/egypt/report-egypt/> (last accessed 6 September 2017).
16. Edward, Said, "Orientalism Reconsidered," *Cultural Critique*, No. 1, Autumn 1985, pp. 89–107.
17. El-Enany, Rasheed, "Rasheed El-Enany on Modern Arabic Lit: Not Quite a Renaissance," interview by Hazem Zohny in *Egypt Independent*, 12 December 2009, <http://www.egyptindependent.com/news/rasheed-el-enany-modern-arabic-lit-not-quite-renaissance> (last accessed 15 September 2016).
18. Adonis, *An Introduction to Arab Poetics*, trans. Catherine Cobham (Austin: University of Texas Press, 1990).
19. Adonis, *Muqaddima lil-shiᶜr al-ᶜarabi* (Beirut: Dar al-ᶜAwda, 1979), 3rd edn.
20. Al-Aswani, ᶜAlaʾ, *Chicago*, trans. Farouk Abdel Wahab, Harper perennial edn (New York: HarperCollins, [2007] 2009).
21. The narrator describes the Egyptian president as an aged man with an artificial smile, who dyes his hair and is grooming his son for the presidency. This story conjures up the reality not only within contemporary Egypt, but also in a number of other postcolonial states whose leaders and officials follow the same pre-modern dynastic tactic of transmitting their power to their descendants.
22. Al-Aswani, ᶜAlaʾ, *Shikagu* (Cairo: Dar al-Shuruq).
23. Samia Mehrez, as is discussed in the introduction to this study, details how the Egyptian state and self-appointed religious and social authorities restrain innovation and freedom of creative expression in Egypt in the name of religion and traditional values. For more information, see Mehrez's *Egypt's Culture Wars: Politics and Practice* (Cairo: AUC Press, 2008).

24. Friedman, Susan Stanford, "Migrations, Diasporas, and Borders," in David G. Nicholls (ed.), *Introduction to Scholarship in Modern Languages and Literatures* (New York: Modern Language Association of America, 2007), 3rd edn, pp. 260–93.

4

Heart Deserts: Memory and Myth between Life and Death in Asharaf al-Khumaysi's *Manafi al-rabb* and Miral al-Tahawi's *The Tent*

As much as the desert surrounds the constitution of Arab identity, culture, and mythical heritage, in addition to inspiring its classical literary expression,[1] choosing the desert as a theme, setting, or character is not a common artistic strategy in Arabic novelistic production in general. Emerging in the early twentieth century, the Arabic novel has been identified as the genre of the modern *par excellence*, as it captures the complex dimensions of modern political, social, and cultural upheavals within Arab states during colonial and postcolonial times by focusing primarily on urbanized settings[2] where the turmoil of colonialism is intensified.[3] A few modern Arabic novels, however, venturesomely set their events in the desert in an attempt to conjure up a world vision and consciousness that counter the effects of self-splitting modernity and its handmaiden, colonialism. These include the Palestinian author Ghassan Kanafani's *Ma tabaqqa lakum*, 1966 (*All That's Left to You*, 1990), the Saudi writer ᶜAbd al-Rahman Munif's *al-Nihayat*, 1978 (*Endings*, 1988), and the Libyan writer Ibrahim al-Kuni's *Nazif al-hajar*, 1990 (*The Bleeding of the Stone*, 2002).[4] The Egyptian novel, as part of the larger body of the Arabic novel, seems to have also distanced its spatial and cultural characters from the desert and its nomadic linkages by anchoring Egyptian modern selfhood to imaginings and conjectures deeply entrenched in Egypt's agrarian roots as well as its urbanized spaces in colonial and postcolonial contexts.[5] However, Ashraf al-Khumaysi's *Manafi al-rabb*, [2013] 2015 ("God's Exiles") and Miral al-Tahawi's *al-Khibaʾ*, 1996 (*The Tent*, 1998) counteract this literary approach towards modernity (similar to what *Ma tabaqqa lakum*, *al-Nihayat* and *Nazif al-hajar* do) by departing from urban centers and turning to the desert. What distinguishes these two contemporary works from their progenitors is how they hinge on the unique historical and cultural backgrounds of Egypt's western and eastern desert regions respectively.

In this chapter, I examine *Manafi al-rabb* and *The Tent*, and their innovative, multi-faceted use of the desert motif. Contemporary authors do not merely employ the desert as a spatial setting for their works, but as a symbolic labyrinth, a mythical center, and a simultaneous path and destination, in which different trajectories of human existence, fulfillment, and despair are postulated. *Manafi al-rabb* represents perceptions and rituals of life and death among the religiously diverse inhabitants of Egypt's western desert, and more specifically those of al-Waʿira, a fictional isolated oasis there, where the novel's main character, the elderly Bedouin Hujayzi, goes on a quest for bodily incorruptibility after death. Following his dialogues and negotiations with Sheikh Mazid at the village's mosque and with Monk Yuʾannis at the neighboring Coptic monastic community, Hujayzi reckons that his pursuit of postmortem bodily imperishability is not to be fulfilled in either Muslim or Christian burial practice, but rather by his eating from a mythical distant orange tree in the desert. *The Tent* transfers its readers to a young Bedouin girl's world, in which the boundaries between myth and reality are blurred. Fatima's incessant attempts to alleviate the anguish resulting from her domestic confinement and lack of autonomy are halted by a physical disability, which allegorically signifies her powerlessness in altering her melancholic condition. The two novels immerse the reader in the desert as a mythical center, in which the figure of the Bedouin is deeply rooted both in body and spirit and in which alternative meanings of life and existence and, thereby, human relations are configured.

When all things are considered regarding the novel as the genre of the modern, the uncanniness and infiniteness of desert existence, spatially and historically, have constituted an inexhaustible and bountiful source for imaginary and symbolic artistry, and novelistic creation is no exception. The Syrian Arabic literature critic Salah Salih enumerates the ways in which the desert possesses imagination-inducing properties that deem it extremely fertile and valuable for creative representations. First, its bewilderingly acute horizontal and vertical stretches strike one with awe, and overwhelm the naked eye with their infiniteness and magnitude. In the desert, any subject can find out how small and feeble they are. Second, the desert's diurnal and seasonal temperatures range from extremely high to extremely low, leading to an exceptional temperature discrepancy between day and night and between different seasons. These extreme climatic conditions, in addition to the rarity and unpredictability of the desert's rainfall, have confounded its inhabitants and inspired their rich reservoir of myths and imaginative explanations for such extreme conditions. Third, the desert is an ideal place for the occurrence of the natural mirage phenomenon, in which human vision is distorted and experiential reality shattered. When unable to distinguish between reality and illusion, the human imagination breaks free, and bursts with a myriad possible scenarios for what could be taking place in the surrounding atmosphere. As Salih puts it, those who experience desert mirages both doubt and, at one and the same time, believe everything. Fourth, the amalgamation of animist (African and Pharaonic) mystical heritages, as well as those of the Abrahamic religions in their birthplace, the desert, have led to their converging in a unique spiritual regional heritage that constitutes "a challenge to the contemporary human mind and a catalyst for creativity, thought kindling, and imagination leaps"[6] (Salih 1997: 9).[7]

In a 2014 interview by Anders Hastrup for the Louisiana Channel,[8] al-Kuni expounds his artistic vision of the desert as a novelistic setting, one which contradicts and challenges the predominant perception of the novel as "*ᶜamal madīniyy*" (an urban work)[9] (al-Kuni 2014). Al-Kuni argues against seeing the city as the novel's only home "*waṭan al-riwāya*," and alternatively believes that the novel may find a home in any place where a human being relates to others (ibid.). In this respect, in a place like the desert that is uninhabitable due to the absence of water as the source of life, as al-Kuni characterizes it (ibid.), it is befitting to liken the desert to what Homi Bhabha calls the "third space," or "non-place" (Bhabha 1994: 53, 352),[10] as well as a spiritual oasis where relationships between humans, on the one hand, and between humans and other desert inhabitants such as flora and fauna on the other, take unexpected turns and forms. In this "non-place," binaries and feuds between perceptibly different entities within our world are re-inscribed following their displacement in the desert realm, that other world where myth blurs reality and spirit negotiates with body to accommodate the confusion and uncertainty resulting from their feuding existences. In that sense, translating novelistic characters to the desert realm allows new reconfigurations and interpretations of structures of power, overdetermined social and cultural representations of human life, and what Homi Bhabha calls "history's most intricate invasions" (Bhabha 1992: 141)[11] in the postcolonial world.

In light of al-Kuni's philosophy of the desert, we can understand how these authors' novelistic undertaking to escape to and seek refuge in the desert realm may stem from their dissident stances towards sweeping modernization—which is genealogically fathered by colonialism—and its denial to humanity of spirituality and freedom. They carry this out by translating their readers to the untrodden desert terrain where spiritual perceptions of and correlations between the self and the other are untainted by, and defy, the unbalanced power relations of modern colonial and post-independence times. The authors of these works do not depict the desert in the narrow sense of realistic geographical alignment with their novels' events. For example, the desert is not solely (a) a portrayal of the danger-filled cross-desert road between Gaza and Jordan in Kanafani's *All That's Left to You*, (b) the natural landscape of the vast Arabian Peninsula desert in Munif's *Endings*, or (c) the distinct mountainous terrains characteristic of the Libyan Sahara in al-Kuni's *The Bleeding of the Stone*. In fact, the desert, in these three works, acquires many more characteristics, that transcend its identification as a specific landscape and the precise geographic location of the respective novels' depicted groups and peoples. Despite the many presumed commonalities between the desert terrains in these novels—as Salih explains, the vast Sahara terrain extending from the Arabian Peninsula to North Africa is, after all, one unified magnitude separated by the very thin channel of the Red Sea (Salih 1994: 8)—each is shaped in a distinct, creative way as a means of delineating the particularities of the human experiences within each of these desert parts.

Kanafani, in *All That's Left to You*, portrays the desert as a setting for Hamid's danger-filled trip to reunite with his displaced mother in Jordan, who could not return with her children to their home in Palestine following the 1948 war. The author tells the story in three distinct voices, Hamid's, his sister Mariam's, and that of the desert, which is creatively painted with the characteristics of a female figure that erotically caresses the youthful footsteps and warm breath of Hamid, turning herself into a vessel for his passionate desires. On his desert trip or quest to find his mother, Hamid breaks his bondage to modern, linear time when he rids himself of his wristwatch by throwing it in the sand. The watch's regular ticking is, in turn, swallowed up in the desert's depths and muted by the desert's unfathomable temporality.

In *Endings*, Munif not only embodies the desert as the natural environment and ruling organism of Bedouin communal life in a fictional village called al-Tiba, but also juxtaposes the village's traditional past—during which the desert either abounds with life in its flora and fauna, or snares every living being under its treacherous sand or its mercilessly burning sun—with the changes incurred by the encroachment of city dwellers and their breaching of the balanced existence of desert life. Munif captures the dreadful consequences of these changes for al-Tiba by opening the whole novel with the keyword "*al-qaḥṭ*" (drought), which he repeats numerous times throughout its pages. The third-person narrator recounts the many droughts al-Tiba people were able to survive prior to the unprecedentedly devastating one that begins the narrative. This demarcates the beginning of the end of life as al-Tiba had always known it.

The Bleeding Stone is set in the North African Libyan Sahara, and draws on the mythical and traditional beliefs, as well as the cosmic outlook, of its indigenous population, *al-ṭawāriq* (Tuareg).[12] The novel revolves around the existence of two competing desert entities: the spirits of the desert plains embodied in its gazelles and those of the desert mountains embodied in its *waddan* (mouflon). They having warred unceasingly with each other from time immemorial, a third entity, man, was sent as a curse from the gods above to destroy them both. The premise indicates the magical realist nature of the novel, as miriam cooke categorizes it in her essay "Magical Realism in Libya"[13] (cooke 2010: 20), in which the desert is not a place but a spiritual existence that can either be impoverished, merciless, and cruel, or bountiful, redemptive, and fulfilling. Set during the Italian colonial period followed by the period of American interest (and therefore presence) in Libyan natural oil reserves, the novel lends itself not only to unravelling colonial and postcolonial power relations, but also to creatively projecting them from the purely spiritual vantage-point of the desert realm. Al-Kuni enriches the spiritual character of his novel with *al-ṭawāriq*'s mythical and cultural reservoir, which extends from the 10,000-year-old rock engravings and sculpture found in the Libyan Sahara's historical sites (Weisburg 2015: 47)[14] to the area's diverse Christian and Sufi mystical heritages. The multi-layered conflict portrayed in the novel, especially that between man and the *waddan*, a sacred animal that symbolically functions both as man's savior and as his executioner, highlights the emblem behind the quintessential human condition articulated repeatedly by the main character, Asuf: "la yushbiʿu ibn adam illa al-turāb" (al-Kuni 1990: 130–46)[15] ("Only through dust will the son of Adam be filled") (al-Kuni 2013: 129–32).[16] Asuf's expression invokes the Hadith by the Prophet Muhammad, transmitted by ibn ʿAbbas, in which man is described as neither content nor satisfied until his inside is filled with dust, namely until he dies. Musa Lashin interprets the Hadith as follows: "If man [Adam's son] possessed two valleys of money, he would desire a third; nothing fills man's inside except dust and God forgives those who repent" (Lashin 2001: 202–3).[17] At the end of the novel, Asuf is predictably slaughtered by his fellow man, Qabil, the flesh eater.

Sharif Elmusa's 2013 study, "The Ecological Bedouin: Toward Environmental Principles for the Arab Region," extrapolates ecological ethics from three Arabic desert novels, in which the desert is employed as the primary leitmotif and the figure of the Bedouin is represented as an inherently environmental "conservationist" (Elmusa 2013: 9).[18] Elmusa describes the desert's significance in Arab consciousness and its value in its literary, and more specifically its novelistic, articulations of the ethical treatment of the regional flora and fauna. He observes how the desert functions as the backdrop, or, in his words, "the shadow of Arab civilization" (ibid. p. 13), the fount of its "cultural memory," as well as the site of Arabs' interactions with other civilizations (ibid. p. 13):

> Its geographic preponderance aside, the desert is a home of that region's cultural memory; its language, poetry, and sacred texts; monasteries and castles; camels and tents; palm trees and palm date fruit; triumphs and defeats of the battlefield . . . It may not be surprising therefore that the fourteenth century Arab polymath Ibn Khaldun (1332–1406 AD) linked the rise and fall of ʿ*umran*, or civilization, to what he considered its "primitive" antecedent, the Bedouin. Today, as the desert is stripped of its "desertness," novelists are trying to preserve its imaginative cultural value. (ibid. p. 13)

Historically, the desert had been home to numerous peoples and groups, but, Salih notes, except for the Nubian, Tuareg, and Garamentes populations there is no accurate record of what groups inhabited the Sahara and where, especially before the time of the Roman Empire. This uncanny past existence of a multitude of unknown peoples "contributed to establishing a belief amongst the current Sahara inhabitants that their original ancestors from time immemorial were from the jinn, who have retired to the invisible realm due to several treasons committed by humans. In addition, the current inhabitants believe that the human and jinni tribes are both descendants of one origin" (Salih 1997: 7).

That dual uncanniness and otherworldliness of the desert has fueled al-Kuni's novelistic imagination. He writes about its "spiritual" existence vis-à-vis that of "materialistic" civilization as follows:

> The question of the desert is primarily an existential question. The desert is not a desert but in actuality a symbol for human existence, because if we reflected for a little, we would discover that this desert, rich with spiritual presence, is a paradise; a paradise of existence . . . and that civilization and city in the absence of spirituality are hell. This is an oxymoron. (al-Kuni 2014)[19]

The desert, in this sense, aesthetically constitutes an ever-present spiritual entity that envelops man and his existence. It is also used as a mythical center in which myths of the self and the other, whether human or non-human, are questioned. In the following analysis, I demonstrate how *Manafi al-rabb* and *The Tent* challenge the materialistic changes wrought by colonization, civilization, and westernization on man by aesthetically transposing them to the spiritual desert domain, where man's spiritual goodness (nature) and depravity (culture) are juxtaposed. I argue that al-Khumaysi's and al-Tahwai's uncommon aesthetic decision to turn to the desert attests to the new consciousness that their novelistic efforts galvanize when they cast off the restraints of the Egyptian center and wander in the Egyptian desert to seek alternative meanings of life, death, and human existence at times of prevailing materialism.

Manafi al-rabb—Ashraf al-Khumaysi

The events of *Manafi al-rabb* are set in al-Waʿira, an isolated fictional oasis in the western Egyptian desert. The nearest town, Mut, to and from which characters journey to fulfill tasks and desires, is about one hundred kilometers away. Although al-Waʿira is fictional, its neighbor, Mut, invokes the name of the real capital of al-Wahat al-Dakhila Governorate (al-Dakhila Oases) located in present-day Egypt. The word "Mut" captures the historic significance of the ancient Egyptian goddess Mut or Maut, the wife of Amun,[20] in addition to being a homophone of the Arabic root *m-u-t* (death), which is a major thematic preoccupation of the novel. On the one hand, the desert trail to and from Mut, which the characters tread, metaphorizes the journey towards death and mysterious after-death existence, and, at one and the same time, the return journey from death back into earthly life and the insights sojourners bring from the realm beyond, the realm of death. On the other hand, the symbolic value of Mut as a female deity derives from her depiction, in the places where she is worshipped, as a protectress vulture, a lioness, and the eye of Ra, the sun god (Lohwasser 2001: 62–4, 70–1).[21] In this respect, she represents an all-encompassing, mighty, and spiritual entity that is present in the sky (a vulture), on land (a lioness), and in the force of the sun's heat in Egypt's western expanse: all features present in the desert and its environmental dictates. Mut is therefore analogous to the desert in galvanizing the oxymoronic qualities of nurture, protectiveness, and spirituality that culminate in promising to those who seek it (the desert/Mut) relief and fulfillment, but at the same time, it is a wild force that prevails over land and air and threatens to incinerate the accursed with its burning eye, the sun ("Mut" 2001).[22]

In the following section, I will explore how Mut as death (*mut*) imbues the novel, how characters are simultaneously enchanted and terrified by it. Then, I will explore the discoveries characters make on their danger-filled journeys to and from Mut, and how these discoveries alter their perceptions.

In Death We Unite

The concurrence of drastic polarities within the desert region, or rather planet, as al-Kuni refers to it (quoted in Salih 1997: 8), is exemplified by its extreme climatic conditions, the mirage-like experiences it provides, its astounding spatial realizations, its unique conflation of the world's most ancient cultural heritages, and its magnificent manifestations of life in the midst of its deadly environment. These simultaneities have naturally permeated the Sufi aesthetic tradition, which originated in the desert, and have become integral to representations of the desert in Arabic literature. Adonis, the acclaimed Syrian poet and critic, describes Sufi aesthetics as resting "on contradictions":

> This means that the object can only explain its essence by contradicting it. Death in life and life in death, day in night and night in day. The opposites meet in complete oneness: movement and stillness, reality and imagination, the strange and the familiar, the lucid and the obscure, the interior and exterior.
> The Sufi unites the interior and exterior, the self and the object, hidden reality and enlightened reality, so in order to attain the state of exalted inspiration, this state will not be revealed to a specific individual but to all individuals. This oneness between the visible world and the invisible world is the oneness of two opposites, and it is one of the basic tenets of the aesthetic of Sufi writing. (Adonis 2005: 117)[23]

Adonis's description of Sufi writing and its natural congruity with desert depictions only sheds more light on the aesthetic approach al-Khumaysi takes in *Manafi al-rabb*, in which the amalgamation of such desert extremes in al-Waʿira forms a harmonious unity of opposites and presents an integral mosaic of disparities that fuels characters' imaginations with nuanced accounts of existence.

Salih explains how, historically, such an experience of opposite conditions has led desert inhabitants to denote the essence of their persistent existence—despite the desert's severity and hostility to life, and their fatalistic bond with it—via a wholesome mythological belief that unites them with another world, namely the spiritual realm of jinn:

> a legendary curse descended on this legendary space to force it out of inhabitable geographies by depriving it of the most important reasons for life (water). The curse has kept that space uninhabitable as a sort of a cogent testimony that marks the forehead of planet earth, to remind its children of

their long, dreadful inheritance of divine wrath . . . from which there is no escape except through death and return to the dream "*waw*,"[24] the beautiful destination, and the lost paradise that is impossible to reach without death. (Salih 1997: 11)

In light of Salih's explanation of the desert's inhabitability, death becomes part and parcel of its space. It is embedded in its terrains only to relieve humans from suffering and to initiate their long-awaited dream, the true life after death. In the section "The Aesthetic Dimension" in his important study *al-Sufiyya wa-l-surryaliyya* (1995) (*Sufism and Surrealism*, 2005), Adonis displays how, in the Sufi tradition, "death is not death so much as another life" (Adonis 2005: 119), and how it "eliminates life in this world and sets up life in the other world. The other life is death with respect to the shadow—this world, but it is life with respect to the light—the other. Absence from shadow is only presence in light. So death is light: death is the existence of truth" (ibid. p. 127).

In *Manafi al-rabb*, the idea of death as an alternative life and way of existence imbues the novel on so many levels that any attempts to separate it from characters' lives in al-Waʿira are thwarted and made fruitless. This can be seen in: (1) Hujayzi's fascination with corpses and mummification as well as his concomitant eagerness for death and the life beyond; (2) the occurrence of multiple characters' deaths and resurrections; (3) the spatial metaphorization of Mut and the desert as the loci for life pursuits and annihilation at one and the same time; and (4) the desert monks' ascetic choice of disdaining earthly life and killing their bodily vigor and desires in pursuit of light in the life beyond. The novel even opens with a death vision when Hujayzi, the elderly Waʿira man who has lived for more than one hundred years, wakes up to a prescient awareness of his death three days thence. The novel's events do not unfold chronologically, but are organized in a constellation of disorderly flashbacks that reveal Hujayzi's Bedouin life, values, and preoccupations. It does not take long for the reader to learn about Hujayzi's simultaneous fascination with and awe of death and corpses. For example, Hujayzi mesmerizes his family and grandchildren with his death stories, as his only son, Bakir, testifies: "Hujayzi, like children, in the gathering of winter nights, loves stories. As soon as one of the children asks him to tell a story, he is ever ready.

His stories are always intriguing; we do not know from where he comes up with them, but his best are the scary ones, in which death is the protagonist" (al-Khumaysi [2013] 2015: 87).[25] Besides, on the rare occasions on which he becomes sexually attracted to his wife, Sarira, he sensually imagines her as a corpse that is being carefully prepared for mummification, with her warm guts being removed from her body and with her heart and two lungs extracted in one pull from her chest (ibid. pp. 140–1). He muses, "I saw Sarira as a corpse that was moving" (ibid. p. 142). Hujayzi's espousal of death in his storytelling and sexuality exhibit his intention to translate himself as well as those he interacts with by means of artistic communication—linguistic and sexual—from their world of the here and now to the transcendental realm of death, where they gain access to "life in the universal internal world" (Adonis 2005: 134).

As a desert novel, *Manafi al-rabb* allows its characters to embrace the values of the indigenous monotheistic religions, and yet it entitles them to challenge these religions' established fixities by planting them on the unpredictable desert "planet" that drives them to question their senses and beliefs. F. F. Moolla explains how Abrahamic religions ascribe contradictory qualities to the desert: how the desert is both "the locus for the vision of the transcendent" and "the divine" and "the locus of uncertainty and danger . . . exile" as well as "trial" (Moolla 2015: 180–1). He writes:

> The desert in the monotheisms is a wilderness untouched by human habitation, but which is the dwelling place instead of demons, the devil or jinn. In the Abrahamic monotheisms thus, since the desert is the locus of uncertainty and danger, the desert is the primal space of exclusion, exile and banishment, most prominently of Cain, the agriculturalist, who murdered his nomadic pastoralist brother, Abel. The desert is a space of trial, most significantly of Hagar, the African slave wife of Abraham, and Ishmael, their son, mythical root of the line of the Arabs. But there are positive connotations to the desert in monotheisms. The desert is an environment where the air is considered to be purer, lighter and healthier and where solitude outside of the city allows self-realization through connection with the divine. This is a theme strongly developed in the monasticism of the 4th century Desert Fathers who withdrew into the deserts around Alexandria in

Egypt. It is also a theme continued in the early history of Islam where the Prophet Muhammad's meditations in a cave in the desert outside of the city of Mecca provided the spiritual preparation for the first revelations. (ibid. pp. 180–1)[26]

Considering the antithetical accounts that monotheisms convey regarding the desert, it is no surprise that Hujayzi himself, as a desert dweller, is defiant regarding religious fixities and searches for truth independent of what humanity has developed and established in terms of religious beliefs and practices. He freely embraces and rejects them in his search for unity and harmony between life and death. He is skeptical towards the common religious belief that the dignity of the dead and the beginning of their new lives are conditional on their burial in a grave or a tomb. He dismisses Sheikh Mazid's assertion that "the tomb is the first of after-life dwellings" (al-Khumaysi [2013] 2015: 112) and that "the grave is a dwelling you prepare for in your life: If you do good deeds, it will become a *rawḍ* [garden] from heaven . . . But if you lead your life committing sins without repentance, the tomb, God forbid, will be a hole from hell" (ibid. p. 113). Despite the undoubted burial of all who die in al-Waʿira, Hujayzi defies the belief, saying, "who said that the dignity of the dead is in their burial? It is only the living who say so. I will believe it when I hear it from a dead person!" (ibid. p. 110). In this sense, after rejecting the predominant belief among Muslims in al-Waʿira concerning burial and tombs, Hujayzi is inclined to adopt other ways and beliefs in his quest for incorruptibility and burial aversion, such as those of Monk Yuʾannis' and his small ascetic community. He muses: "What is the problem? Perhaps this monk's religion will solve my problem. I will follow their Christ and will see if he is able to save my body after death or not! After all, Monk Yuhanna is the one who preserved the water in al-Waʿira's well" (ibid. pp. 226–7).

Hujayzi's rejection of underground burial can be interpreted in two ways. First, his rejection of becoming united with the soil when his body decomposes aligns with the familiar Bedouin disdain for peasant attachment to soil, which is evident in Sheikh Mazid's sermon at the funeral of Saʿdun's wife and son. Sheikh Mazid blames their death in a house fire on the Bedouin decision to settle in the desert, grow dates and olives, and live in houses rather than tents (ibid. pp. 44–5). Second, Hujayzi's unyielding quest for postmortem bodily incorruptibility is driven fundamentally by his desire to evade the inevitable separation of the dead from the living that comes with burial. The narrator observes, "Hujaizi escapes death because it is mere loneliness. He loves company. The living will not accept him in their midst if he decomposes. If he is able to evade decay and rotting, the living will not have an aversion toward leaving his body in their midst" (ibid. p. 151). Thus, Hujayzi's embrace of death while alive and insistence on existing among the living while dead is an affirmation of *Manafi al-rabb*'s novelistic fusion of contradictions—life and death—in its wholesome form, per the Sufi aesthetic tradition. His pursuit of a ghostly existence at his home and among the living is a "movement away" from the binary between life and death (Bhabha 1994: 21) to occupy an in-between space and time in which the "private and public, past and present, the psyche and the social develop an interstitial intimacy. It is an intimacy that questions binary divisions through which such spheres of social experience are often spatially opposed" (Bhabha 1994: 19).

Moreover, from a Fanonian perspective, Hujayzi's revocation of burial and desire to be present among the living can be read as a pursuit of their recognition of his continued existence after death. He urges them to purge themselves of the defilement of indulging in the "here and now" of their immediate world and the limits of "thingness," in the same way a body is purged of its spoiling guts for the sake of its overall mummification and preservation. Frantz Fanon discusses the desire to "be considered" in a disregarding, materialistic world, writing:

> As soon as I desire I am asking to be considered. I am not merely here-and-now, sealed into thingness. I am for somewhere else and for something else. I demand that notice be taken of my negating activity; insofar as I pursue something other than life; insofar as I do battle for the creation of a human world—that is a world of reciprocal recognitions. (Fanon 1967: 218)[27]

By the same token, Hujayzi's reassertion of the ancient, antiquated practice of mummification, which is frowned upon by the surrounding religious cultures, can be interpreted as a "negating activity" that realigns religiously prescribed time and space to make room for his presence as unrepresented past (Bhabha 1994: 18). It also casts doubt on existing beliefs that perpetuate the false separation between life and death, interiority and exteriority, and thereby the inability to achieve a state of greater consciousness and "exalted inspiration" (Adonis 2005: 117) that is made visible to all individuals indiscriminately.

God's Exiles

The novel suggests that several characters are trapped in what its title, *manafi al-rabb* (God's Exiles), denotes, and are therefore impeded from reaching that exalted consciousness that enables them to understand the truth about existence so that they achieve union with the transcendent spirit of the divine. The questions to pose here are: are these exiles spatial or spiritual?; are they self-inflicted or outwardly so? In the following section, Hujayzi's as well as other characters' lives are examined to find answers to these questions. Although the novel centers itself on the desert, the heart of spirituality, its characters' lives are evidently conditioned by the materialistic world, which leads to their being distracted from pursuing the true, beyond life inscribed in the desert's natural laws. In other words, the novel alludes to a form of spiritual exile and fear of death resulting from indulgence in earthly desires. As much as death prevails in the characters' conversations, they do not hesitate to express their fear of it. For example, Saʿdun says on one occasion, "I hate death" (al-Khumaysi [2013] 2015: 34) after seeing a dead bird in his house. Although Saʿdun is married to the love of his life, Zulaykha, they fail to conceive together and insist on having a child irrespective of the damage that this stilted pursuit might cause to their union. Later, Saʿdun takes a second wife, who gives birth to his only son. Evidently, that child becomes a source of his family's suffering and spiritual growth. While Zulaykha dies of grief over her lost love shortly after the child's arrival, Saʿdun loses both that newborn son and his mother in a house fire. At that moment, Saʿdun realizes the spiritual exile he has sent himself into by insisting on memorializing his earthly name through procreation and lineage rather than preserving the immense love and union he and Zulakha had.

Subhi, who later adopts the ascetic ordination name of Monk Yuʾannis, is another character who lives in spiritual exile owing to materialistic conditions. Monk Yuʾannis's dialogues with Hujayzi reveal his having suffered as a young man from extreme poverty and the religious intolerance that ravaged his home village (ibid. pp. 232–3). Young Subhi decides to flee his hostile hometown environment and travel to the nearest metropolis, Asyut, only to find a different type of hostility, this time on the basis of economic achievement. His rich Coptic merchant employer disdainfully warns young Subhi of broaching the subject of marrying his eligible daughter, due to Subhi's poverty. After the merchant's death, Subhi's feeling of inadequacy and low self-worth persists even after the daughter, Sirin, offers her love to him. Subhi harshly declines Sirin's offer and suppresses his desire for her. However, in a later erotic moment, Subhi penetrates Sirin's body in a bloody scene that ends with her death. Devastated by guilt, Subhi flees the cruel world of his material and sensual existence to seek spiritual refuge in the desert. He embraces asceticism in self-imposed solitude, choosing to kill his body and its senses in an attempt to unite with the divine. However, living under the natural laws of the desert, he reaches a state of consciousness in which he realizes that the torment he inflicted on his spirit when he murdered the epitome of his love, Sirin, is due to the materialistic conditions that engulf their world, and that his lost union with Sirin forestalls his attempts at union with the transcendent divine spirit.

Hujayzi's quest for incorruptibility is fundamentally a quest to achieve balance and harmony between life and death and between body and spirit. In his exploration of the available Muslim and Christian beliefs and practices about the afterlife imparted by both Monk Yuʾannis and Sheikh Mazid, Hujayzi realizes that neither of these approaches to religion promises harmony between life and death, which is signified by the two characters' inability to pledge postmortem bodily imperishability to Hujayzi. Adonis discusses, how among the Sufis, it is necessary to fuse what is physically "perceptible" with the "imperceptible," the "inner" world of the self with the "outer" world, and "the real" with "the figurative" in the form of man's "creative imagination." This process of artistic conjoining takes place in the human being and enables him or her to apprehend and internalize in their imagination what is beyond the here and now (Adonis 2005: 137). Elaborating on the mutual significance of the body and imagination in reaching this mystical knowledge and creating transcendental poetics from a human source, Adonis writes:

> Creative imagination makes the body transparent, since it itself becomes the other world that Sufi gnosis attains. The body becomes an element

for generating the imaginative structure of the place, and becomes a Sufi dimension and song of the interior, which reflects upon the exterior place, restructuring it in its image. Poetry in this sense is the imaginative dimension that restructures the exterior world in the image of its creator, the internal world.

The Sufi develops the macrocosm in his body, which is the microcosm—in such a manner that he makes his body live, after it has become transparent, through the action of the creative imagination itself as the original, the primordial domain of what is possible. (ibid. pp. 137–8)

In the light of the Sufi perception of the body, we can understand the aesthetics behind Hujayzi's demand to revere the body and reject its burial and isolation from the living after death as well as the suppression of its livelihood while still alive. It is a way of existence and an aesthetic rooted in believing that "[t]he body, basically and fundamentally brings together the allegoric and the material in its figurative form . . . and thus the body is the domain of the possible, a place in which what is perceptible by the senses can be transformed" (ibid. p. 138).

Journeys to Life En Route to Mut

After identifying the spiritual exile of some of the characters, in the course of the novel's events—fragmented and unchronological though they are—readers are still able to see characters being released from materialistic entrapment, especially on their journeys to and back from Mut. Saʿdun's, Ghunayma's, and Hujayzi's journeys on the desert trail to and from Mut are metaphors for their death and rebirth, as major eye-opening events take place there. Thereafter, every character is able to apprehend what would otherwise be hidden from its limited perception. When Saʿdun takes the trail to Mut with his wife, Zulaykha, seeking fertility treatment to conceive a child, their pursuit is of no avail and they return disappointed. However, after they consume the fruit of the orange tree they have decided to rest under, they arrive at a physical and spiritual union they have never achieved as a couple prior to that moment (al-Khumaysi [2013] 2015: 274–80). While Ghunayma is on the Mut trail a deadly sandstorm erupts, and he is forced to fight its deadly conditions to save his life. During the night, an extraordinarily beautiful woman named Jalah appears to him to keep his body warm and protected. She introduces herself as part of the large Persian army that accompanied her (ibid. pp. 256–61). When Ghunayma wakes up, he realizes Jalah and the whole army faction have been buried under the sand during the desert storm. Confounded between reality—historically, the Persian army had once trod Egypt's western desert (between 525 and 404 BCE) with its men, women, horses, and wagons to fight Libyan armies[28]—and delusion, Ghunayma finds Jalah's green head covering as evidence of her reality to him (ibid. p. 292). Ghunayma, in this instance, finds life in the experience of death, and his future in reliving history.

It is on the outskirts of the oasis, at the beginning of the path to Mut, where the bodies of his dead friends, Saʿdun and Ghunayma, are isolated from the dwellings of the living, that Hujayzi finds solace, comfort, and harmony between life and death. Hujayzi demonstrates his ability to hold conversations with them while dead, a sight that stuns his son, Bakir, but affirms Hujayzi's proximity to their spiritual, beyond world. It is on the path to Mut that Hujayzi finds the mythical orange tree, which he believes will when eaten confer on his body its scent and repel the process of decay. Hujayzi's eating of the mystical fruit is creatively relayed from two inextricable perspectives, a metaphysical one relayed by an omniscient, anonymous narrator and a realist other perspective relayed by Hujayzi's son, Bakir. While the omniscient narrator describes Hujayzi's reaction to the magnificent sight of the mystical tree fruit as well as the appearance of the mystical character of al-Muʿazzi (the Consoling One), Bakir relays his bewilderment at his father's attempts to reach out for and communicate with what he cannot see or hear. This creative narrative approach precludes the reader from distinguishing what is communicated as mystical knowledge from positivist knowledge/experiential reality. As soon as Hujayzi reaches the mystical orange fruit, al-Muʿazzi runs to him on a radiant black horse with a beautiful woman riding behind him (ibid. p. 401). The consoling knight allays Hujayzi's fears of burial and draws attention to the eternity of his memory:

> Even if your body is buried, your legacy will not be. I know the day that your story will inspire a writer's heart. He will write it as a detailed chapter, filled with wonders. News about the story will spread across the globe,

so that people know in all ages to come the story of "Hujayzi, the son of Shadid al-Waʿiri," God's true follower, who abstained from life to live it forever and who fought forgetting for a hundred years to win remembrance as long as the world exists. (ibid. p. 404)

Al-Muʿazzi's words encapsulate the philosophy behind Hujayzi's life quest for immortality, which al-Muʿazzi translates to the realm of artistic endeavor. Hujayzi's quest to conjoin the opposites of life and death inspires creative writing fusing human bodily experience with imagination, thereby immortalizing and memorializing life quests such as Hujayzi's across different times and spaces.

The Tent

The Tent transports the reader to the Egyptian desert region, east of the Nile Valley and the Delta, where the fertile farmland gradually recedes. The uniqueness of this geographical setting provides *The Tent* with the spatial expanse and aesthetic scope necessary to creatively mediate the cultural disparities between the indigenous Pharaonic and agrarian communities of the Nile River valley, on the one hand, and the nomadic population dispersed across the north-eastern desert region on the other. Moreover, this geographic location, being remote from the overpopulated Egyptian metropolis, functions aesthetically as a space for *al-lā maʾhūl* (the deserted/unpopulated) and thereby translates readers spiritually and existentially from their world of familiar surroundings to a deserted, untrodden spatial microcosm where alternative meanings of physical and spiritual existence are manifest.

In her 1997 article "al-buʿd al-ithnugrafi lil-ʿamal al-riwāʾi" (The Ethnographic Dimension in Fiction: A Testimony), Miral al-Tahawi reflects on her authorial experience in aesthetically representing such unique space with the particularities of its communities' modern history in *The Tent*. Although her priority was the aesthetic value of her novelistic endeavor, she understood that the ethnographic dimension could add value to the novel, highlighting the intersection of that geography's culture with regional women's histories (al-Tahawi 1997: 146).[29] She writes:

> The novel does not postulate a place as much as it does a people shaped by the place's culture and transformed by its changes. They interact with the

place in ebbs and tides until the place creates within itself disjunctive dualities of values. The valley lying between two desert wings is not a geographic reality as much as it is a representation of the conflict between a patriarchal agrarian culture and a pastoral matriarchal one: nomadism and urbanism, moving and settling, freedom and authority. These dualities are capable of creating a narrative of life conflict, thereby determining my primary creative concern. (ibid. pp. 147–8)[30]

By focusing on the element of people "shaped" and "transformed" by the culture of the place they dwell in, *The Tent* represents the historical and cultural experiences a Bedouin family undergoes over a generation, while paying close attention to its female members. These changes are also suffused, albeit allusively, with the modern colonial experience Egypt (and concomitantly its Bedouin population) underwent at the turn of the twentieth century. *The Tent* highlights the impact of colonialism on Bedouins through the interventions of a character named Anne in the family's affairs. Anne is portrayed as an Orientalist ethnographer from Europe, who immerses herself in Egypt's nomadic life to record habits, customs, and cultural heritage—"She listed her interests: horses, hawks, hunting, woman" (al-Tahawi [1998] 2003: 99)—but whose infiltration into the Bedouin family's traditional household has irreversibly altered its customs.

The novel depicts the life span of the youngest female in the Bedouin family, Fatima, who witnesses her family's transformations firsthand, and through whose voice the novel's events are narrated. Fatima demonstrates astounding storytelling abilities and a fertile imagination that awe everyone who knows her, and undoubtedly the reader. The novel opens with Fatima's articulation of her dilemma as an anguished five-year-old with a consciousness, visions, stories, and interactions that are mystifyingly beyond her years, if not beyond comprehension—a situation that leads her family and household members to believe Fatima must be possessed by otherworldly spirits and demons. As Fatima's narration develops, the reader realizes that Fatima is not at all possessed by out-of-this world spirits, but rather, her fecund imagination yields rich pictures and stories of transcendental desert life, which is no longer physically accessible to her following her ancestors' exchange of their traditional nomadic life for settlement in Egypt's cultivable land. This imaginative narrative style choice attests not only to the Bedouin's mournful removal from her traditional desert environment, but also to her unyielding attempts to invoke that background and heritage so as to acclimatize herself to her seclusion behind the walls of her new settled dwelling. In addition, the aesthetic decision to narrate the novel's events from Fatima's ever-fascinating imagination and constantly evolving awareness, rather than, for example, as a memory flashback from her mature self, supplies elements of anticipation, involvement, admiration, and sympathy from the reader to the growing character of Fatima, whose first-person perspective on the history of oppression and violence that she and other female characters undergo takes the form of a compelling personal testimony.

Mutual Centrality of Women and Desert

The centrality of female figures runs parallel to that of the desert in *The Tent*, thus allowing them to reflect one another in conditions and traits. The women in Fatima's narrative consciousness possess the same significance and force that the desert does in her imagination, as both entities are portrayed as defying man's manipulative attempts to undermine their value or suppress their creative power for materialistic gains. The novel inventively conjures up ghostly remnants of times in which women, embodied in the character of the Bedouin matriarch Hakima, and the desert, embodied in the mythical desert-dwelling characters of Musallam, Zahwa, and Saqima (Sigeema), enjoy autonomy and freedom. Although the novel focuses on Fatima's female family members, a multiplicity of other women, whose ethnicities, classes, and ages differ greatly, are portrayed side by side with their Bedouin counterparts. These diverse women's lifestyles and practices, as well as Fatima's herself, are aesthetically assembled in a novelistic mosaic of Fatima's inspirational narratives and pictures, which in their turn obscure pre-established narratives and pictures of these women's statuses and hierarchies based on their ethnicity, seniority, and class. Fatima's narrative subverts such preconceived female dynamics on two levels. First, it portrays the noble status of Bedouin females and its accompanying physical confinement as an affliction and a curse by which women of other ethnicities, who are perceived as subordinate to Bedouins, are not necessarily tormented. Second, it suggests that female activities like sewing, beading, singing, hair braiding, animal tending, cooking, and storytelling, activities that are traditionally seen as minor if not degrading, are shared acts of female liberation and empowerment, across all female groups.

Powerful Women across Time in the Bedouin Household

In the time span of the novel's events, which seem to take place in approximately the first half of the twentieth century, there is no portrayal of a golden age per se for Bedouin women. However, at least during Fatima's early childhood, there are remnants of a ghostly age in which matriarchs enjoyed a superior status, not only to junior female household members, but also to their adult male children. Al-Tahawi mentions that the nomadic culture is historically a matriarchal one (al-Tahawi 1997: 147); however, the novel demonstrates that the Bedouin culture's interactions with its patriarchal agrarian counterpart has impacted the role of women and diminished their authority over time. The character of Grandmother Hakima—whose name literally means "female ruler"—captures the shadows of an aged authoritarian matriarch from the past, whose perspective on the female offspring in her family is filled with disdain for her own gender, a view that indicates the demise of female reverence in past Bedouin tradition.[31]

Hakima is the only Bedouin woman who has "the main gate opened for her" (al-Tahawi [1998] 2003: 7). However, in Fatima's eyes, her "gold-capped teeth" and dark-blue cloak make her resemble "*al-ghūla*" (the ghoul) (al-Tahawi [1996] 2010: 15), and her unceasing curses and unjust view of her granddaughters and the female servants as "*khilfat-l-suʾ*" (miserable offspring) (ibid. p. 16) generate on their part resentment and detestation of her ghostly authoritarian figure. At the opposite end of Bedouin women's hierarchy lies Fatima's mother, whose inability to keep a male child qualifies her, in Hakima's words, as "*jallābat-il-khilfa al-ḥarām*" (al-Tahawi [1996] 2010: 17); "She's given birth to nothing but bad luck" (al-Tahawi [1998] 2003: 9), another indication of women's diminishing status and suffering. Young Fatima describes one of the ominous mornings in her mother's room:

> It would be a morning like all previous mornings, full of tension and anxiety. Either my mother wouldn't open the door of her room, or, if she did open it, she would watch us with apprehensive eyes. Her pale, emaciated

figure, the thin veins on her eyelids, and her nose swollen from floods of tears, choked my heart with sadness. (ibid. p. 3)

The fearful image of unjust authority illustrated in the grandmother figure and the immense pain experienced by the mother constitute a source of anxiety and distress for young Fatima and chase sleep away from her eyes. She thinks: "sleeplessness eats fear, and sleep is full of nightmares, and the darkness is a cloak" (ibid. p. 24). Fatima, as a witness of cultural change, is bewildered by the discrepancy between the subordinate positions she, her mother, and female siblings occupy in relation to their all-powerful, authoritarian grandmother. She wonders if the grandmother belongs to the same gender: "Was she really a woman? She was the mother of us all. Our great demon mother who wrapped herself in men's scarves" (ibid. p. 7). Wearing "men's scarves" implies Hakima's gender-status crossing from the female subordinate realm to the superior male counterpart, which is only possible due to her senior age, which guarantees her loss of bodily vitality and sexual vigor. As novelistic time passes, and towards the end of the novel, this gender-status crossing is underlined once more when Safiyya, the eldest Bedouin sister, occupies her grandmother's position, but in an even more drastically ghostly context of matriarchy, as by the time Safiyya attains seniority status the house is already in a shambles and all signs of the family's nobility and wealth are obliterated: "The wooden guest house was blackened by years of smoke and dirt, and time had settled its dust on the tent and carpets too" (ibid. p. 125).

The economy and management of the Bedouin household involve women who are physically confined to the house, such as the ailing Bedouin mother and her four female children, as well as women, who belong to other ethnicities—not necessarily superior to the Bedouin's—but are not cloistered. For example, Sasa comes from a peasant background, yet has freedom to leave the house for chores. Muha (Mouha) is a local gypsy, who, despite her ties to the house as a servant, also enjoys freedom to leave its gates, ride animals, smoke cigarette stubs, and sing with other gypsy girls in the desert. The European ethnographer, Anne, does not dwell in the Bedouin household, and yet her disruptive interference in its affairs attests to the colonial moment the novel is set in. The mythical female characters, Zahwa, Sigeema, and the seven daughters of Naʿsh, dwell in Fatima's imagination and assist her in escaping from the house, albeit fantastically, to their liberating habitat in the nearby desert and its open sky.

As women characters defy their physical confinement by engaging in creative activities, so do their desert-dwelling mythical counterparts, whose lives challenge humans' sensual and experiential understanding. For example, the two noble Bedouin sisters, Fuz and Rayhana, sew and bead dresses and table cloths from the fine Damascene-dyed fabric their father buys during his trips (al-Tahawi [1996] 2010: 17), and so do Mouha and Sasa, who sew scraps of cloth together and spin cheap dark-colored wool to make hair-braid extensions (ibid. pp. 23–4). The novel, thus, through shared activity, albeit with materials unequal in monetary worth, mediates the two girl-pairs' ethnic and economic difference and aligns their creative and liberating activities regardless of their class asymmetry.

Fatima, the Outcast, Inquirer, and Harbinger of Change

The novel depicts Fatima as unwelcome in either pair's activities. Despite her "ʾ*amīra*" (princess) status, at least in her father's eyes (ibid. p. 40), her older sisters refuse to reveal their secrets to her due to her younger age. In like manner, Muha and Sasa, the house servants, deny her participation in their games due to her superior class. Fatima, thus, is portrayed as the outcast who envies both pairs for being able to escape the cloister through shared group activities. She recalls, in one of her sleepless nights: "Fuz and Rayhana lay in one another's arms, sharing their secrets. I was furious. Even in their sleep they had secret conversations which I could not join in" (al-Tahawi [1998] 2003: 2). Similarly, Fatima's entreatment of Mouha and Sasa to allow her to play with them always goes unheard: "'Mouha . . . where are you going? Play with me.' She looked at me indifferently, then she left me" (ibid. p. 17). As it happens, most of Fatima's attempts to communicate with her family and household members are futile because they do not appear to hear her voice. For example, the mother does not respond to Fatima's question: "'Are you asleep, Mother? Are you asleep?' She didn't answer and I jumped up beside her" (ibid. p. 20).

Fatima's exacerbated isolation and overlooked existence in her own house offers a foreboding of her community's dismay at the unwanted change to which her character and lifetime bear witness. As a child, Fatima spends long periods of time sitting by the iron rods that block one of the large windows to give an account of the somewhat lively economy of the household with its filled grain store rooms, its gate huge enough to allow a whole caravan of camels to pass through, its livestock stables, and its guest house, all nestled within a big, black mud fence (ibid. pp. 21–2). In her mature years, she observes the abandonment and degeneration of the house: "The main gate was ajar. The dust had piled up and now it couldn't move. It was no longer opened and closed" (ibid. p. 125).

Young Fatima craftily draws attention to the thorns and wild plants blocking her from reaching the beautiful mastic and lemon trees in her yard, which are known to grow locally in the sunny, dry Mediterranean south. The wild plants and thorns symbolize the Bedouin cultural restraints that prohibit Fatima from enjoying the Mediterranean environment in which she is newly settled. Nonetheless, Fatima transcends these thorny boundaries with the aid of two influential women, Anne and Sardub (henceforth Sardoub). On the one hand, the only trees made accessible to her, from whose top she can see the "rich black earth" with "plots of green" (ibid. p. 15), are, ironically, some foreign, unfamiliar trees named *busianus*, gifted to her father by Madame Anne (ibid. p. 23). On the other, Fatima finds her refuge and dream world on Sardoub's warm lap, as only there is she able to visualize the free, joyful world of peasants, next to whom the sun's golden rays reflect on sand dunes. She muses:

> The peasants were there. Sometimes I heard them singing and saw them strolling gracefully in their brightly colored clothes. The sun glanced the tops of hills along the horizon and the sand dunes reflected its dazzling rays. Finally I had something to do. I came down from the treetop into Sardoub's folded lap, where I lay my head for a while and dozed off. I felt I was falling deeper and deeper into a bottomless well. (ibid. p. 15)

In this passage, some of the historical and thematic concerns of *The Tent* are vividly exhibited in Fatima's restless search for the *joie de vivre*. While the *busianus* trees, gifted by Anne, signify the impact of foreign intervention—as the harbinger of modernity—on Bedouin lifestyle, these foreign trees also provide Fatima with a position from which to view for herself the merits of peasant life, irrespective of the hostile Bedouin stance towards civilization and settlement. In other words, what both Anne and Sardoub metaphorically present to Fatima controverts her Bedouin heritage and jointly leads to her self-split. Miral al-Tahawi explains that while the presence of Anne's character in the novel serves to convey a mere historical truth about the historical change brought about by the presence of Europeans, her creative focus was on the place where Bedouin and peasant spaces (the desert and cultivable land) and their cultures intersect and/or clash (al-Tahawi 1997: 146). She writes about the long-held Bedouin view of peasants as follows:

> Bedouins were enjoying the familiarity of the desert while reaping the spoils of abrupt raids on the bounties of the valley. These raids concerned Egypt's peasants and turned Bedouins into an enemy on many levels. The animosity was fueled by the scorn Bedouins harbor towards all that is agrarian since they perceive it as submissiveness and a shameful resignation from the pride the Bedouin holds valuable to his existence. (ibid. p. 148)

From her perspective, Fatima ridicules that long-held, disdainful Bedouin opinion of peasants by, first, sighting them enjoying life, and second, dreaming about their free world in the comfort of Sardoub's lap, who is a peasant herself. Yet, on one level, Fatima's sense of "falling" into a "bottomless well" while laying her head in Sardoub's lap marks the confusion and uncertainty that come with challenging and changing tradition. On another, the well reference indicates how the novel anchors Fatima's search, confounded though it is, in Arab mythical and oral storytelling heritage. Wells are sources of water and thereby life, but choosing to settle by them is a curse in traditional, nomadic culture (Salih 1997: 19).

In the coming section, I will demonstrate how the influential figures of Sardoub and the mythical desert inhabitants, Musallam, Sigeema, and Zahwa, empower Fatima and relieve her anguish by nurturing her fantasy with both agrarian and desert oral and mythical heritage. Then, I will discuss how Anne, who is depicted as an influential female figure, represents the inevitable colonial history that has embedded itself in this peripheral part of Egypt.

Sardoub is portrayed as a nurturing mother figure and an avid storyteller, in whose arms Fatima can shut her eyes and dream away. Sardoub's desert- inspired legends, like the seven-faced sun and Naʿsh and his seven daughters, ignite Fatima's fantasy with alternative happenings and activities in an unrestricted, external world. However, Sardoub's storytelling is often fragmented and unfinished, reflecting the surrounding cultures' disregard for and suppression of their women's significant life narratives and prompting Fatima to complete them herself. Fatima recounts:

> She stroked my hair and told me a story: "The sun goes round in the sky, and becomes a circle. The sun is a girl and like all other girls she has seven faces and then there is a long night when she buries her last face, the pock-marked face of an old woman lamenting and wailing. Then she runs away behind the Mountains of Oblivion, the mountains of iron and fire. Between us and them are two dams and a well of molten iron which the sun falls into."
> "Who? Who, ya-Mama Sardoub?"
> "The Pharaohs, and the slaves of the cannibals of Namnam and Gog."
> (al-Tahawi [1998] 2003: 6)

Sardoub's story creates an analogy between the sun's journey in the sky from sunrise to sunset and that of a woman during her lifetime. However, the sinking of the sun behind mountains of iron can imply both the final stage of a woman's life and the violent thrust with which women's paths, talents, and endeavors are thrown into oblivion, behind the iron bars of their cloisters. Sardoub says: "Between us and them are two dams and a well of molten iron," a setting that suggests the hardships and obstacles Sardoub and Fatima will have to overcome to unravel these women's hidden lives. At the same time, although sunset implies the end of the sun's daylight cycle, it is also a given that the sun will return with all its might to shine over the desert the following day. Analogously, these women's legacies are to be revived when their younger counterparts acknowledge and commemorate their ancestral accomplishments.

Similarly, Sardoub's other story told to young Fatima of the seven daughters of Naʿsh underscores the overlooked Arab mythical heritage attesting to Arab women's struggles on the one hand and strengths on the other. The Arab legend is a cultural interpretation of the well-known astrological phenomenon of the Pleiades, a constellation of stars that has bewildered humans for thousands of years. Every culture around the globe has attempted to interpret the Pleiades with a powerful legend that reflects its particular cosmic outlook. The Arab legend relates that Naʿsh had seven daughters, but was killed by Suhayl, which is seen as a southern star. Grieving for their father, Naʿsh's daughters pledge that they will not bury him until they have sought revenge on his murderer, Suhayl. They have been seen since time immemorial as the star cluster chasing Star Suhayl southward: four of them are perceived to be virgins carrying their father's *naʿsh* (coffin) and leading the other three sisters/stars in the chase. The legend describes the remaining three sisters as one carrying a child in her hand, another who is pregnant, and a third who is crippled and walking slowly (Salim 2010).[32] The legend conveys these daughters' endless turmoil, chasing their father's murderer, but at the same time, it attests to their unyielding determination and strength.

Sardoub, as a creative storyteller, puts her own spin on the legend, since she fuses it with the experiences she and other females around her have courageously undergone. First, she translates the daughters' chase from the sky to the desert terrain. Then, she portrays them as being chased away rather than chasing, suggesting that the daughters' venture has been altered or rather marred over time by unidentified forces: "Seven daughters Naʾsh had, seven girls. The desert was bleak and desolate and the ground was soft and treacherous. How would they hide their tracks? And the Virgin took her newborn child and fled across the sky after they had pelted her with stones" (al-Tahawi [1998] 2003: 13). While the virgins in the original legend are in the lead in the Pleiades' cluster, the virgin in Sardoub's version is alone, is violently attacked, and is fleeing the "bleak and desolate" desert with her newborn child, suggesting a more tumultuous trajectory and pursuit of refuge. The anguished virgin in Sardoub's narrative can be read as a reflection of Fatima. On the one hand, they both demonstrate courage, tenacity, and a desire to chase truth. They are also both surrounded with creative, powerful women, namely the virgin's strong-willed star sisters, in the Pleiades, and the creative Bedouin, peasant, or gypsy women, in Fatima's household. On the other, their curiosity and attempts to capture the meaning of existence, their own and that of others, set them off on quests and trials in unfamiliar realms and draw doubt, if not disapproval, from their communities. The motif of a virgin carrying a newborn child presents an oxymoron that has been used in the traditional narratives of patriarchal societies to forewarn of what is believed to be deviant behavior by young women and the elicited punitive action from the community.

Both virgins search for refuge from their traditional communities' sanctions. The flight of the virgin and her newborn child parallels Fatima's from her cloister in her imagination, which, in turn, can be seen as Fatima's newborn, impregnated in her fecund mind by the espousal of traditions and cultures other than her own—desert, peasant, and gypsy. Furthermore, the virgin-and-newborn motif vividly evokes the biblical narrative of the Virgin Mary with her newborn. They are believed to have fled from Jerusalem to Egypt's desert terrain after Herod, Jerusalem's ruler at the time, sought to kill the newborn for fear of the prophesied control that infant would have over his kingdom. Analogously, as the biblical newborn presents a threat to Herod's established power, Fatima's newborn imagination, which carries a multiplicity of foreign images and narratives, constitutes a threat to established Bedouin tradition and power structures. Both newborns are therefore viewed as harbingers of undesirable change.

Sardoub does not finish telling her version of the famous Arab legend of Naᶜsh's seven daughters to Fatima, a storytelling approach that both suggests the continuation of the virgin's turmoil and foreshadows Fatima's own suffering when she permanently loses her ability to walk. The incomplete story also leaves Fatima confused about the virgin's fate, but keen to utilize her own imagination to alter or even end the virgin's desolate path as well her own. Fatima's constant evolution in the poetic and narrative forms she uses in recording and articulating her experiences and those of others corresponds with her persistent climbing of the foreign *busianus* treetop, Madame Anne's gift, to observe the intersection of peasant and desert lives outside her house. The climbing of a foreign tree to seek knowledge is ironic and signals Fatima's inevitable slipping from tradition, which is represented in her literal fall from the tree and the subsequent amputation of her leg (al-Tahawi [1996] 2010: 97). Fatima's physical disability, however, marks her loss and helplessness in determining her fate after this violent fall, especially after her father's delegation of Madame Anne to look after her, in the same way as he leaves Fatima's favorite filly, Khayra, to Anne to breed with other horses. Fatima now feels she has become Anne's prey. On the one hand, at Anne's mansion, Anne gives Fatima language and music lessons. She proudly explains to her guests:

"She couldn't even read or write in her own language, and now she knows three languages. She reads a lot. We have worked out a special program for her education. They smiled in astonishment and heaped praise upon her" (al-Tahawi [1998] 2003: 99). On the other, Fatima observes how "Anne smiles greedily. She loved my stories, and nothing delighted her more than listening to them. It was as if she were discovering new and wonderful things with me" (ibid. p. 97). According to al-Tahawi, Anne's character sprang to the author's imagination from the historical actuality of the presence of European ethnographers during modern colonial times, whose mission was to observe and record details about the Bedouin cultural heritage. That historical representation was necessary for underlining Fatima's suffering and self-split (al-Tahawi 1997: 146)

Fatima's stories exhibit how the desert is her imaginative sanctuary. She travels with her imagination to Musallam's, Sigeema's, and Zahwa's tent in the desert as she seeks spiritual and imaginative refuge. She muses:

> Every time I closed my eyes I found them. Every time I surrendered my thick, long hair to Sardoub's tender hand they moved before me in silence. It was as if I had leapt over the high wall, and flown away, moving in and out between the farm buildings until I reached the open land beyond the houses and the wide mud walls. There were the green pastures, and the mountain and low hills. I watched Mouha tending her goats, and I rode the donkey, and I ran and ran across the desert until I saw the seven palm trees. Here was the oasis of Musallam and Zahwa and Sigeema and the little slave. (al-Tahawi [1998] 2003: 1)

Fatima's mythical desert-dwelling characters seem to not merely reflect the experiences of her family and household members, but also transcend the difficulties their real counterparts face thanks to living in the free, untainted-by-civilization desert terrain. For example, Musallam resembles her father in nobility and family-loving traits. Musallam is sketched as an older man, whose "taut, noble cheeks" and "tough lean hands could sharpen jagged rocks" (ibid. p. 4). His interactions with the nomadic guests, who stop by his oasis to eat, drink, and rest during their desert travel, evince timeless Bedouin habits before political and geographical rifts. While his guests boast about their glorious achievements, recall Arab tribal wars, and complain about the Egyptian state soldiers' atrocities in the valley, Musallam does not make lineage claims to any Arab tribe, define himself as a *mashriqi* (Eastern Arab) or *maghribi* (Western Arab),[33] or take pride in having sons (al-Tahawi [1996] 2010: 18–19). In fact, his only answer to all their questions is "I have a wife. She's as light-footed as a gazelle" (al-Tahawi [1998] 2003: 12). Fatima's imagination asserts Musallam's view of Sigeema when she describes her as being "very small, like a child that had been surprised by wrinkles" (ibid. p. 40). Musallam, thus, is a male, albeit mythical, who orients himself primarily towards female love. While Musallam does not heed to his guests' mockery of his selfless love of his wife, Fatima's father succumbs to the cultural pressure to beget a male child and abandons his wife.

Zahwa is portrayed as a gazelle with anthropomorphic traits, who has the ability to exist in different places simultaneously. She reflects Fatima in being a restless spirit that always wanders in the desert. Zahwa's freedom fascinates Fatima, and presents her as an empowered and empowering figure whom Fatima continuously invokes, poses questions to, and seeks to accompany. Nonetheless, Zahwa, as a figurative embodiment of freedom, seems to be an untraceable creature. Fatima muses:

> [Zahwa] "gazed into the distance and then with her finger drew crucified figures writing in the sand. I watched on in admiration and handed her sharp stones and date stumps while she made her pictures . . . Night was falling. She walked away and the soles of her feet left no mark on the ground. The hem of her dress brushed over the sand and no trace of her remained." (ibid. p. 4)

At the end of the novel, just as the Bedouin household dismantles, the mythical family of Musallam, Sigeema, and Zahwa disappears. In Fatima's last fragment of Sigeema's and Zahwa's narrative, she describes their blood drying in the desert sun (ibid. p. 119). The disappearance of these pure desert creatures is symbolic of the obscuring of civilization to desert life. As Fatima grows weary of Anne's persistent demands to tell stories and sing songs ("The story, ya—Fatim, tell the story . . . Carry on, ya—Fatim"), Fatima asks her figurative parallel, Khayra, the filly: "Are you fed up, Khayra, like me? Books and writing paper, pregnancy and labor" (ibid. pp. 101–2). By this means, Fatima sees her fate mirrored in both Khayra's and Zahwa's melancholic end, but nonetheless tries to rewrite that fate that obscured desert heritage before it is erased. Fatima's creative narratives and songs evince al-Tahawi's valuable, yet elegiac endeavor to memorialize a large quantity of Egypt's overlooked Bedouin folkloric heritage in the traditional forms of *majārīd, shitiwa, hajja, ᶜalam,* and *takhārīf,* carefully collected from the Bedouin elderly (al-Tahawi 1997: 150–1).

In conclusion, the aesthetic principality of the desert is vividly corroborated in *Manafi al-rabb* and *The Tent.* While *Manafi al-rabb* challenges the disjunctions between life and death, body and spirit, and reality and myth through Hujayzi's discovery of their connectedness in the magical desert realm, *The Tent* re-inscribes female inspirational and creative enterprise in contemporary male-dominated Bedouin culture. It also juxtaposes the value of women's creative work in Bedouin cultural memory and heritage, as they appear in legends and folktales, with their current subordination. The novels both emphasize the significance of human love and unity between the self and the other by highlighting the destructive effect of the modern cultural conditions that split and disjoin them. They do so, for example, by subverting procreation and child reproduction when they are culturally conditioned and intended to secure materialistic gain or fulfill overdetermined gender roles, rather than solidify human unity. While *Manafi al-rabb* disrupts the idea of procreation when it depicts its characters as having connected with the transcendent divine spirit after losing their children and abandoning their here-and-now world for the life beyond, *The Tent* warns against overlooking women's invaluable contributions and creativity due to prescribed gender hierarchies, by simultaneously invoking and mourning Bedouin ancestral imaginativeness, spiritual purity, traditional art forms, and, more importantly, Bedouin reverence for women.

Notes

1. Salah Salih reminds us of "the special relationship that connects the primary roots of Arab culture and language to the desert on both the artistic and religious-intellectual planes. *Jahiliyya* Arabic poetry and Islam were born in the semi-deserts (steppe) of Najd and the plains of the Arabian peninsula, which constitute, along with the African Sahara, one geographical region" (Salih 1997: 8). For more details, see Salah Salih's study of Arabic desert novels,

"Tajalliyat usturiyya lil-saharaʾ al-afriqiyya al-kubra fi al-riwaya al-ʿarabiyya" (Mythic Manifestations of the Sahara in the Arabic Novel)," in *Alif: Journal of Comparative Poetics, Literature and Anthropology in Africa*, No. 17, 1997, pp. 6–27.
2. The trend of the urbanized novel is so prominent that it has been identified by previous literary observers such as Sabry Hafez and Mara Naaman. For more details, see Sabry Hafez's "The New Egyptian Novel: Urban Transformations and Narrative Form," *New Left Review*, 64, July–August 2010, pp. 46–62, and Mara Naaman's *Urban Space in Contemporary Egyptian Literature: Portraits of Cairo* (New York: Palgrave Macmillan, 2011).
3. The Libyan author and critic Ibrahim al-Kuni rejects delimiting the novel's spatial possibilities to urbanized settings, as will be discussed in more detail in this chapter.
4. Salih's "Tajalliyat usturiyya lil-saharaʾ al-afriqiyya al-kubra fi al-riwaya al-ʿarabiyya" surveys more works, especially from North Africa, that utilize, to varying degrees, the desert and its mythical and cultural heritage. These include, from Libya, Ibrahim al-Kuni's *Rubaʿiyyat-l-khusuf*; from Sudan, Tayeb Saleh's *Mawsim al-hijra, ʾila al-shamal*, Makki Muhammad ʿAli's *al-Saysabana* (1983), and ʿUmar al-Hamidi's *Jazirat-il-ʿawad* (1976); from Algeria, ʿAbdel Hamid bin Haduqa's *Rih al-janub* (1976); from Mauritania, Ahmad Walid ʿAbdel Qadir's *al-ʾasmaʾ al-mutaghayyira* (1981); from Tunisia, Mahmud al-Masʿadi's *al-sadd* (1985); and two novels from Egypt, Jamal al-Ghitani's *al-Zuwayl* (1980), and Sabri Musa's *Fasad al-ʾamkina* (1982).
5. There are only very few examples of Egyptian novels that employ the desert as a primary spatial setting for their events. These include Jamal al-Ghitani's *al-Zuwayl* (1980) and Sabri Musa's *Fasad al-ʾamkina* (1982).
6. Translations from Salah Salih's article in Arabic are my own.
7. Salih, Salah, "Tajalliyat usturiyya lil-saharaʾ al-afriqiyya al-kubra fi al-riwaya al-ʿarabiyya," *Alif: Journal of Comparative Poetics: Literature and Anthropology in Africa*, No. 17, 1997, pp. 6–27.
8. Al-Kuni, Ibrahim, "In the Desert We Visit Death," interview by Anders Hastrup, Louisiana Channel, Louisiana Museum of Modern Art (22 April 2014), <http://channel.louisiana.dk/video/ibrahim-al-koni-desert-we-visit-death> (last accessed 5 March 2016).
9. Al-Kuni recalls learning Georg Lukács's theory of the novel from his essays on Thomas Mann during his studies at the Gorky Institute for literature.
10. Bhabha, Homi, *The Location of Culture* (New York: Routledge, 1994).

11. Bhabha, Homi, "The World and the Home," *Social Text: Third World and Post-Colonial Issues*, Nos. 31/32, 1992, pp. 141–53.
12. *Al-ṭawāriq* (Tuareg) are nomadic groups that populate the south-western Libyan desert in addition to other parts of the North African Sahara and West African Sahel.
13. cooke, miriam, "Magical Realism in Libya," *Journal of Arabic Literature*, Vol. 41, 2010, pp. 9–21.
14. Weisburg, Meg Ferniss, "Spiritual Symbolism in the Sahara: Ibrahim Al-Koni's Nazīf al-Ḥajar," in *Research in African Literature*, Vol. 46, No. 3, Fall 2015, pp. 45–67.
15. Al-Kuni, Ibrahim, *Nazif al-hajar* (London: Riyad al-Rayyis lil-Kutub wal-Nashr, 1990).
16. Al-Kuni, Ibrahim, *The Bleeding of the Stone*, trans. May Jayyusi and Christopher Tingley (Northampton: Interlink Books, 2013).
17. Lashin, Musa Shahin, *Al-Manhal al-hadith fi sharh al-hadith: Ahadith mukhtara from sahih al-Bukhari hasab manhaj al-maʿahid al-azhariyya al-asila* (Cairo: Dar al-shuruq, 2001), 2nd edn, Part IV.
18. The three desert novels that Sharif Elmusa studies are *Endings* by ʿAbd al-Rahman Munif, *The Bleeding of the Stone* by Ibrahim al-Kuni, and *Seeds of Corruption* by Sabri Musa. See Sharif Elmusa, "The Ecological Bedouin: Toward Environmental Principles for the Arab Region," *Alif: Journal of Comparative Poetics*, Vol 33, 2013, pp. 9–35.
19. The English translation is mine.
20. The worship of Mut was popular during the New Kingdom era and centered on Thebes, as well as on where the present-day western oases of Dakhla and Kharja are located.
21. Lohwasser, Angelika, "Queenship in Kush: Status, Role and Ideology of Royal Women," *Journal of American Research Center in Egypt*, Vol. 38, 2001, pp. 61–76.
22. "Mut" in *The Oxford Encyclopedia of Ancient Egypt*, 2001.
23. Adonis, "The Sufi Aesthetic Dimension" in *Sufism and Surrealism*, trans. Judith Cumberbatch (London: Saqi Books, 2005).
24. Adonis expounds the symbolism of the Arabic letter *waw* in Ibn ʿArabi's thought: "When we write the letter *waw* as we pronounce it (*'w-a-w'*), Ibn ʿArabi thinks 'that the first *waw* is the *waw* of the ipseity (*huwia*: essence, identity) and that the second *waw* is that of *kawn* (being), as the letter *alif* [a] interposed is the veil of uniqueness (*ahadia*).'" Ibn ʿArabi, quoted in Adonis, *Sufism and Surrealism*,

trans. Judith Cumberbatch (London: Saqi Books, 2005), pp. 9–10. For more details see Ibn ᶜArabi, *Kitab al-mim wa-l-waw wa-l-nun* [The Book of Letters Mim, Waw and Nun], in *Rasaʾil Ibn ᶜArabi* (Beirut: Dar Sadir, 1997).

25. Al-Khumaysi, Ashraf (2013), *Manafi al-rabb* (Cairo: Al-Dar al-Misriyya al-Lubnaniyya, 2015), 3rd edn.
26. Moolla, F. F., "Desert Ethics, Myths of Nature and Novel Form in the Narratives of Ibrahim al-Koni," *Tydskrif Vir Letterkunde*, Vol. 52, No. 2, 2015, pp. 176–96.
27. Fanon, Frantz, *Black Skin, White Masks* (New York: Grove Press, 1967).
28. Baines, John R. et al., "Egypt from 1075 BC to the Macedonian Invasion," *Britannica Online*, <https://www.britannica.com/place/ancient-Egypt/Egypt-from-1075-bce-to-the-Macedonian-invasion> (last accessed 4 July 2016).
29. Al-Tahawi, Miral, "al-buᶜdu al-ithnughrafi lil-ᶜamal al-riwaʾi: shihada/The Ethnographic Dimension in Fiction: A Testimony," *Alif: Journal of Comparative Poetics: Literature and Anthropology in Africa*, No. 17, 1997, pp. 145–52.
30. Translations from al-Tahawi's article in Arabic are my own.
31. Salih illustrates how desert writers attest to the past social and political superiority of desert females over males by referring to the two sister characters in al-Kuni's quartet novels, *al-Khusuf*, who consume their two male siblings unapologetically (Salih 1997: 20–1). Salih stresses that "leadership was for females in that legendary wasteland" (ibid. p. 21).
32. Salim, Saᶜid, "Suhayl wa 'banat naᶜsh:' Usṭura abadiyya min zaman al-dahsha," *Jaridatu-l-Ittihad*, 30 August 2010, <http://www.alittihad.ae/details.php?id=54725&y=2010> (last accessed 31 August 2016).
33. In her article "al-buᶜd al-ithnugrafi lil-ᶜamal al-riwaʾi: shihada," Miral al-Tahawi explains how Egypt's Bedouins came originally from the Arab tribes that expanded with Islamic *fatḥ* (conquest) into North Africa. Over time, they have become divided between "*ᶜarab al-maghariba*" (Western Arabs) who settled in Egypt's west and "*al-mashāriqa, ᶜarab al-shām*" (Eastern or Levant Arabs), who preferred to settle in the Sinai (al-Tahawi 1997: 148).

Epilogue: New Directions

Identifying and analyzing examples of the new-consciousness novel reveals that their aesthetic forms and impressions are entwined with their innovative socio-political content and character. As this study has illustrated, their collective imagination and literary enunciation of a pluralistic Egypt, in which minority groups' diverse experiences and cultures are given prominence over preoccupations with articulations of collective sameness, attest to the emergence of a distinct critical effort that counteracts the persistent cultural constructions of a homogeneous national self for the sake of a shared national good. The concern of the new-consciousness novel with the intersections of class and/or gender marginalization with other overlooked, yet major, categories of differentiation, and thereby with the socio-political marginalization of certain individuals and groups on the basis of race, ethno-religion, and language, draws attention to the complex levels of inequality in Egyptian society. At the same time, it also creatively envisions inclusive socio-political and cultural spaces from which the multiplicity of Egypt's existing groups can equally, and dynamically, engage in the construction of their polity, irrespective of their lived or created differences.

In the last few years following the most recent and particularly distressing political upheaval launched by the 2011 January revolution, new directions in Egyptian novelistic production have emerged and in their turn have commanded visibility and critical attention. As was discussed in the introduction to this book, the new-consciousness novel constitutes an act of writing that both heralds and signifies the cacophonous revolution in Tahrir Square, as well as other Egyptian streets, where distinctly variant voices cried out in united dissonance for equality and dignity. I argue here that the eruption of the revolution on January 25, 2011 by and of itself represents a parallel act, on both popular and socio-political grounds, that consolidates the new-consciousness novel's heterogeneously expressed sentiments and efforts at changing hegemonic discourses and practices of national sameness. A few questions pose themselves in light of this historical moment. Do the novels produced in the post-2011[1] period align with or break from the new-consciousness novel? How do they operate in Michael McKeon's dialectical framework of historical change and the definitional volatility of the novel? Where do minorities' concerns exist in post-2011 novels? This epilogue will attempt to shed light on these questions by examining the current transitional moment in Egyptian history through sensing its tribulations, uncertainties, and ambivalences in novelistic expression.

Tahrir Square: Ruptures and Continuities

Sherine Fouad Mazloum contends that "the 25 January 2011 Egyptian revolution revived the Egyptians' sense of belonging and commitment to their country" (Mazloum 2015: 207),[2] but also points out Mariz Tadros' acute observation of the "time- and space-bound moral economy of Tahrir Square" (Tadros 2012: 3).[3] Both Mazloum and Tadros acknowledge how Egyptians protested as one collective; but at the same time, each highlights a particular type of contention and discord between the lived Tahrir "moral economy" during the protest days and the distorted power hierarchy that was configured afterwards, since this neither reflected the ethos and efforts behind Egyptians' collective act of revolt nor represented the diversity of its revolutionary participants.

According to Tadros, that moral economy manifested itself in the populist coalition in Tahrir, where diverse groups across the spectrums of gender, class, religious affiliation, age, and political ideology and role made concerted efforts to jointly topple an old regime and effect radical transformations in the Egyptian social structure.[4] Indeed, these diverse masses effected what Tadros calls "rupture with the *status quo*" (ibid. p. 2), and did so twice by succeeding in overthrowing Mubarak and his old regime on February 11, 2011, and, some two years later, the then newly elected president, Morsi, and his government on July 3, 2013. Nonetheless, the revolution's starkly discrepant outcome thus far has invited scholars like Tadros and Mazloum to pay attention to an important issue that can provide an insight into why this time- and space-bound moral economy did not carry on after the overthrow of the two regimes. For Tadros, while the Tahrir moral economy was "civil" (peaceful and secular), the disparities between the societal and political agendas of the diverse revolutionary actors, and, thereby, their unequal relationships with the ruling powers (ibid. pp. 2–7), unraveled as time went on and impeded the sustaining of their collective spirit. That situation unpremeditatedly created a power vacuum and assisted conventional power holders to quickly reclaim their former central positions in both the state and civil society.

The marginalized groups' hopes for reforms and equality have, thus, been truncated despite their pivotal role in effecting "rupture with the *status quo*" and continuing to seek accountability from the state. A case in point is that of women, the largest minority group in Egypt, and the impediment of their rights to gender equality, personal freedom, and self-representation by one appointed government after another, after (as before) 2011. Drawing parallels between the two major popular revolutions in Egypt, in 1919 and 2011, Mazloum highlights the fact that, while Egyptian women were part and parcel of each revolution rising against social and political oppression, "the nationalist discourses, at times, reproduced women's oppression" (Mazloum 2015: 211). In the same way as Egyptian feminists of the early twentieth century, like Huda Shaʿrawi (1879–1947), were let down by their fellow male revolutionaries when they were not granted the right to vote, in post-2011 Egypt women suffered "setback," if not "betrayal," when their demands for social and political reforms regarding "the whole gender thing" were rejected despite their being "hailed as 'half the society' rising to alleviate oppression" (ibid. p. 210). Positioning her study between discourses on essentialism and anti-essentialism with respect to both feminism and nationalism, Mazloum examines three narratives by Egyptian women writers about their experiences in Tahrir Square during the first eighteen days of the revolution: Ahdaf Soueif's (b. 1950) memoir *Cairo: My City, Our Revolution*, 2012; Mona Prince's (b. 1970) testimony *Ismi thawra*, 2012 (My Name is Revolution); and Donia Kamal's (b. 1987) novel *Sijara sabʿa*, 2012 (A Seventh Cigarette). Mazloum argues that these women writers, by combining the acts of writing and revolting, "'effected' their construction of a sense of Egyptianness. Being in the *midan* (in reference to Tahrir Square) provides the material dimension for the three writers to reconstitute themselves as part of the revolution that is making changes on the ground" (ibid. p. 209).

As each writer navigates her position towards, in Mazloum's words, "the dilemma of whether *the personal is political*" (ibid. p. 212) in these narratives, each articulates a unique perception of the "self" in relation to the "collective" within Tahrir Square. According to Mazloum, Soueif, in her memoir, envisions the "I" as inseparable from, if not homogeneous with, the collective and communal "we," but only on the basis of shared goals and desires rather than who that "I" and "we" define themselves to be (ibid. p. 214), whereas Prince's testimonial narrative of Tahrir days is presented from a first-person "I," that cautiously refrains from identifying with the collective in fear of aggression, recalling the assault incidents some women experienced in the *midan* (square) (ibid. p. 219). Kamal, in her fictional narrative, fluctuates between her individual experience and space and her desire for involvement with the collective in Tahrir (ibid. p. 216). Mazloum's analysis insightfully recognizes an "oscillating pattern of inclusion and exclusion which serves to show that Egyptians are not one and the same" (ibid. p. 215), and surmises that each writer's political stance in the *midan* emanates from her transformative involvement and interaction with the larger collective (ibid. p. 219).

The Novel: New Directions

By the same token, witnessing the social and political tribulations during the Tahrir Square days and afterwards, novelists after 2011 capture both the continuities and the ruptures and discontinuities within these historical conditions by producing new aesthetics that inventively mirror new socio-political engagement and popular forms of dissent. Since it is the task of literary critics to keenly watch such novelistic expressions while they are taking shape, translating their realities onto the literary and figurative plane and responding to their surrounding incomprehensibilities, and since the scholarly aims of this book are to attempt to do precisely this in order to understand the novel as a historical product that dynamically interacts with the process of historical change, reading a few examples of the post-2011 novel will serve to illustrate the view they present in dialogue with the new-consciousness novel.

The post-2011 novels examined here are *Jirafit*, 2014 (Graphite) by Hisham al-Khashin (b. 1963), *al-Tabur*, 2013 (*The Queue*, 2016) by Basma ᶜAbd al-ᶜAziz (b. 1978), and *ᶜUtarid*, 2015 (*Otared*, 2016) by Muhammad Rabiᶜ (b. 1978). These novels have in common that they are permeated by uncertainty and despair, if not the outright dystopian reflection of a cruel, disavowing reality that refuses to yield to popular efforts at social and political reform. However, each of them constitutes a distinct effort at approaching this reality and figuratively reconstructing it from a unique perspective in order to actively engage readers as citizens in pondering and deliberating on their socio-political conditions from that proposed angle. Whether or not readers align their viewpoint(s) with that/those of the novelists should not influence our understanding of the concerns or aims of the writing. As it happens, what elicits, and enhances, the act of writing is the writer's ability to use their right of freedom of expression and right to comment on their surroundings through the creative written word. At the same time, the summoning of readers to take part in ruminating on their human condition, through their act of reading, stimulates them as a collective to exercise their power of agency and serves as a reminder of their capacity to shape their own history—especially at moments of despair, but also in terms of continuous efforts at dissenting from the status quo.

Jirafit invokes a promising historical past of cultural efforts at gender equality by setting its events between the 1920s and 1950s, during which time a group of young Egyptian women were the first to be sent to Europe by the Egyptian government to study abroad. The narrative revolves around the life of its main character, Nawal ᶜArif, who is one of two Egyptian women selected to study at the Sorbonne University in Paris. The other student, who constitutes one of the major influences on Nawal's life and thought, is a fictional portrayal of the real historical figure of Durriyya Shafiq (1908–75), the Egyptian feminist and activist whose key role in amending the Egyptian constitution in 1956 guaranteed women's suffrage as well as securing their right to education and political self-representation. My examination of *Jirafit* shows its attempts at conjuring up a long, but triumphant journey by Egyptian women towards gender equality during the crucial historical period of nationalist formation in the first half of the twentieth century. I argue that *Jirafit*'s novelistic undertaking serves to inspire the contemporaneous socio-political endeavors—one decade into the new millennium—to continue to improve the status and conditions of women as Egypt's largest marginalized group as well as to avert potential regression of the gender-equality cause due to the rise of antagonistic political agendas. At the same time, the eminence of the Western influences on both Nawal and Durriyya, as well as delimiting feminist influence and support within Nawal's domestic environment to her pro-feminist father, Hamid, may seem to overshadow the role of traditional female figures and thereby cast doubt on the novel's feminist project. I argue, however, that towards the end of the novel a reconciliatory moment occurs, during which the amalgamation of flashes of the incidents of suffering Nawal has experienced and her inspiration by the diverse individuals she has interacted with, be they female or male, Egyptian or Western, inflames her revolution against the status quo and the social restraints hindering her self-fulfillment. In *The Queue*, overall popular morale post-2011, as well as collective action after "rupture with the *status quo*" are aesthetically reconfigured in the seemingly meaningless act of waiting. The novel depicts numerous characters from all walks of life standing in an endless queue waiting helplessly for an authoritative gate to open so that they can get permissions to resume normal life. I argue that this depiction of this absurd waiting at that gate is an allegory of the perpetual waiting for the state to implement the reforms it promised after Mubarak's and later Morsi's overthrow. My analysis shows that the act of waiting is by no means meaningless or ineffectual. On the contrary, the diverse characters' ability to endure the irrational and cruel absurdity of the situation evidences their unyielding spirit, which strives to conquer any social or political adversity. Of the post-2011 novels I choose here to represent novelistic production after the political upheaval, it is safe to say that *Otared* presents the bleakest picture of Egypt and Egyptians. Set in 2025, the novel is bathed in imaginings of Egypt as a place with hellish resemblances and of Egyptians as utterly dehumanized. The novel is essentially a tale of war, foreign occupation, and waste, in which acts of cannibalism, rampant and heartless killings of innocent people, debilitating and incurable ailments, pedophiliac assaults, and sexual violence towards women are pervasive. My analysis demonstrates how Rabiᶜ's utilization of the thematic device of dystopian society not only enables him to relay a negative vision of Egypt's unfathomable current socio-political conditions—by projecting them in a dismal future—but also functions as a cautionary-tale instrument, whereby readers can take heed of the bleakness awaiting them if they do not act upon their present conditions.

Jirafit

While the novel primarily revolves around the personal life of Nawal, it interweaves its developments with the changes in women's political status in Egypt in order to unsettle attempts to separate the personal from the political. On a secondary, but parallel level of the novel's events, the author interlaces the rise of two seemingly competing cultural formations, that is, the secular and the religious dimensions of public and national life in Egypt, while obscuring their conceptualized divides to demonstrate their interconnections and their shared influence in shaping contemporary Egyptian history.

The novel's events are told by a third-person narrator, from whose perspective and voice readers can see and hear the actions and voices of its women, men, and racially diverse characters. At the same time, al-Khashin interposes the epistolary form as he allows readers to directly access the voices and thoughts of Nawal and of Hamid, her father, through their exchange of written letters during her stay in Paris. This formal device not only aesthetically captures the novel's view of the significance of the written word in recording—without mediacy—both Nawal's and Hamid's self-perception, gender identity, and special father–daughter relationship and dialogue, but also serves to accommodate, in narrative form, that special space of freedom of self-expression, facilitated by Nawal's father's endorsement of her right to gender equality, education, and the opportunity to live, study, and attain a global consciousness in Paris.

While the historical persona of Durriyya is not the main character of the novel—Nawal is—Durriyya's social and political status stands both as a reflection of and in contrast to Nawal's, a position that frames Durriyya as a transcendent model for Nawal. The similarities the narrator draws between the two characters, besides their being the first two Egyptian females to be funded by the Egyptian government to study at the Sorbonne, include the following. They have both lost their mothers, Nawal at birth and Durriyya at the age of twelve, and both went to French schools, Nawal to Collège de la Mère de Dieu in Cairo and Durriyya to Collège Notre Dame des

Apôtres in Tanta. Moreover, while their fathers were the persons who stood behind them in defying tradition by supporting their opportunities to study abroad, their grandmothers, respectively, objected (Al-Khashin 2014: 52).[5] The absence of their mothers as potentially empowering female figures mystifies the existence of maternal influence on Nawal's and Durriyya's thought formation, and instead emphasizes, on the one hand, the stark difference in socio-cultural perspective, and the generational gap, between the grandmothers and their aspiring granddaughters; and on the other, the positive influence of the young women's pro-feminist father figures who defy social conventions to promote their daughters' education and independence. In addition, both Nawal and Durriyya are imaginative artists who are capable of using their imagination to produce art; graphite drawing for Nawal and poetry composition for Durriyya. The portrayal of their shared creativity underscores the significance of the artistic imagination in fostering their freedom of thought and expression on social and political levels.

As much as the two characters seem to rhythmically orbit in the same universe, Nawal is portrayed as falling behind Durriyya in public and domestic achievements. The narrator seizes every opportunity in which Durriyya interacts with Nawal, or any other character, to assert her individuality and extraordinary characteristics, while alluding to Nawal's subsequent mixed feelings of admiration and jealousy—due to a sense of inferiority. For example, on board the ship taking them to France, Mukhtar Safwat, the government employee accompanying the student delegation, admires Nawal's graphite drawing and introduces himself to both Nawal and Durriyya. The narrator describes how Durriyya responds "in calmness and confidence [saying] 'it's [a] pleasure to meet you,'" whereas Nawal "remains the same: in a state of astonishment and fluster before her decision to emulate her friend. With faint murmur and repetitive words as though she is a parrot mimicking Durriyya, she says "'pleasure to meet you'" (ibid. p. 55).[6] On a different occasion, the narrator observes Nawal's sense of limitation as she compares herself to Durriyya: Nawal "realized that she did not possess similar, or even half, the perseverance Durriya had" (ibid. p. 126). This juxtaposition between the two characters' attitudes and abilities bathes Durriyya's figure in mythical light, an inspirational icon that Nawal looks up to and attempts to emulate, but in so doing she fails, at least temporarily, until she is enabled by her own personal experiences, domestic, educational, romantic, and artistic.

The narrator denotes that Durriyya's achievements are in the public eye by recounting the nation's celebration upon her return from France and the completion of her degree. Nawal's return, by contrast, is neither public nor triumphant. With the recent death of Nawal's father—an incident that marks a rupture in Nawal's path towards self-actualization—her reception was limited to two family members, her cousin, Bahija, and her husband, Hilmy, who are portrayed as a traditional couple with assigned gender roles: Bahija is a wife and mother who did not finish her education so as to assume the role of creating and caring for a family, whereas Hilmy is his family's sole provider, whose involvement in the religious movement the Muslim Brotherhood as a means of reforming his society and polity suggests the entwined espousal of tradition and cultural heritage in both his domestic (private) and his political (public) attitudes and inclinations. In the absence of Nawal's father's support in challenging societal and cultural expectations and, thereby, the assigned gender role for his daughter, Nawal's reception by Bahija and Hilmy betokens her initial confinement to domestic wife and mother duties. Soon after Nawal's return, her grandmother and uncle arrange for her marriage to her cousin, Kamil, who squanders his father's wealth in gambling and later amasses a new fortune by supplying food provisions to the British colonial personnel camping in Maadi, Cairo, during World War II. Nevertheless, that seeming delimitation of Nawal's domestic and social conditions propels her expansive growth in artistic creativity and expression through the medium of graphite drawings.

At this juncture, it is important to examine the aesthetic function of Nawal's graphitic drawings in mirroring her life journey. The narrator observes how, at the beginning of Nawal's stay in Paris, her "drawings—which are still graphitic and without color—became a blend of her estrangement and alienation and a reflection of what fascinates her in the City of Light" (ibid. p. 88). The narrator here alludes to the rich grades and effects graphitic drawings can create and, therefore, the layers of messages Nawal's art can convey to its viewer. As graphite is a type of crystalline carbon that is also regarded as a mineral, with different pencils and crayons and by using different pressure techniques graphite artists can draw a variety of dark shadows as well as sparkled lines. Nawal's graphitic impressions, that vacillate between dark and metallic shades, reflect the duality of her feelings towards Paris, where she experiences dark and light moments. Nonetheless, the narrator's reference to the colorlessness of Nawal's art underscores a kind of one-dimensionality for Nawal's still-life creative production at that point in her life, a perspective that signifies her precursory status, in which, due to feelings of nostalgia and cultural estrangement, she reacts with reserve to her new world rather than embracing some of its readily available freedoms such as Durriyya's attitude demonstrates. Durriyya challenges the authority of the Ministry of Education over her educational choices, whereas Nawal is deterred by her fear of contravening the status quo and continues to study geography, the subject preselected for her instead of art, her real passion. Throughout Nawal's life experiences, whether they are seemingly fulfilling or not, she undertakes graphite drawings to express her despondencies and aspirations.

In addition to Durriyya and Nawal's father, there are two other inspirational and supportive figures—Claude and Mukhtar—whose admiration for Nawal and support for her art at its different phases of maturity present a gestural impetus for her personal growth. For example, Claude, the young artist she meets in Paris, with his artistic inclinations, nomadic lifestyle, and revolutionary spirit—similar to Durriyya's—becomes another center of Nawal's attention and attraction. He encourages her to break free from her inhibitions and pursue the study of art, but she refuses to foster discontent. Then, he proposes an alternative opportunity for her to work closely with an established Parisian artist while gently prodding her spirit to action by commenting that "this is only a reconciliatory, not a revolutionary solution" (ibid. p. 112). In addition, Mukhtar Safwat remarks favorably on what he perceives to be Nawal's worthwhile effort to embrace modern ways while preserving tradition (ibid. p. 132). His intention of marrying Nawal and his legal assistance later in freeing her from her arranged marriage suggest the merits and restorative powers of her selective synthesis of the liberties that modernity offers while conserving traditional ways of life with the aim of maintaining a distinct identity. Like Durriyya and Claude, Mukhtar exhibits revolutionary inclinations. While he is in Paris and attending an event for Egyptian immigrants with Nawal, in commemoration of the 1919 Egyptian Revolution, the guest speaker, who is also a politician, defends the Egyptian people's good-naturedness against their then-tarnished reputation as "revolutionary and uncivilized" (ibid. p. 119) after their revolution. Mukhtar denounces the politician's statement and says to Nawal: "They are denying us the right to revolt against injustice as if revolution is a disgrace" (ibid. p. 119). Mukhtar resigns from his government post and studies law instead. Despite Claude's and Mukhtar's positive influence on Nawal and their pursuit of her affection, she does not marry either of them.

Nawal's transformative moment, in which she replaces her state of acquiescence with that of revolution, is triggered by her husband's domestic tempest, during which he disparages her and her artistic achievements and tears some of the graphite drawings that narrate her suppressed dreams and desires. Nawal is left shocked by Kamil's senseless act, and, at the same time, motivated to frantically assemble her graphitic drawings—whether torn or intact—and retrieve the one Claude drew of her before she left Paris. Recovering that past image of herself, captured by Claude's experiential and imaginative knowledge of her, serves as a reminder of the inextinguishable flame she possesses inside herself as a catalyst for her revolution against the status quo. The collage of her drawings—whether painted with soft tonal effects by her pencil or with hard lines that relate times of pressure—constitutes a symbolic repossession of her memories in their entirety, and enables her to legibly see, as a whole, the impact of everything she has encountered and everyone she has known during her life. She sees her dead grandmother's face with a regretful expression, her uncle as a helpless man after Kamil squandered his wealth, her cousin Bahija burdened by Kamil's appropriation of her inheritance, Claude encouraging her to revolt, Durriyya with a wry smile blaming her for not standing up for what she desires, and an apparition of her youngster, whom she named after Durriyya, as an adult blaming her for not securing her freedom, and finally her father encouraging her to fight for her dreams (ibid. p. 209).

Following Nawal's realization of the value and meaningfulness of her life experiences as a whole, the novel more succinctly merges fiction with history and correlates Nawal's personal accomplishments with the public ones achieved by Egypt's women activists like Durriyya Shafiq and Seiza Nabarawi (1897–1985). The narrator conveys Nawal's involvement, in February 1951, in the historical endeavor by the Egyptian Feminist Union, founded by

Huda Shaʿrawi (1879–1947) and Nabarawi, to establish Egyptian women's suffrage and right to self-representation. The novel concludes with Nawal merging into the march of Durriyya and other women towards the building of the Egyptian Parliament while shouting "equality, equality" (ibid. p. 215). Only then, the narrator remarks, does Nawal feel equal to her friend and icon, Durriyya (ibid. p. 217).

At the other end of the cultural formations, there is a parallel subplot around Nawal's cousin's husband, Hilmy, who becomes one of the founding members of the Muslim Brotherhood. In the same way as the main plot correlates Nawal's personal life with her public counterpart, this subplot aims at demonstrating how religious and secular nationalist formations are interconnected and jointly influence Egypt's social and political domains. On one level, *Jirafit* distinguishes between Islam as a traditional religion and its politicization by highlighting the religious and socio-political attitudes of Hajj ʿAbd al-ʿAlim al-Ahwani, Hilmy's father, and his practices vis-à-vis his son's. Hajj ʿAbd al-ʿAlim is portrayed as a moral, nationalist, and religiously unbiased man, who opposes the British colonial presence and whose faith is anchored in the Sufi Islamic tradition. His friendships with religiously diverse people are portrayed as standing the test of time as well as the growing sectarian tension in Egypt surrounding the rise of exclusionary nationalisms. Hilmy's allegiance to the emergent Muslim Brotherhood and his embrace of politicized Islam signify a shift from his father's overall principles and attitudes. For example, the father immerses himself in Sufi circles in the ancient Cairo district of al-Husayn by listening to sermons that call for the avoidance of hard-heartedness and the nominal remembrance (*dhikr*) of God that is not accompanied with love and compassion for the other, whether they be Muslim or non-Muslim (ibid. p. 184). In addition, the narrator captures the plethora of mystical sounds in the background of Hajj ʿAbd al-ʿAlim's interactions with the Sufi mystics in al-Husayn by reciting some verses from *al-Burda*, a poem by the seventh-century Sufi poet al-Busiri, in which he praises Prophet Mohammad for his compassion and for mystically curing him of an ailment.[7] At the same time, the son's overall attitude and actions, after pledging allegiance to the Muslim Brotherhood, seem to center on either promoting the growth of the emergent group or assisting in achieving its political objectives, at the expense of his domestic and social obligations. For example, he refrains from moving permanently to Cairo, as he promised his in-laws, to join his wife, Bahija, after he was urged to remain by Hasan al-Banna in Ismailia, near the Suez Canal—where the European colonial presence was predominant, a situation that results in his father's dismay at his choices. Moreover, al-Khashin portrays a conflict between the father's traditional Sufi approach to Islam and his son's politicized one, especially through referencing al-Banna's influential thought and lectures on Hilmy. As Hasan al-Banna's character is a fictional portrayal of the real founder of the Muslim Brotherhood, al-Khashin utilizes excerpts from one of al-Banna's essays in *Majallat al-Nadhir* (issue 18, of September 1938), in which al-Banna argues about the value of mastering "*ṣinaʿat al-mawt*" (the industry of death). Those who master that *ṣinaʿa* strive to earn a dignified and honorable death that will render not only their death but also their life on earth worthwhile and most rewarding (ibid. p. 150). This excerpt alludes to the focus of al-Banna's thought on "*sabil al-jihad*" (path of struggle), which is regarded as his way of criticizing "the spiritual quiescence of official Islam and the Egyptian political establishment in general, together with their inability to counter western secularization and materialism" (Mura 2012: 70).[8] The novel, thus, exhibits how al-Banna's ideological message of Islamization is anti-colonial and nationalist, but that it may also have shaped militant thought. During Hajj ʿAbd al-ʿAlim and Hilmy's joint visit to their lifelong Jewish friends, Binyamin and Ifrayim, in Harat al-Yahud (the Jewish Alley), a bomb explodes and injures their friend's son on his Bar Mitzvah. At that horrific moment, Hilmy realizes that he might have unknowingly helped execute that militant act of violence.

At the same time, the novel consolidates both secular and Islamist cultural formations with regard to the centrality of women's roles, in advocating social and political reform of the status and rights of women in Egypt. It does this by shedding light on another influential female Islamic activist, Labiba Ahmad (1870–1951), who appears as one of the inspirational characters in Nawal's life. Through her cousin Bahija's and her husband Hilmy's circle of acquaintances in the Muslim Brotherhood and Sisterhood, Nawal is introduced to Labiba Ahmad and her daughter, Zaynab ʿAbduh. Zaynab is not only the first President of the Muslim Sisterhood, but also, like Nawal, a talented artist, who was sent by the Egyptian government to study in

Europe. During a visit to Labiba Ahmad's house for a religious lesson, Nawal becomes impressed with Zaynab's paintings and sculptures, and is encouraged by Zaynab herself to teach at the School of Art Education (Al-Khashin 2014: 177–8). The novel, thus, pays tribute to Labiba Ahmad's and Zaynab ʿAbduh's thought and feminist endeavors, which are premised on Islamic reform rather than radicalism. The novel also reconfigures the founding narrative of the Islamist political movement the Muslim Brotherhood—which is generally considered a male-dominated movement—by highlighting the pivotal role Labiba and Zaynab have played in its beginnings. According to Beth Baron, Labiba was not only al-Banna's senior, but also an elite woman, who actively participated in the nationalist and feminist movements of the first half of the twentieth century, such as Mustafa Kamil's Watani (Nationalist) Party and Saʿd Zaghlul's and Safiyya Zaghlul's anti-colonial efforts, in addition to demonstrating with women in 1919 in protest against British rule. Yet her feminist and nationalist ideology and activism were distinctly anchored in the idea of a societal return to Islam, rather than in emulation of the West and its secularist modernity. Her Islamist ideology, writings, and philanthropic and educational efforts through her establishment of the Society of Egyptian Ladies' Awakening demonstrate that her activism was centered around feminist issues like the right of women to work as doctors and artists (as her own daughters did), women's sexuality, and women's relationships with family members. This novelistic perspective provides evidence that female Islamic activists are "thinkers and activists in their own right, and critical participants during the formative years of the movement" (Baron 2001: 226–41).[9]

The Queue

Published in 2015, the novel is primarily concerned with capturing the angst and uncertainty that has gripped people's spirits in the aftermath of the 2011 revolution through the allegorical portrayal of what seems like an eternally closed and impenetrable gate, in front of which people from all walks of life stand in an endless queue for a senselessly infinite period of time. The Gate allegorizes an encompassing, authoritarian system, whose surveillance and control of every absurd detail in the lives of the people in the queue impact their ability to conduct their day-to-day affairs, from filling out prescriptions from public pharmacies to issuing permits for eye exams and filing a complaint for unavailable *baladi* (local) bread. The Gate disqualifies individuals from getting a telephone landline or resuming employment because of what it ludicrously deems misconduct. It accordingly halts their normal activities until they are proven to be true citizens and are granted the Certificate of True Citizenship—through its administration of an obscure, if not undetermined, process of scrutinization. That excessive hold on people's livelihoods and existence transports readers to a realm beyond reality, where their fantasies tread in magnified authoritarianism and exacerbated anguish. Through that seeming discontinuation of life and normal activities, readers join everyone else in the queue in their state of bewilderment, uncertainty, and anticipation. I argue that, on one level, waiting in the queue is no hiatus; it is permeated with critical communication and expression of protest against the surrounding conditions. On another level, the organizational system of the queue represents a spatio-temporal juncture in which people gather, connect, and compare views and positions. The queue can also be perceived as a chain structure with a domino effect, whereby people's lives and fates are tied together and, as a result, they are collectively vulnerable to any event that can dismantle their queue. At the same time, people's ability to maintain the integrity of their queue signifies their civil unity as well as their shared responsibility in keeping that order and structure, whereas their varying styles of activism and points of interaction in (and outside of) the queue—during the waiting—exhibit, first, disparate subversive acts of rebellion that are aimed at hounding the Gate out of its deafness and muteness, so that it listens to their needs and, secondly, the nuances of people's attempts at taking matters into their own hands.

The novel is told from a third-person perspective, which echoes the diversified tones of all the characters waiting in the queue, and also that of the Gate with its stern and incomprehensible statements and decrees. The Gate seems to have a life and agency of its own: "The Gate had come into power many years earlier, in the wake of a popular uprising known as the First Storm" (ʿAbd al-ʿAziz 2016: 8).[10] It "had materialized and insinuated itself into everything, people didn't know where its affairs ended and their own began" (ibid. p. 31). The narrator correlates that self-materialized power with the hard and mute magnitude of the concrete structure behind the Gate: "a strange crimson octagonal structure, slightly higher than the concrete walls that extended from it on either side ... If it weren't for the people who'd once entered it and told of all the rooms and offices inside, anyone gazing up at it would have imagined it to be a massive block, solid and impenetrable" (ibid. p. 35). *The Queue* is set in a fantastical time and space that imply a Cairo wasteland in the post-2011 period. There are no neighborhoods with names, only neutrally numbered districts with no historical or common reference. Cafés and stores downtown are all closed with iron bars after having been attacked by robbers. Streets are filled with "empty tear-gas canisters," "multi-colored munitions," "fissures" in the asphalt, and remnants of "pungent gas" odors (ibid. pp. 107–8). These are all remains of what became known as the Disgraceful Events" (ibid. p. 33), in response to which not only did the Gate close its doors and cease to fulfill citizens' needs, but also a "full range of security units soon appeared, too" (ibid. p. 22): the Deterrence Force, the Concealment Force, and the Quell Force. The narrator expounds how the Disgraceful Events had led to such a bleak context:

> Ordinary people rose up, defeated the security forces on the streets, overcame the old guard's defenses, and nearly forced the ruler to surrender. But unfortunately—or perhaps it was fortunately?—things hadn't continued as they'd begun. The movement had fractured before it was able to overthrow the regime. Some people used the gains they'd made to secure their own position and power. Others continued the fight against the regime, leaving a path of destruction in their wake. Some armed themselves in anticipation of a counterattack. Still others were wary because the ruler might manage to remain in power, and slipped away to make their own private deals with him. Soon the situation unraveled, and different groups who had taken part in the First Storm accused one another of betrayal. They were so entrenched in their own conflicts that they forgot about the ruler, who started to rally his inner circle and regained influence on the ground. While the people were distracted with their squabbles, the old guard regrouped and began to rebuild. Not long after this, the Gate appeared. (ibid. pp. 8–9)

As much as this excerpt from the beginning of the novel delineates so astutely how a triumphant uprising by ordinary people against their tyrannical regime was soon fractured by their "own conflicts" and divisions—a situation that led the "old guard" to "regroup" and the Gate to come into existence—the novel nonetheless conjures up a continuation of that popular movement in the people's concentrated activities within the site of the queue, as they determinedly continue to negotiate their differences. The queue, thus, constitutes the nucleus of novelistic activities and narrative time.

While the Gate represents a personification of authoritarian power, whose personnel are portrayed as individuals with machine-like traits and demeanors, the types of people in the queue, by contrast, as the narrator describes them "were women and men, young and old people, professionals and the working class. No section of society was missing, even the poorest of the poor were there, not separated from the rich by any means. Everyone was on equal ground. But they all had the same look about them, the same lethargy" (ibid. p. 90). In the case of each individual sharing the malady of oppression, their story and position in the queue metaphorically reflect their unequal relation to the Gate and correspondingly their disparate demands of it. The novel creatively establishes a variety of lines of communication across the queue depending on people's positions and movements. For example, Inas (Ines), the young teacher from Cairo seeking a Certificate of True Citizenship, interacts with Shalabi (Shalaby), the poor peasant who stands in front of her, to seek compensation from the Gate for his cousin's death while serving his country. Ines contests Shalaby's constructed narrative about his cousin's heroism during the Disgraceful Events, after learning that he shot a fellow citizen as a blindly obedient conscript in the security forces. Ines' destabilization of Shalaby's narrative and, inevitably, his claim for compensation demonstrates not only citizens' divergent interests and demands given their socio-economic status, gender, and background, but also the ensuing distrust, one-sided conclusions about each other's religiosity and morality, and repudiation of the validity of each other's claims. The narrator describes how Shalaby, in turn, "felt as though his words were tainted. Every time he told his story he glanced around, looking for her, afraid she would butt in like last time, ruining it and turning him into the laughing stock of the queue" (ibid. p. 162). He even regarded Ines as "probably corrupt, morally and otherwise—no scruples, no religion, not even wearing a respectable headscarf ... It was possible that she had participated in the Disgraceful Events, too; he'd heard rumors that there were women saboteurs" (ibid. p. 78).

The individuals standing in the queue include two anonymous characters, the man in the "*galabeya*" and the woman with short hair and a black skirt, who represent two poles of activism on site. On the one hand, the man in the *galabeya* holds weekly religious lessons for the queue community and supports the High Sheikh's fatwa against boycotting "businesses owned by God-fearing believers." These include Violet Telecom, which is believed to tap people's phone conversations to provide them to the Gate's surveillance operations. The woman with the short hair, on the other hand, launches an oppositional campaign to boycott Violet Telecom and discredit its consumer-friendly promotions. With the help of Ihab (Ehab), the journalist, she prints out leaflets that include statements and a "passage from the Greater Book, which urged people to respect and defend personal privacy" (ibid. p. 135). In these competing styles of activism, religion is utilized to both persuade and dissuade people from using the same telecom company, a situation that reveals the ambivalence of using religious rhetoric in mobilizing people politically.

Umm Mabruk (Um Mabrouk) is a poor and hardworking mother of three, whose health conditions have been deteriorating due to chronic ailments. Um Mabrouk not only stands in the queue to apply for subsidized healthcare from the Gate for her sick daughter, but also stands out in the midst of the queue community for her entrepreneurial and innovative spirit. Since she cannot afford not to work, in order to make money she constructs a makeshift café, from which she sells drinks and snacks to the queue community. Moreover, she is uneducated, and yet her attitude and actions demonstrate her discernible understanding of the skills and talents of all the people in the queue, but especially the women, with whom she forms exceptional solidarity. For example, she does not part from Ines' side, and always asks her to read her the circulated leaflets and newspapers. She also invites the woman with the short hair to her makeshift café and offers her free drinks because she always carries a small radio that "remained a steadfast source of news" (ibid. p. 168). Notably, the queue members gathering around the woman with short hair, according to the narrator, compete in number with those attending the weekly lesson of the man in the *galabeya*. This setting encourages people across the queue to come and buy drinks from Um Mabrouk, but more importantly, as the narrator describes:

Little discussion groups sprang up and slowly grew larger, frequented by students, lecturers, and ideologues alike. Soon they became social meeting points that attracted everyone with a desire to hear and debate the latest on the Gate, or with questions on more distant developments. Um Mabrouk's gathering place became the mouth of a river that filled the queue with news and rumors. Sometimes they were invented from within and shipped upstream, while other times the queue accepted rumors arriving from far-off places. (ibid. pp. 168–9)

In this way, Um Mabrouk's stand—with the help and collaboration of Ines and the woman with the short hair—creates a forum in which the people of the queue can share disjointed news as well as their views, even if disparate. While Ines and the woman with the short hair are outspoken, Um Mabrouk does not eschew supporting and defending their opinions in the face of opponents. The portrayal of such strong-willed and courageous women characters and their pivotal role in propelling free speech and negotiation among the different people of the queue invoke the significance of women's courage and solidarity in voicing their opposition as well as their ability to mediate conflict and bring disparate parties to the same discussion table.

Yahia (Yehya) is a central member of the queue community, whose body metaphorizes the site and "map of the battle" (ibid. p. 25) between the people and the Gate. According to the narrator, Yehya "was a different kind of man, steadfast and stubborn . . . he was carrying a government bullet inside his body. He possessed tangible evidence of what had really happened during the Disgraceful Events, and was perhaps the only person still alive who was to prove what the authorities had done" (ibid. p. 116). Yehya had been shot in the pelvis by the Gate's security during the Disgraceful Events, but despite his injury he stood in the queue like everyone else "so resolutely" (ibid. p. 17) to obtain a copy of the X-rays that may hold the Gate accountable for its violation of its citizens' bodies. The Gate, instead of taking responsibility, denies the occurrence of such assaults, hides any medical records that prove the existence of such bullets in its citizens' bodies, and prohibits medical facilities from extracting the bullets. Yehya's endurance symbolizes the citizens' tenacity and resolution to hold their regime accountable for their wellbeing, whereas the Gate's persistent denial of its violations not only adds salt to their wounds, but also culminates in death, as will be demonstrated.

Among the characters who are directly involved in Yehya's dilemma is Dr Tariq (Tareq), the attending physician at the time of Yehya's hospital admission. Tareq ordered the X-rays and can confirm the existence of a bullet in Yehya's pelvis, but, fearing being incriminated by the Gate, he refrains from helping Yehya. Tareq is also the only person who has access to Yehya's hospital file, which he keeps in a locked drawer in his office desk at the hospital. The narrator gradually discloses the content of each of the file's six documents, which become mysteriously updated with Yehya's latest movements every time Tareq reviews the file. Document 4, ironically, states one of Yehya's disorders, a deriding diagnosis of his "belief he can alter reality" (ibid. p. 102). These ghostly intrusions and evaluative additions to Yehya's file increase Tareq's insomnia and paranoia about the Gate's insidious infiltration of everybody's life, including his: he "realized that he was on the same path as Yehya, and that one of these days he might merit a document just like this one" (ibid. p. 104). Towards the end of the novel and after a long period of hesitation at Tareq's end, he decides to effect a change; however, the day he determines to operate on Yehya and remove the bullet, he reads a sinister update in Yehya's file stating that he has already succumbed to the bullet wound. There and then the novel ends. Tareq's belated understanding of the entwined paths his and Yehya's lives are taking stands as a forewarning of his own death due to his failure in responding to Yehya's urgent health needs. In other words, with Yehya's death, and with the ideas of tied fates and the chain effect on which *The Queue* is premised, readers can anticipate not only Tareq's own end, but also that of the rest of the characters in the queue, unless someone or something can effect real change in this bleak situation.

Otared

Set primarily in 2025, *Otared* creatively captures a horrific future of Cairo that develops from and extends beyond the events of the Egyptian revolution of 2011. In that future, Cairo is occupied by a foreign army that belongs to the Knights of Malta, which is inspired by the existence of a real religious and international order known by the same name and whose roots date back to the middle of the eleventh century in Arab-ruled Jerusalem.[11] Historically, that order was exiled across the globe by different rulers at different historical times—from Jerusalem in 1291 and Rhodes in 1523 to Malta in 1798—before it settled in Rome in the nineteenth century, where it currently has headquarters. It holds a unique status under International Law, by which it is acknowledged as a sovereign entity with no affiliated territory (Keating 2011).[12] While, in the Middle Ages, a religious order with charitable and/or military assignments, like the Knights of Malta, was not a surprising existence,[13] its fictional invocation casts a gloomy shadow over Cairo, if not the whole world, in which religiously driven militarisms and armies can raid territories for nationalist expansion. In *Otared*, an already socially and politically demolished Cairo falls easily in 2024 to the forces of the Maltese Army, who choose the heart of Cairo, its Nile River, as the site of their military base.

Situated as part of the resistance movement in Cairo Tower in al-Jazira, the site of the occupation forces and their ships becomes an eyesore for ʿUtarid (Otared), a former police colonel, who secedes from an acquiescent Egyptian police force, along with other police officers, to fight this foreign army. Otared's resistance group reclaims West Cairo from the occupation forces and operates sniping stations that aim at Egyptian corrupt civilians and regime officials, who collaborate with the occupation forces. Otared's resistance effort gradually transforms into a mission of sniping at citizens indiscriminately with the vision that he might be saving them from the inevitable anguish and violence lurking in their meaningless existence: leading to a more desolate dystopia in Cairo as well as within his soul.

Otared reverses to two other periods in Cairo's past that reflect similarly grim contexts, that of 2011–14 CE and the other in AH 455. The former period invokes the historic period of the 2011 revolution in Egypt, but captures it from Otared's perspective, while the latter constitutes the temporal background of a different set of sinister events revolving around the inexplicable death of a young man named Sakhr al-Khazarji. I argue that the three sets of sinister events in Cairo across those different chronologies mirror one another in being permeated with violence, death, and utter despair, in order to underline a fateful existence in a dystopia that cannot be circumvented in Egypt.

The novel's events that take place in 2025 and between 2011 and 2014 are narrated from a first-person perspective by its central character, Otared. At the same time, the events that take place in AH 455, also in Cairo and particularly in al-Muqattam, are told by an anonymous narrator, who witnesses the gruesome and inexplicable deaths of a multitude of people rushing to see a false miracle: that one of their own, young Sakhr al-Khazarji, who has just died and whom they "marked" as the "Son of Death" (Rabiʿ 2016: 197),[14] is resurrected back to life. Not only Sakhr's resurrection becomes an illusion, but also the lives of the multitudes rushing to witness his mythical return to life. The anonymous narrator himself seems to die numerous times—either by being stampeded by the masses flocking to see Sakhr or by being struck by the guards violently dispersing the multitudes (ibid. p. 201)—and is resurrected, only to experience another horrific death. This oxymoronic pattern of resurrecting into life for the sole purpose of experiencing death again reinforces the futility and purposelessness of an irredeemable existence. The anonymous narrator says: "And I bethought me that I had lived a just life in hell . . . And I considered my prayers and my fasting and I laughed, for there is no prayer here, nor fasting, nor ever any lightening of torment. All that I possess is patience and all that I fear is hope" (ibid. p. 214). The same feeling of hopelessness and experience of eternal hellish cycles are echoed by Otared at the end of the novel. He alludes to himself as a policeman who has led "many different lives in many hells," while narrating his account of ominous events in 2014 in the downtown streets of Cairo, Qasr al-Aini, Mohamed Mahmoud, and Talaat Harb. He says:

> Then I saw that I had been a policeman in the world, and saw that I had been a policeman in many different lives in many hells, and a million million images passed before me in which I saw everything: how I had tormented people and been tormented by them.
> And I saw that hell was eternal and unbroken, changeless and undying; and that in the end, all other things would pass away and nothing besides remains. And I knew that I was in hell forevermore, and that I belonged there. (ibid. p. 341)

Given the resonance within the two narrators' testimonies and their parallel experiences, reading that the anonymous narrator from AH 455 is Otared himself—while they are leading different lives—is not only plausible, but an effective device that stresses the inescapability of the living hell during these disastrous times in Cairo.

Otared, preoccupied with the negation of life and the persistence of death, opens with a section called "A Beginning," which as one reads it only indicates an ending to humanity as we know it: a murder and a human flesh-eating scene that Otared is called to. Otared's description of the sight and smell of days-old cooked human flesh, fecal matter, and drying blood immediately summons up readers' horror and disgust. Throughout the novel, the senses are creatively and effectively evoked to convey implausible levels of atrocity within Cairo. Examples include the faceless "cockroaches," a group of teens who wrap their faces with newspapers and sexually assault women with unimagined frenzy, whether they are living, dying, or, even, corpses—especially after hundreds of men and women are regularly brutally and purposelessly shot on Cairo's streets. Otared expounds this abominable behavior as follows:

> Their loud shouts and laughter were clearly audible, but muffled by the sheets of newspaper wrapped haphazardly around their heads. They reminded me of the corpse robbers I'd seen stripping clothes months ago: the same skinny young bodies covered in scars. The three of them were laughing, and shouting, and letting off ringing snorts, in a frenzy of high spirits, bouncing around hysterically, sprinting off and deliberately smashing their bodies into the walls, into one another, into the terrified whores who stood there trembling. (ibid. p. 128)

This inconceivable horror and aggression committed against women and their bodies pervade the novel. Another example is the one-eyed garbage man, who holds captive two homeless sisters to repeatedly rape them "as violently as he was able . . . accompanied by tearing flesh and flowing blood" in his repugnantly smelling garbage shelter (ibid. p. 237). The depiction of such aggression solicits not only readers' abhorrence, but also incredulity towards the possible societal and moral conditions that could allow such acts.

As much as *Otared* evokes the senses in capturing the smells and sights of decay and deterioration in Cairo, it also presents the ways characters' senses are voluntarily or involuntarily numbed or blocked to suggest the intolerability of their suffering. For example, Zahra is a young schoolgirl whose father goes missing during the fateful 2011 events and never picks her up from school. This leads her compassionate teacher, Insal, to take her to his home and wife while attempting to search for the father. After a fruitless search in police reports accounting for the injured during the events, Insal moves his search to morgues to find the father among the unidentified corpses of the killed. The narrator describes Zahra's unendurable agony during the deadly search as follows:

> The chaos of smells was oppressive and bewildering. Zahra could make out fear, anxiety, anger, and sickness. She sniffled out sweat and feet and hair. And over these lay the powerful, heavy odor of antiperspirants and fragrances, while the reek of formaldehyde and disinfectant blanketed the lot. From an unseen spot, some corner Zahra couldn't quite locate, came the faint scent of uncertain hope. This was a memory of her father's smell. (ibid. p. 182)

Locating a "faint scent of uncertain hope" in the deathly familial and familiar scent of Zahra's father figuratively and grimly situates hope in death, but, more importantly, leads Zahra's mouth, nose, ears, and eyes to be gradually shut and blocked with her expanding and overgrowing skin until she can no longer interact with her cruel world.

While Zahra's shutting organs and senses are an involuntary means of alleviating her suffering, Otared and other individuals in the resistance group voluntarily resort to narcotics to distort their sense of the foreign occupation, sheer violence, and decaying morality among officials and civilians alike. At the beginning of the novel, Otared relates how he and his fellow resistance officers stationed in the Cairo Tower "took turns smoking the [hash] joint" (15). After the Tower Group operations are dismantled due to their losing hope of liberating Cairo, Otared resorts to a new synthetic narcotic called Karbon, which causes him to descend to a lower realm of "blackness" and "nothingness," in which he attempts to perceive whether he is alive or dead, in motion or still, only to conclude he "was nothingness . . . I tried recalling what had happened that day, where I was and what I was, but I had forgotten language and memory" (ibid. p. 133). Karbon's effect dispossesses Otared of his sense of the world around him; he is neither able to recollect the painful incidents around him nor communicate them to others through the medium of language. Similarly, the use of masks in *Otared* stands out as another device for blocking characters' perception and senses. It can be seen as both a means of masking feelings and as protection from known and unknown dangers. Otared and the rest of the resistance officers are required to wear masks to disguise their identity, with a persona of their choice, like people on the streets. He observes how, strangely, he grows inseparable from his mask: "I wasn't substituting the mask for my face as I'd first thought, but putting a barrier between myself and everyone around, though they were my colleagues and friends . . . Like me, I saw them go into decline, hanging onto their masks . . . nothing would stick in my mind but details of those borrowed identities" (ibid. p. 59). Instead of helping the group members achieve success in their mission by protecting their identity, the masks detach the group members from one another personally, dismantling their unity and leading their resistance effort to fail.

At this juncture, it is worth noting that within its dystopian configuration of Cairo, *Otared* sheds light on the responsibility of the police force—through the representation of Otared's experiences and acts, the disunity of his resistance group, and their collective spiritual wasteland—in the hell Cairo is transformed into during and after the 2011 events. It does so by underlining, at least at the beginning of the novel, Otared's location of anti-colonial efforts solely in a group of police officers—to whom he belongs—while, by and large, removing army officers and civilians from that exclusively nationalist undertaking. Otared recalls how all Egypt's government officials and agencies, such as the president, have "stepped down" and how "operations by all branches of the Egyptian armed forces have been halted" as soon as the Maltese forces have "inflicted severe defeats" on Egypt (ibid. p. 28). He continues:

> The resistance belonged to us, and to us alone; a huge organization run by the cream of the cops, whose first and only purpose was to expel the occupier. The fact is, I couldn't have cared less about the army officers. They were finished the first day of the occupation, and they'd stay that way unless we said otherwise. What bothered me was the credulousness of the civilians in our ranks . . . I learned they were just throwing their lives away, and it was only when I saw that the overwhelming majority of Egyptians were living under occupation in perfect contentment that I felt sympathy for them—there are people who still care about this country, I told myself. (ibid. pp. 34–5)

Otared's description not only figuratively reconstitutes the actual power structures of contemporary Egypt, where the Armed Forces are known as Egypt's most powerful political entity and the police force as a supplementary entity; it also undermines civilians' nationalism and resistance efforts. Furthermore, Otared's reflection on how "[t]ruly wonderful" the January days were in 2011, when killing was only "permitted to dispose of terrorists, troublemakers, fifth columnists, and demonstrators, with the unconditional support of the people, the prosecutor general, and the judiciary" (ibid. pp. 70–1), repudiates, all the more, justification of the brutal killings of any of the above imagined groups on the basis of an ad-hoc determination of their affiliation. *Otared* thus metaphorically stands as a cautionary tale of the bleak future that could await Cairo if violence and exclusivist nationalisms persist in the layers of its forces, agencies, and society.

Post-2011 Egypt in Novels: "Unruly Politics"

Following this examination of *Jirafit*, *The Queue*, and *Otared* as examples of novelistic production that capture Egypt in light of the recent revolutionary events and developments in 2011 (and afterwards), it can be said that they all highlight a prevalent sense of popular anguish and uncertainty, if not sheer despair at older power relations persistently finding their way back into Egyptian political and social schemes. At the same time, like new-consciousness novels, *Jirafit*, *The Queue*, and *Otared* do not lack unrelenting efforts to denounce the country's deteriorating conditions—albeit from newer angles and using forms of expression that befit their socio-political preoccupations during these specific moments of historical rupture. Mariz Tadros invites intellectuals to examine forms and spaces of "unruly politics," where citizens continue to subvert authority and continue their protest (Tadros 2013).[15] I argue that these novels demonstrate forms of unruly politics and continuous popular protest in their innovative aesthetics. However, they do so by shifting from the preoccupation of new-consciousness novels and their focus on complex minoritarian experiences in Egypt at the intersections of race, ethno-religion, and gender. The examples of post-2011 novels, as demonstrated above, tend to highlight, instead, subtle shades of difference within Egyptian society, in which the experiences of women and lower socio-economic classes are at the forefront—while still emphasizing the impact of social and political injustices on the larger population of Egypt. This shift in novelistic focus under the new historical conditions and the ever-changing socio-political context invokes McKeon's observations on the novel as a historical product: it interacts fully and responsibly with the dictates of the here and now.

I argue that, in their unruly politics and figurative attempts to bring everyone back to the negotiating table, *Jirafit*, *The Queue*, and *Otared* combine to offer an emphatic symbolic return to Egypt's modern center, Cairo, as a space and setting for their events, in particular its downtown area, where modern definitions of Egyptianhood have been formed and contested since the inception of the modern national self, as Mara Naaman puts it (Naaman 2011: 71).[16] During and after the revolutionary events of 2011, Cairo and its downtown area have all the more acquired expansive symbolic values following newer articulations of what Egyptianhood entails having emerged there at that time and having been negotiated since. Therefore, the choice of these exemplary novels to locate their events and characters in Egypt's urban center *par excellence*, whether clearly depicted as Cairo (as in *Jirafit* and *Otared*) or as an anonymous central city divided into digital districts (as in *The Queue*) backdrops their proposition of ways to resume negotiations, activism, and collective revolutionary effort among the different characters within their novelistic planes. At the same time, the examples depart from attempts to change perspective and pay attention to other marginalized directions from which *other*, alternative expressions of Egyptianness can be generated.

While articulating a joint concern with social and political injustices, each novel presents its particular understanding of the dissonance arising from the variant voices of opposition to the ever-renewed status quo in Egypt. *Jirafit* is bathed in historical light that is intended to invoke an inspirational period of feminist activism in Egypt in the first half of the twentieth century. The delicate shades of Nawal's graphite drawings metaphorically stand for her cumulative experiences across time and space as an Egyptian woman finding her way towards her right to social and political equality with men. This novelistic endeavor can be seen as a cultural endorsement of the on-the-ground negotiations towards complete gender equality and comprehensive social and political reforms that serve the particular needs of Egypt's women. *The Queue* belongs to the vein of absurdist realism, in which readers recognize the ridiculed portrayal of the details of the 2011 revolution and the struggles Egyptian people continue to face with the ruling authority. Its allegorical depiction of the impenetrable gate that refuses to answer to its citizens' demands is creative, but the astute representation of din within the queue community (in their relentless dialogues and interactions), as well as the unequal distance of individuals in the queue from the gate (in their near or far positions from it), are even more innovative. *Otared* metaphorically functions as a cautionary tale of what Cairo's future might look like unless real changes come into effect. It is set primarily in a Cairo of 2025, and readers are transported to a dystopian city that is recognizable in terms of familiar streets, bridges, buildings, and the Nile River and yet unrecognizable in its deterioration, its inhabitants' moral decay, and the pervasiveness of despair, violence, and death. *Otared*, through the narrative account(s) of its central character, presents the hellish experiences of a police officer in Cairo during and in the years following the bleak events of 2011–14. Portraying a foreign occupation and the secession of a resistance force that is exclusive to police officers, the novel exposes the spiritual dystopia existing within the people constructing such formations, and their inability to reclaim themselves or their city.

The analysis of *Jirafit*, *The Queue*, and *Otared* has illustrated thematic commonalities in these examples of post-2011 novelistic production in Egypt, including in how these works respond to their particular historical moment. Their unique aesthetics and means of engaging figuratively with the ongoing revolution and the unruly politics of protest testify to McKeon's "definitional volatility" theory of the novel, according to which new trends dissolve into the antithesis of their predecessor. However, in so doing, they borrow from former trends, and, as is the case with the post-2011 examples, they return to former novelistic spatial settings in urban centers. Seeing these novels in dialogue with new-consciousness novels highlights their departure from preoccupations with marginalized spaces and minority cultural experiences at the intersections of race, gender, ethno-religion, culture, and language. While this can be seen as a type of underrepresentation of and diffused treatment of imagined differences and thereby practices of differentiation in Egypt, it illustrates the dialectical process of historical change, in which the focus now is on summoning the collective and bringing everyone back to the table of political negotiation—while downplaying their imagined differences.

Notes

1. I refer to the period following the eruption of the Tahrir revolution as the post-2011 period. I intentionally refrain from using other temporal markers—such as post-Arab Spring or post-revolution—as I find them reductionist, if not unrepresentative of the ongoing social and political engagements and efforts of Egyptian citizenry. While the former assumes that the historical transitions that Egypt has undergone since 2011 would translate into a prescribed democratization process, the latter assumes that the revolution has ended, whereas in reality the masses continue to hold one appointed government after the other accountable for its practices.
2. Mazloum, Sherine Fouad, "To Write/To Revolt: Egyptian Women Novelists Writing the Revolution," *Journal for Cultural Research*, Vol. 19, No. 2, 2015, pp. 207–20.
3. Tadros, Mariz, "Introduction: The Pulse of the Arab Revolt," *Institute of Development Studies Bulletin*, Vol. 43. No. 1, 2012, pp. 1–15.
4. Tadros explains further what she means by the "time- and space-bound moral economy of Tahrir Square," in which Egypt's diverse groups laid aside their different political interests in that specific space and during those specific days. She writes:

   > The slogans that were used in Tahrir Square served to reinforce the emergence of a new narrative or script that would help unify the people, such as "Muslim Christian one hand" and "Not the [Muslim] Brothers, not the parties, our revolution is a youth revolution" which was deployed to override deep rifts in political society . . . This moral economy was civil both in the sense of being civilised (its non-violent, peaceful nature in the face of police brutality and infiltrators and thugs) and in the sense of not assuming a politicized religious character . . . It was also one where gender norms of engagement were reconfigured: women, veiled and unveiled, moved freely in late hours of the day, without being subjected to any harassment. (Tadros 2012: 10)

5. Al-Khashin, Hisham, *Jirafit* (Cairo: Maktabat al-Dar al-ᶜArabiyya lil-kitab, 2014).
6. All translations from *Jirafit* are my own.
7. The Egyptian-born poet al-Busiri (1213–94), also known as Muhammad bin Saᶜid al-Sinhaji, wrote a poem in praise of the Prophet Muhammad. The poem

is named after Prophet Muhammad's *burda* (garment). In the oral tradition, it is told that al-Busiri was ill but that during his sleep he saw the Prophet Muhammad in a vision, in which the Prophet took care of him and covered him with his garment to heal him. For more details see "Qasidat al-burda al-Khalida ʿala marr al-ayyam …," <http://habous.gov.ma/daouat-alhaq/item/4078> (last accessed 27 August 2017).

8. Mura, Andrea, "A Genealogical Inquiry into Early Islamism: the Discourse of Hasan al-Banna," *Journal of Political Ideologies*, 1 February 2012, Vol. 17, No. 1, pp. 61–85.

9. Baron, Beth, "An Islamic Activist in Interwar Egypt," *Women, Philanthropy, and Civil Society*. ed. Kathleen D. McCarthy (Bloomington: Indiana University Press, 2001), pp. 225–44.

10. ʿAbd al-ʿAziz, Basma, *The Queue*, trans. Elisabeth Jaquette (New York: Melville House, 2016).

11. The Knights of Malta's beginnings in Jerusalem were primarily of a charitable nature, as it originated as a group of monks who cared for sick Christian pilgrims in Jerusalem under the name of the Sovereign Military Hospitaller Order of Saint John of Jerusalem. For more information see Joshua E. Keating's article "Who Are the Knights of Malta—and What Do They Want?," *Foreign Policy*, 19 January 2011, <http://foreignpolicy.com/2011/01/19/who-are-the-knights-of-malta-and-what-do-they-want/> (last accessed 27 August 2017).

12. Keating, Joshua E., "Who Are the Knights of Malta—and What Do They Want?," *Foreign Policy*, 19 January 2011, <http://foreignpolicy.com/2011/01/19/who-are-the-knights-of-malta-and-what-do-they-want/> (last accessed 27 August 2017).

13. For more information on the history of the Knights of Malta and their mission, see Abbé de Vertot's *The history of the Knights Hospitallers of St. John of Jerusalem, Styled afterwards, the Knights of Rhodes, and at present, the Knights of Malta*. Translated from the French of Mons. L'Abbe de Vertot, Vol. I, London, 1775. *Eighteenth Century Collections Online*. Gale. Binghamton University Libraries—SUNY.

14. Rabiʿ, Muhammad, *Otared*, trans. Robin Moger (Cairo: Hoopoe, AUC Press, 2016).

15. Tadros, Mariz, "Egypt's Unfinished Transition or Unfinished Revolution? Unruly Politics and Capturing the Pulses of the Street," Work in Progress Paper on the website of Institute of Development Studies, May 2013, <http://www.ids.ac.uk/files/

dmfile/EgyptsUnfinishedTransitionorUnfinishedRevolutionMTadros2013. pdf> (last accessed 12 May 2017).

16. Naaman, Mara, *Urban Spaces in Contemporary Egyptian Literature: Portraits of Cairo* (New York: Palgrave Macmillan, 2011).

Bibliography

ᶜAbd al-ᶜAlim, Dina (2009), "Muᶜtazz Futahya: yahud ma qabl al-thawra lisu khawana" (Muᶜtazz Futayha: The Jews from the pre-revolution period are not traitors), *Al-Yawm al-Sabiᶜ*, 3 August 2009, <http://www.youm7.com/story/2009/8/3/124053/‏معتز-فتيحة-يهود-ما-قبل-الثورة-ليسوا-خونة‎> (last accessed 15 September 2016).

ᶜAbd al-ᶜAziz, Basma (2013), *al-Tabur*, Cairo: Dar al-Tanwir.

ᶜAbd al-ᶜAziz, Basma (2016), *The Queue*, trans. Elisabeth Jaquette, New York: Melville House.

Adonis, Ali Ahmed Said (1990), *An Introduction to Arab Poetics*, trans. Catherine Cobham, Austin: University of Texas Press.

Adonis, Ali Ahmed Said (1979), *Muqaddima lil-shiᶜr al-ᶜarabi*, 3rd edn, Beirut: Dar al-ᶜAwda, 1979.

Adonis, Ali Ahmed Said (2005), "The Aesthetic Dimension," in *Sufism and Surrealism*, trans. Judith Cumberbatch, London: Saqi Books, pp. 115–42.

Aikhenvald, Aleksandra and Dixon, Robert (2001), *Aerial Diffusion and Genetic Inheritance: Problems in Comparative Linguistics*, New York: Oxford University Press, 2001.

Ajami, Fouad (1995), "The Sorrows of Egypt," *Foreign Affairs*, Vol. 74, No. 5, pp. 72–88.

Al-Aswani, ᶜAlaʾ (2006a), *The Yacoubian Building*, trans. Humphrey Davies, New York: Harper Perennial.

Al-Aswani, ᶜAlaʾ (2006b), *ᶜImarat yaᶜqubiyan*, 9th edn, Cairo: Maktabat Madbuli.

Al-Aswani, ᶜAlaʾ (2007), *Shikagu*, Cairo: Dar al-Shuruq.

Al-Aswani, ʿAlaʾ [2007] (2009), *Chicago*, trans. Farouk Abdel Wahab, Harper Perennial edn, New York: HarperCollins.

Al-Ghitani, Jamal (2005), "Nuqtat ʿubur," in ʿAlaʾ al-Aswani, *The Yacoubian Building*, 8th edn, Cairo: Maktabat Madbuli, pp. 350–1.

Al-Ghitani, Jamal (2009), *The Zafarani Files*, trans. Farouk Abdel Wahab, Cairo: AUC Press.

Al-Hakim, Tawfiq (1964), *ʿAwdat al-ruh*, Cairo: Maktabat al-Adab.

Al-Hakim, Tawfiq [1947] (1989), *Maze of Justice: Diary of a Country Prosecutor*, trans. Abba Eban, foreword by P. H. Newby, London: Saqi Books.

Al-Hakim, Tawfiq (1990), *Return of the Spirit: Tawfiq al-Hakim's Classic Novel of the 1919 Revolution*, trans. William M. Hutchins, Washington, DC: Three Continents Press.

Al-Hakim, Tawfiq [1937] (1965), *Yawmiyyat naʾib fi-l-aryaf*, Cairo: Maktabat al-Adab.

Al-Hufi, Nashwa (2006), "'ʿAlaʾ al-Aswani: Katabtu '*The Yacoubian Building*' wa ʾana ʾastaʿiddu lil-Hijra ʾila niyu ziland," *al-Sharq al-awsat*, 22 March, <http://archive.aawsat.com/details.asp?article=354235&issueno=9976#.V_UQ_xQ5aB8> (last accessed 5 October 2016).

ʿAli, Idris (2001), *al-Nubi*, Cairo: al-ʿAlamiyya Press.

Al-Kharrat, Idwar (2002), *Rama and the Dragon*, trans. John Verlenden and Ferial Jabouri Ghazoul, Cairo: AUC Press.

Al-Kharrat, Idwar (1980), *Ramah wa-l-tinnin*, Beirut: al-Muʾassasa al-ʿArabiyya lil-Dirasat wa-l-Nashr.

Al-Khashin, Hisham (2014), *Jirafit*, Cairo: Maktabat al-Dar al-ʿArabiyya lil-kitab.

Al-Khumaysi, Ashraf [2013] (2015), *Manafi al-rabb*, 3rd edn, Cairo: Al-Dar al-Misriyya al-Lubnaniyya.

Al-Kuni, Ibrahim (2014), "In the Desert We Visit Death," interview by Anders Hastrup, Louisiana Channel, Louisiana Museum of Modern Art (22 April 2014), http://channel.louisiana.dk/video/ibrahim-al-koni-desert-we-visit-death (last accessed 5 March 2016).

Al-Kuni, Ibrahim (1990), *Nazif al-hajar*, London: Riyad al-Rayyis lil-Kutub wal-Nashr.

Al-Kuni, Ibrahim [2002] (2013), *The Bleeding of the Stone*, trans. May Jayyusi and Christopher Tingley, Northampton: Interlink Books.

Allen, Roger (2009), "Fiction and Publics: The Emergence of the 'Arabic Best-Seller,'" *The Middle East Institute Viewpoint: The State of the Arts in the Middle*

East, pp. 9–12, <https://www.mei.edu/sites/default/files/publications/state-arts-middle-east.pdf> (last accessed 15 September 2016).

Al-Qurʾan al-Karim (1935), Misr: ʿAbd al-Hamid Ahmad Hanafi.

Al-Saʿdawi, Nawal [1975] (1979), *Imraʾa ʿinda nuqtat al-sifr*, 2nd edn, Beirut: Dar al-Adab.

Al-Saʿdawi, Nawal (1986), *Memoirs from the Women's Prison*, trans. Marilyn Booth, London: Women's Press.

Al-Saʿdawi, Nawal [1984] (1986), *Mudhakkirati fi sijn al-nisaʾ*, 2nd edn, Cairo: Dar al-Mustaqbal al-ʿArabi.

Al-Saʿdawi, Nawal (1983), *Woman at Point Zero*, trans. Sharif Hatata, London: Zed Books.

Al-Tahawi, Miral (1997), "al-buʿdu al-ithnughrafi lil-ʿamal al-riwaʾi: shihada/The Ethnographic Dimension in Fiction: A Testimony," *Alif: Journal of Comparative Poetics, Literature and Anthropology in Africa*, No. 17, pp. 145–52.

Al-Tahawi, Miral [1996] (2010), *al-Khibaʾ*, 2nd edn, Beirut: Dar al-Adab.

Al-Tahawi, Miral (2010), *Bruklin hayts*, Beirut: Dar al-Adab.

Al-Tahawi, Miral [1998] (2003), *The Tent*, trans. Anthony Galderbank, Cairo: AUC Press.

Al-Zayyat, Latifa (1960) (1989), *Al-Bab al-mafuth*, Cairo: al-Hayʾa al-Misriyya al-ʿAmma lil-Kitab.

Amin, Galal (2011), *Egypt in the Era of Hosni Mubarak, 1981–2011*, Cairo: AUC Press.

Amin, Galal (2013), *Madha hadatha lil thawra al-misriyya*, Cairo: Dar al-Shuruq.

Amin, Galal (2000), *The Open Door*, trans. Marilyn Booth, Cairo: AUC Press.

Appiah, Kwame Anthony (2006), *Cosmopolitanism: Ethics in a World of Strangers*, New York: Norton.

"Azazel" (2012), *Encyclopædia Britannica Online*, <http://www.britannica.com/EBchecked/topic/46745/Azazel> (last accessed 15 September 2016).

Bakhtin, Mikhail [1934–5] (1981), "Discourse in the Novel," in Michael Holquist (ed.), *The Dialogic Imagination*, trans. Caryl Emerson and Michael Holquist, Austin: University of Texas Press, pp. 259–422.

Baron, Beth (2001), "An Islamic Activist in Interwar Egypt," in Kathleen D. McCarthy (ed.), *Women, Philanthropy, and Civil Society*, Bloomington: Indiana University Press, pp. 225–44.

Bayyumi, ʿAmr (2008), "Muʾallif Riwayat *Azazeel* yuʾakkid anna waqaʾiʿaha haqiqiyya wa yutalib al-ʾnba Bishuy biʾiʿadit qiraʾtiha," *Al-Masri al-Yawm*, 26

July, <http://today.almasryalyoum.com/article2.aspx?ArticleID=114789> (last accessed 15 September 2016).

Beinin, Joel (1996), "Egyptian Jewish Identities: Communitarianisms, Nationalisms, Nostalgias," *Contested Polities: Stanford Humanities Review (SEHR)*, Vol 5, Issue 1, February, <http://web.stanford.edu/group/SHR/5-1/text/beinin.html> (last accessed 15 September 2016).

Benjamin, Walter [1968] (2000), "The Storyteller," in Michael McKeon, *Theory of the Novel: A Historical Approach*, Baltimore: Johns Hopkins University Press, pp. 77–93.

Benjamin, Walter (1968), "The Work of Art in the Age of Mechanical Reproduction," in Hannah Arendt (ed.), *Illuminations*, trans. Harry Zohn, New York: Harcourt, Brace & World, pp. 217–52.

Bhabha. Homi (1994), *The Location of Culture*, New York: Routledge.

Bhabha. Homi (1992), "The World and the Home," *Social Text: Third World and Post-Colonial Issues*, Nos 31/32, pp. 141–53.

Booth, Marilyn (1993), *My Grandmother's Cactus: Stories by Egyptian Women*. Austin: University of Texas Press.

Booth, Marilyn (2013), "Locating Women's Autobiographical Writing in Colonial Egypt," *Journal of Women's History*, Vol. 25, No. 2, Summer, pp. 36–60.

Caiani, Fabio (2005), "Representations of Egypt in Some Works by Idwār al-Kharrāṭ," *Journal of Middle Eastern Literatures*, Vol. 8, No. 1, January, pp. 35–52.

cooke, miriam (2010), "Magical Realism in Libya," *Journal of Arabic Literature*, Vol. 41, pp. 9–21.

Cornwell, Graham H., and Atia, Mona (2012), "Imaginative Geographies of Amazigh Activism in Morocco," *Social & Cultural Geography*, Vol. 13, No. 3, pp. 255–74.

Deleuze, G, and Guattari, F. (1986), *Kafka, Toward a Minor Literature*, trans. Dana Polan, foreword by Reda Bensmaia, Minneapolis: Minnesota University Press.

Du Bois, W. E. B. [1903] (2007), *The Souls of Black Folk*, ed. Brent Hayes Edwards, New York: Oxford University Press.

East, Ben (2012), "Award-winning Book from Youssef Ziedan Gets Translated into English," *The National*, 26 March, <http://www.thenational.ae/arts-culture/books/award-winning-book-from-youssef-ziedan-gets-translated-into-english> (last accessed 30 July 2012).

El-Enany, Rasheed (2006), *Arab Representations of the Occident: East–West Encounters in Arabic Fiction*, London: Routledge.

El-Enany, Rasheed (2009), "Rasheed El-Enany on Modern Arabic Lit: Not Quite a Renaissance," interview by Hazem Zohny in *Egypt Independent*, 12 December, <http://www.egyptindependent.com/news/rasheed-el-enany-modern-arabic-lit-not-quite-renaissance> (last accessed 15 September 2016).

Elmusa, Sharif (2013), "The Ecological Bedouin: Toward Environmental Principles for the Arab Region," *Alif: Journal of Comparative Poetics*, Vol 33, pp. 9–35.

El-Shobaki, Amr (2011), "Ending Sectarianism in Egypt." *Egypt Independent Online*, 14 January, <http://www.egyptindependent.com/opinion/ending-sectarianism-egypt> (last accessed 16 September 2016).

Fanon, Frantz (1967), *Black Skin, White Masks*. New York: Grove Press.

Fanon, Frantz [1963] (2007), "On National Culture," in Tejumola Olaniyan and Ato Quayson (eds) *African Literature: An Anthology of Criticism and Theory*," Malden: Blackwell, pp. 251–61.

Fanon, Frantz [1963] (1966), *The Wretched of the Earth*, trans. Constance Farrington, preface by Jean-Paul Sartre, New York: Grove Press.

Faraj, ʿAbd al-Nabi (2003), "Idris ʿAli: Jil al-sittinat inkasaru b-inkisar batalihim alladhi habasahum fi maʿmaʿat al-siyasa," *Al-Sharq al-Awsat*, 29 September, <http://www.aawsat.com/details.asp?section=19&article=195200&issueno=9071#.U2EqfV5GqDo> (last accessed 30 April 2014).

Faraj, Khalid (2016), "Muʿtazz Futayha baʿd al-hukm bi-habs Rana al-Subki: Man yarfaʿ hadhihi al-nawʿiyya min al-qadaya 'tufayliyyat,'" *Al-Watan*, <http://www.elwatannews.com/news/details/927658> (last accessed 19 September 2016).

Friedman, Susan Stanford (2007), "Migrations, Diasporas, and Borders," in David G. Nicholls (ed.), *Introduction to Scholarship in Modern Languages and Literatures*, 3rd edn, New York: Modern Language Association of America, pp. 260–93.

Futayha, Muʿtazz (2008), *Akhir yahud al-iskandariyya*, 2nd edn, Cairo: Dar Uktub.

Hafez, Sabry (2010), "The New Egyptian Novel: Urban Transformation and Narrative Form," *New Left Review*, 64 (July–August), pp. 46–62.

Halsall, Paul, "Galerius and Constantine: Edicts of Toleration 311/313," *Internet Medieval Sourcebook*, Fordham University Center for Medieval Studies website, <http://sourcebooks.fordham.edu/halsall/source/edict-milan.asp> (last accessed 22 September 2016).

Haqqi, Yahya [1940] (1984), *Qindil umm hashim*, 5th edn, Cairo: Dar al-Maʿarif.

Haqqi, Yahya (1973), *The Saint's Lamp and Other Stories*, trans. Muhammad Mustafa Badawi, Leiden: Brill.

Hasan, Sayyid Mahmud (2010), "Baʿd haya ʿasiba: Wafat al-katib Idris ʿAli,"

Al-Ahram Online, 1 December 2001, <http://www.ahram.org.eg/Books/News/50974.aspx> (last accessed 20 July 2012).

Haykal, Muhammad Husayn [1914] (1967), *Zaynab: Manadhir wa akhlaq rifiyya*, Cairo: Maktabat al-Nahda al-Misriyya.

Haykal, Muhammad Husayn (1989), *Mohammed Hussein Haikal's Zainab: The First Egyptian Novel*, trans. John Mohammed Grinsted, London: Darf.

Helm, Robert (1994), "Azazel in Early Jewish Tradition," *Andrews University Seminary Studies Journal*, Online Archive, Vol. 32. No. 3, Autumn, pp. 217–26.

Honeywell, Arthur J. (1996), "Plot in the Modern Novel," in Michael J. Hoffman and Patrick D. Murphy (eds), *Essentials of the Theory of Fiction*, 2nd edn, Durham, NC: Duke University Press, pp. 147–57.

Ismail, Sherif H. (2015), "Arabic Literature into English: The (Im)possibility of Understanding," *Interventions*, Vol. 16, No. 6, pp. 916–31.

Ibrahim, Sunᶜallah [1981] (1983), *Al-Lajna*, Beirut: Dar al-Kalima.

Ibrahim, Sunᶜallah (2001), *The Committee: A Novel*, trans. Mary St. Germain and Charlene Constable, Syracuse: Syracuse University Press.

Jacquemond, Richard (2008), *Conscience of the Nation: Writers, State, and Society in Modern Egypt*, trans. David Tresilian, Cairo: AUC Press.

Jameson, Fredric (1982), *The Political Unconscious: Narrative as a Socially Symbolic Act*, Ithaca: Cornell University Press.

Kanafani, Ghassan (2004), *All That's Left to You: A Novella and Other Short Stories*, trans. May Jayysi and Jeremy Reed, introd. Roger Allen, Northampton: Interlink Books.

Kanafani, Ghassan (1966), *Ma tabaqqa la-kum*, Beirut: Dar al-Taliᶜa.

Keating, Joshua E (2011), "Who Are the Knights of Malta—and What Do They Want?" *Foreign Policy*, 19 January, <http://foreignpolicy.com/2011/01/19/who-are-the-knights-of-malta-and-what-do-they-want/> (last accessed 27 August 2014).

Khalil, Menna (2012), "The People and the Army Are One Hand: Myths and Their Translations," in Samia Mehrez (ed.), *Translating Egypt's Revolution: The Language of Tahrir*, Cairo: AUC Press, pp. 249–75.

Krämer, Gudrun (1989), *The Jews in Modern Egypt, 1914–1952*, Seattle: University of Washington Press.

Lalami, Laila (2009), "Introduction" to Tayyib Salih's *Season of Migration to the North*, trans. Denis Johnson-Davies, New York: New York Review Books.

Lashin, Musa Shahin (2001), *Al-Manhal al-hadith fi sharh al-hadith: Ahadith mukht-*

ara from sahih al-Bukhari hasab manhaj al-maʿahid al-azhariyya al-asila, Part IV, 2nd edn, Cairo: Dar al-shuruq.

Latourette, Kenneth Scott (1975), *A History of Christianity Volume 1: To A.D. 1500*, rev. edn, foreword by Ralph D. Winter, New York: Harper San Francisco.

Levine, George [1981] (2000), "From the Realistic Imagination: English Fiction from Frankenstein to Lady Chatterley," in Michael McKeon (ed.), *The Theory of the Novel: A Historical Approach*, Baltimore: Johns Hopkins University Press, pp. 613–31.

Levine, George (1996), "Realism Reconsidered," in Michael J. Hoffman and Patrick D. Murphy (eds), *Essentials of the Theory of Fiction*, 2nd edn, Durham, NC: Duke University Press, pp. 234–45.

Lodge, David (1996), "Mimesis and Diegesis in Modern Fiction," in Michael J. Hoffman and Patrick D. Murphy (eds), *Essentials of the Theory of Fiction*, 2nd edn, Durham, NC: Duke University Press, pp. 348–72.

Lohwasser, Angelika (2001), "Queenship in Kush: Status, Role and Ideology of Royal Women," *Journal of American Research Center in Egypt*, Vol. 38, pp. 61–76.

Lukács, Georg (1963), *The Historical Novel*, trans. Hannah and Stanley Mitchell, preface by Irving Howe Boston: Beacon Press.

Mahfuz, Najib [1957] (1972), *Al-Sukkariyya*, Beirut: Dar al-Qalam.

Mahfuz, Najib [1956] (1983), *Bayn al-qasrayn*, Cairo: Maktabat Misr.

Mahfuz, Najib (1957), *Qasr al-shawq*, Cairo: Maktabat Misr.

Mahfuz, Najib (1991), *Palace of Desire*, trans. William M. Hutchins and Olive E. Kenny, New York: Doubleday.

Mahfuz, Najib (1990), *Palace Walk*, trans. William M. Hutchins and Olive E. Kenny, New York: Doubleday.

Mahfuz, Najib (1992), *Sugar Street*, trans. William Maynard Hutchins and Angele Botros Samaan, New York: Doubleday.

Mamdani, Mahmood (1996), *Citizen and Subject: Contemporary Africa and the Legacy of Late Colonialism*, Princeton: Princeton University Press.

Mazloum, Sherine Fouad (2015), "To Write/to Revolt: Egyptian Women Novelists Writing the Revolution," *Journal fir Cultural Research*, Vol. 19, No. 2, pp. 207–20.

McKeon, Michael (2000a), "Genre Theory," in Michael McKeon (ed.), *Theory of the Novel: A Historical Approach*, Baltimore: Johns Hopkins University Press, pp. 1–4.

McKeon, Michael (2000b), "Generic Transformation and Social Change: Rethinking the Rise of the Novel," in Michael McKeon (ed.), *Theory of the Novel: A Historical Approach*, Baltimore: Johns Hopkins University Press, pp. 382–99.

Mehrez, Samia (2008), *Egypt's Culture Wars: Politics and Practice*, New York: Routledge.

Memmi, Albert (1991), *The Colonizer and the Colonized*, trans. Howard Greenfeld, introd. Jean Paul Sartre, Boston: Beacon Press.

Moolla, F. F. (2015), "Desert Ethics, Myths of Nature and Novel Form in the Narratives of Ibrahim al-Koni," *Tydskrif Vir Letterkunde*. Vol. 52, No. 2, pp. 176–96.

Munif, ᶜAbd al-Rahman (1978), *Al-Nihayat*, Beirut: Dar al-Adab.

Munif, ᶜAbd al-Rahman (2007), *Endings*, trans. Roger Allen, Northampton: Interlink Books.

Mura, Andrea (2012), "A Genealogical Inquiry into Early Islamism: The Discourse of Hasan al-Banna," *Journal of Political Ideologies*, 1 February, Vol. 17, No.1, pp. 61–85.

"Mut" [2001] (2005), in Donald B. Redford (ed.), *The Oxford Encyclopedia of Ancient Egypt Online*, <http://www.oxfordreference.com.proxy.binghamton.edu/view/10.1093/acref/9780195102345.001.0001/acref-9780195102345-e-0481?rskey=sqoYDH&result=1> (last accessed 9 May 2016).

Naaman, Mara (2011), *Urban Spaces in Contemporary Egyptian Literature: Portraits of Cairo*, New York: Palgrave Macmillan.

Nkrumah, Gamal (2014), "Knocking on Nubia's Door," *Al-Ahram Weekly*, 6 February, <http://weekly.ahram.org.eg/News/5313/32/Knocking-on-Nubia's-door.aspx> (last accessed 30 September 2014).

Nur, Hasan (2007), *Dawwamat al-shamal*, Cairo: Al-Dar al-ᶜAlamiyya lil-Tibaᶜa wal-Nashr.

Qasim, Muhammad Khalil (1968), *Al-Shamandura, Awwal riwayah nubiyya fi tarikh al-adab al-ᶜarabi*, Cairo: Dar Al-Kitab Al-ᶜArabi.

Rabiᶜ, Muhammad (2016), *Otared*, trans. Robin Moger, Cairo: Hoopoe, AUC Press.

Rabiᶜ, Muhammad (2015), *ᶜUtarid*, Cairo: Dar al-Tanwir.

Rifᶜat, Alifa (1991), *Jawharat Firᶜawn*, Cairo: Dar al-Hilal.

Rudwin, Maximilian (1931), "The Devil in Literature," *The Open Court*, Vol 45, No. 896, January, The University of Southern Illinois Open Library website, pp. 56–64, <http://opensiuc.lib.siu.edu/cgi/viewcontent.cgi?article=4352&context=ocj> (last accessed 21 September 2016).

Said, W. Edward (1985), "Orientalism Reconsidered," *Cultural Critique*, No. 1, Autumn, pp. 89–107.

Salih, Salah (1997), "Tajalliyat usturiyya lil-saharaʾ al-afriqiyya al-kubra fi al-riwaya al-ʿarabiyya," *Alif: Journal of Comparative Poetics: Literature and Anthropology in Africa*, No. 17, pp. 6–27.
Salim, Saʿid (2010), "Suhayl wa 'banat naʿsh:' Ustura abadiyya min zaman al-dahsha," *Jaridatu-l-Ittihad*, 30 August, <http://www.alittihad.ae/details.php?id=54725&y=2010> (last accessed 31 August 2016).
Sartre, Paul (1991), Introduction to *The Colonizer and the Colonized* by Albert Memmi, trans. Howard Greenfeld, Boston: Beacon Press, pp. xxi–xxix.
Selim, Samah (2004), *The Novel and the Rural Imaginary, 1880–1985*, Albany: State University of New York Press.
Shalabi, Khayri (2010), *Istasiyya*, Cairo: Dar al-Shuruq.
Shalan, Jeff (2002), "Writing the Nation: Emergence of Egypt in the Modern Arabic Novel," *Journal of Arabic Literature*, Vol. 33, No. 3, pp. 211–47.
Spaulding, Jay (1982), "Slavery, Land Tenure and Social Class in the Northern Turkish Sudan," *The International Journal of African Historical Studies*, Vol. 15, No. 1, pp. 1–20.
Spivak, Gayatri (1996), *The Spivak Reader: Selected Works of Gayatri Spivak*, New York: Routledge.
Tadros, Mariz (2012), "Introduction: The Pulse of the Arab Revolt," *Institute of Development Studies Bulletin*, Vol. 43, No. 1, pp. 1–15.
Tadros, Mariz (2013), "Egypt's Unfinished Transition or Unfinished Revolution? Unruly Politics and Capturing the Pulses of the Street," Work in Progress Paper on the website of *Institute of Development Studies*, May, pp. 6–13, <http://www.ids.ac.uk/files/dmfile/EgyptsUnfinishedTransitionorUnfinishedRevolutionMTadros2013.pdf> (last accessed 12 May 2017).
Tahir, Bahaʾ [1995] (2000), *al-Hubb fil-manfa*, Beirut: Dar al-Adab.
Tahir, Bahaʾ (1996), *Aunt Safiyya and the Monastery: A Novel*, trans. Barbara Romaine, Berkeley: University of California Press.
Tahir, Bahaʾ (1991), *Khalti Safiyya wa-l-Dayr*, Cairo: Dar al-Hilal.
Tahir, Bahaʾ (2001), *Love in Exile*, trans. Farouk Abdel Wahab, Cairo: AUC Press.
Tahir, Bahaʾ (2009), *Sunset Oasis*, trans. Humphrey Davies, London: Sceptre.
Tahir, Bahaʾ (2006), *Wahat al-ghurub*, Cairo: Dar al-Hilal.
Talahite, Anissa (2007), "North African Writing," in Tejumola Olaniyan and Ato Quayson (eds), *African Literature: An Anthology of Criticism and Theory*, Malden: Blackwell, pp. 38–45.
Tamraz, ʿAlya (2010), "Nashir 'Akhir yahud al-Iskandariyya:' 'hasasiyyat al-mawduʿ' awqafat tahwil al-riwaya ila film," *Al-Masri al-Yawm*, 19 October.

Tucker, Judith (1978), "While Sadat Shuffles: Economic Decay, Political Ferment in Egypt," *MERIP Reports*, No. 65, March, pp. 3–9, 26.

Young, Robert J. C. (2001), *Postcolonialism: An Historical Introduction*, Malden: Blackwell.

Walkowitz, Rebecca L. (2006), *Cosmopolitan Style: Modernism beyond the Nation*, New York: Columbia University Press.

Weisburg, Meg Ferniss (2015), "Spiritual Symbolism in the Sahara: Ibrahim Al-Koni's Nazīf al-Ḥajar," *Research in African Literature*, Vol. 46, No. 3, Fall, pp. 45–67.

Wilken, Robert L. (1965), "Tradition, Exegesis, and the Christological Controversies," *Church History*, Vol. 34, No. 2, June, pp. 123–45.

Wills, Garry (2011), "The Trials of an Unquiet Heart," *New Statesman*, 18 April 2011, pp. 24–7.

Zaydan, Yusuf [2008] (2009), ᶜ*Azazil*, 6th edn, Cairo: Dar al-Shuruq.

Zaydan, Yusuf (2012a), *Azazeel*, trans. Jonathan Wright, London: Atlantic Books.

Zaydan, Yusuf (2012b), "al-Asʾila al-taʾsisiyya: Hal taqum bi-miṣr dawla diniyya?," *Al-Masri al-Yawm*, 22 May, <http://www.almasryalyoum.com/node/859261> (last accessed 27 July 2012).

Zohny, Hazem (2009), "Rasheed El-Enany on Modern Arabic Lit: Not Quite a Renaissance," *Egypt Independent*, 12 December, <http://www.egyptindependent.com/news/rasheed-el-enany-modern-arabic-lit-not-quite-renaissance> (last accessed 15 September 2016).

Index

ᶜAbd al-ᶜAziz, Basma (or Abdel Aziz, Basma), 162, 172
ᶜAbd al-Nasir, Jamal (or Abdel Nasser, Gamal), 8–11, 14, 43, 48
Adonis (or Ali Ahmed Said), 113–14, 117, 132–4, 137–8
Al-Aswani, ᶜAlaʾ (or Al-Aswany, Alaa), 2–3, 5, 29–31, 98–102, 104–18, 120
Alexandria, 2, 19, 25, 33, 43, 56–7, 63, 67, 69, 72–6, 79, 81–2, 85–6, 88–94, 110, 134
Al-Ghitani, Jamal (or Al-Ghitani, Gamal), 19–20, 101
Al-Hakim, Tawfiq, 16–18, 21
ᶜAli, Idris (or Ali, Idris), 2–3, 5, 31–2, 42, 44–50, 52–6, 58, 63–4
Al-Kharrat, Idwar (or Al-Kharrat, Edwar), 19, 21–2
Al-Khashin, Hisham, 162, 164–5, 170
Al-Khumaysi, Ashraf, 2, 5, 34, 124, 130–2, 134–5, 137, 139
Al-Kuni, Ibrahim (or Al-Koni, Ibrahim), 34, 100, 124, 126–31
Allen, Roger, 99–100; *see also* best-seller
Al-Sadat, Anwar (or Sadat, Anwar), 8–11, 14, 21, 46
Al-Saᶜdawi, Nawal (or El-Saadawi, Nawal), 22–4, 26, 99
ambivalence, 47, 49, 159
Amin, Jalal (or Amin, Galal), 10
Al-Tahawi, Miral (or Al-Tahawy, Miral), 2–3, 5, 25, 34, 124, 141–2, 144, 146, 148–54
Al-Zayyat, Latifa, 22–4

Amazigh, 2, 31–2, 42–6, 56–62, 64
  Tamazight, 43
  see also Assiwans
ancien régime, 16, 26, 101, 108
Appiah, Kwame, 4, 33, 72
Assiwans, 64
  Issiwan, 43, 46, 56, 58–9
asymmetries of power, 1, 27, 99; *see also* inequality

Bakhtin, Mikhail, 15; *see also* heteroglossic (polyphonic)
Bedouin 34, 46, 125, 128–9, 133, 135, 142–3, 144–54
  Bedouin woman, 2–3, 144
Benjamin, Walter, 44, 52, 54–5, 92
best-seller, 5, 99
beyond, 126–7, 136
  life beyond, 133, 154
  place beyond, 114
  realm beyond, 131, 172
  see also desert *and* Sufi aesthetic tradition
Bhabha, Homi, 126–7, 136
  third space, 126
Booth, Marilyn, 23–4

cacophony, 14; *see also* clamor *and* dissonance
Caiani, Fabio, 22
Cairo, 13, 16, 19–20, 25–6, 29–30, 43, 45–6, 51, 55–7, 63, 91, 98–9, 102–5, 108, 110–11, 117, 120, 160, 164, 166, 169–70, 173–4, 177–85

Cairo (*cont.*)
  downtown Cairo, 13, 29, 98, 102, 110–11
    see also Tahrir Square (*midan*)
  center, 34, 56–7, 73, 99, 102, 116, 120, 125, 130, 137, 167, 184–5; *see also* margin
clamor, 13–14, 77
collective sameness, 158
communal life, 17–18, 128; *see also* traditional past
class, 2, 19–20, 26–9, 30–2, 64, 91, 98, 101–6, 108, 110–11, 120, 143, 146, 158–9, 174
  class differences, 19, 28, 105
  see also socio-economic inequality
colonialism, 23, 57–9, 124, 127, 142
cooke, miriam, 128
corruption, 10, 98, 108, 115
cosmopolitan style, 34, 84; *see also* critical cosmopolitanism
critical cosmopolitanism, 73–4, 86; *see also* Rebecca L. Walkowitz
cultural production, 6, 9, 12; *see also* novelistic production

decentered consciousness, 2, 3, 26, 93; *see also* new consciousness
Delueze, Gille, 3
demonstrations, 13; *see also* protests *and* Tahrir Square (*midan*)
desert, 33–4, 56, 87, 124–35, 137–43, 145–6, 148–54
  desert novel 129, 134
  Egyptian desert 34, 131
  see also Bedouin
diabolical muse, 78–9, 85
dialectical process, 7, 15, 185; *see also* Michael McKeon
dialogues, 30, 34, 125, 137, 185
diegesis, 53–4; *see also* mimesis
difference, 1–2, 4, 16, 19, 20, 23, 27–30, 32, 44–7, 49, 51, 54–5, 60–4, 67, 72, 74, 87, 89, 91–3, 98–9, 101, 103–5, 111–12, 120, 146, 158, 165, 174, 183, 185; *see also* discordance
differentiation, 23, 27–8, 30, 32, 35, 44, 58, 62, 64, 111, 158, 185; *see also* marginalization
discordance, 4, 14
dissent, 13, 21, 30–1, 161

poetical and political dissent, 111
popular dissent, 21
dissident voices, 13–14, 115
dissonance, 20, 159, 184
diversity, 29, 43, 46, 81, 86, 120, 159; *see also* heterogeneity
double consciousness, 34, 86
Du Bois, W. E. B., 86; *see also* double consciousness
dystopia, 178, 185
  dystopian society, 163

Egypt, 2–6, 8–23, 25, 27, 28–31, 33–4, 42–8, 50, 53–7, 62–4, 67–77, 81–3, 85–9, 93, 99, 101–5, 109–11, 115–20, 124–5, 131, 135, 140, 142, 148, 151, 154, 158, 160, 163–4, 168–70, 178, 182–5
Egyptian novel, 1–2, 5, 25
Egyptianhood, 184
Egyptianness, 161, 184
Egyptian army, 19
  Free Officers, 11
  military, 8, 10, 12, 59, 70–1, 92, 101–3, 105, 112, 178
El-Enany, Rasheed, 63, 110
Elmusa, Sharif, 129
El-Shobaki, Amr, 69
ethnicity, 1–2, 17, 26, 35, 120, 143
essentialism, 2, 4, 23, 160
  anti-essentialism, 160
  counter-essentialism, 22–3
  see also exclusivism
exclusion, 1, 30, 111, 134, 161
  exclusionary nationalist discourses, 86
  exclusionary nationalisms, 94, 169
  exclusivism, 2
  possessive exclusivism, 4, 109
  see also homogeneity
exile, 46–7, 75, 78, 84, 115, 134, 137, 139

Fanon, Frantz (Fanonian), 23, 58, 136
feminist novel, 22–3, 26, 163
Futayha, Muʿtazz, 2, 32, 67, 68, 85, 87, 93

gender, 1–2, 24–8, 35, 62, 81, 89, 98, 101, 120, 144–5, 154, 158–60, 162–4, 166, 174, 183–5; *see also* gender inequality
genre, 1, 4–7, 16, 22, 24, 27, 124–5
  generic instability, 6
  literary genre, 5
  novelistic genre, 5, 7, 16

Graeco-Roman Empire, 76–7
Guattari, Félix, 3

Hafez, Sabry, 6, 22, 25–6
Haqqi, Yahia (or Haqqi, Yehia), 16
Haykal, Muhammad Husayn (or Mohammed Hussein Haikal), 16–18
heterogeneity, 16, 29, 98, 111
 heterogeneous, 1–2, 14, 46, 159
 see also homogeneity
heteroglossic (polyphonic), 16
historical change, 7–8, 91, 148, 159, 161, 185; *see also* historical transformation(s)
historical conditions, 5, 42, 44, 68, 161
historical transformation(s), 1, 6, 8
homogeneity, 55, 108; *see also* collective sameness
homosexuality, 99, 105–6
Honeywell, Arthur J., 54–5; *see also* plot(s)

Ibrahim, Sun ͨallah (or Ibrahim, Sonallah), 19–20
identity, 16–17, 21, 30, 33, 43, 46, 49–53, 60, 72, 77, 86, 111, 124, 164, 167, 182
 national identity, 16, 43, 49
imagination, 26, 55, 74, 80, 87, 101, 125–6, 130, 132, 138–9, 141–3, 150–3, 158, 165
 collective imagination, 158
 fantasy, 148–9
 literary imaginary, 4
 national(ist) imaginary, 18, 22
 political and cultural imaginaries, 2
immigration, 27, 45
 immigrant, 1–2, 20, 30, 90, 114, 116, 118–19, 167
imperialism, 8, 32, 59, 65
inclusion, 30, 111, 161; *see also* exclusion
inequality, 26, 158
 gender equality, 25, 160, 162–4, 184
 socio-economic inequality, 26
intellectuals, 9, 11, 12, 17, 21, 80, 117, 119, 183; *see also* writers
intersections, 2, 26, 88, 158, 183; *see also* negotiations
Islamism, 8–9, 108

Jacquemond, Richard, 6, 8–9, 11, 15, 21, 23–5
Jameson, Frederic, 5

Kanafani, Ghassan, 124, 127
Krämer, Gudrun, 68, 86

Levine, George, 100; *see also* realism
linguistic defamiliarization, 53
literary establishment, 22–3, 25
literary history, 6, 15, 19
Lodge, David, 53; *see also* diegesis

Mahfuz, Najib (or Mahfouz, Naguib), 19
Mamdani, Mahmood, 44, 49, 58–9; *see also* identity *and* differentiation
margin, 31, 46, 56–7, 63, 77, 99
marginalization, 2, 23–4, 68, 86, 158
Mazloum, Sherine, Fuad, 159–61
Memmi, Albert, 60
memory, 33, 124, 129, 140, 143, 154, 181
 cultural memory, 129, 154
McKeon, Michael, 5–7, 11, 14, 159, 184–5
Mehrez, Samia, 6, 12–14
mimesis, 53–4
minority, 21, 25, 43–5, 48–9, 53, 55, 68–9, 93, 109, 158, 160, 185
 Coptic minority, 69
 ethnic minority, 43, 48, 55
 ethno-religious minority, 93
 Jewish minority, 68
 Kenuz-Nubian minority, 53
 minor literature, 3
modernity, 16, 19, 20, 30, 55, 111, 124, 147, 167, 171
modernization, 127
see also tradition
monastic tradition (Coptic), 33, 72
 monks, 33–4, 46, 72, 74, 77–8, 83–4, 134–5, 137–8
Moolla, F. F., 134
Mubarak, Husni (or Mubarak, Hosni), 10–13, 42, 69, 70–1, 159, 163
Munif, ͨAbd al-Rahman (or, Abdel Rahman, Munif), 124, 127–8
Mursi, Muhammad (or Mohamed Morsi), 12, 70, 159
Muslim Brotherhood, 10–12, 68–71, 166, 169–71
mythical center, 34, 125, 130
 labyrinth, 34, 125
 see also desert
myths, 21, 50, 126, 130

nationalism, 16–17, 19, 21–2, 48, 87, 94, 160, 169, 183

negotiations, 30, 34, 106, 111, 125, 184; *see also* dialogues
new consciousness, 1–2, 4–6, 8, 14–16, 22, 26–9, 31, 33, 42, 130, 158–9, 161, 183, 185; *see also* decentered consciousness
novelistic production, 5–6, 14–15, 19, 22–3, 26, 55, 100, 124, 158, 163, 183
Nubia, 31–2, 43, 45, 48–50, 53, 55, 63–4
Nubian, 2–3, 5, 21, 29, 31–2, 42–56, 63–4, 105, 130
  Kenuz Nubians, 50–3
  Kenzi, 28, 32, 53–5, 64

otherness, 42
  Egypt's others, 45

peasant(s) (*fallaḥ*), 17–19, 25, 58, 102–3, 109–10, 135, 145, 147–8, 150–1, 174
  Egyptian peasantry, 16, 18, 103
plot(s), 54, 64
  subplots, 28–9, 103, 106, 169
pluralism, 13
  pluralistic Egypt, 1
post-2011 novel(s), 159, 161–3, 183
postcolonial state, 14, 25, 32, 49, 64, 99, 107–8
protests, 14, 39; *see also* dissent

Rabiᶜ, Muhammad, 162–3, 179
race, 1–2, 17, 26–8, 32, 45–6, 59–60, 65, 81, 87, 89–90, 93, 98, 101, 112, 134–6, 138, 147, 153, 158, 167–9, 173–4, 176, 183, 185
realism, 21, 10–11
  magical realism, 128
religion, 1–2, 9, 11, 17, 19, 26–8, 30, 32, 35, 51, 65, 67, 69, 71, 74, 77, 81, 89, 94, 101, 107–8, 110–12, 114, 117, 119–20, 135, 138, 158, 169, 174–5, 183, 185
revolution, 10, 18, 30–1, 42, 68–70, 102–3, 105–7, 117–20, 158–61, 163, 167–8, 171, 177–8, 184–5
  January revolution (2011), 42, 158

Said, Edward, 2, 4, 109; *see also* decentered consciousness *and* possessive exclusivism

Salih, Salah, 125–7, 130–3, 148; *see also* desert
sectarianism, 69–72, 77
secularist modernity, 171
Selim, Samah, 103; *see also* peasant(s) (*fallaḥ*)
Shalan, Jeff, 16–8
Siwa, 31–2, 42–3, 46–7, 56–8, 63–4; *see also* Amazigh
spirituality, 127, 130–1
Spivak, Gayatri, 23; *see also* gender *and* counter-essentialism
street censorship, 117
Sufi aesthetic tradition, 132, 136; *see also* Adonis

taboo(s), 22, 113–14
Tadros, Mariz, 159–60, 183; *see also* unruly politics
Tahir, Bahaʾ, 2–3, 5, 31–2, 42, 44–7, 56–65
Tahrir Square (*midan*), 12–4, 158–61
theology (Christian), 74, 77, 84
  Christological debate (thought), 75–6, 83
  fifth-century schism (CE) 67, 72
  Nestorian thought, 78
tradition, 5–8, 12, 16, 30, 33, 54–5, 72, 75, 79–80, 83, 91, 101, 111, 114, 132–3, 136, 144, 148, 151, 165–6, 169
  traditional past, 128
transnational, 30, 43, 73
  transnational identity, 43
  transnational negotiations and dialogues, 30
  transnational thought, 73

unruly politics, 183–5

Walkowitz, Rebecca L., 33–4, 68, 73, 83, 86
writers, 3–4, 8–9, 13–16, 19, 21–6, 33, 46–7, 72–3, 100–1, 110, 117, 160–1
  women writers, 22–5, 160

Zaydan, Yusuf (or Youssef Zeidan), 2–3, 5, 32, 67–8, 70–1, 74–5, 77–9, 81–4

EU representative:
Easy Access System Europe
Mustamäe tee 50, 10621 Tallinn, Estonia
Gpsr.requests@easproject.com

www.ingramcontent.com/pod-product-compliance
Lightning Source LLC
Chambersburg PA
CBHW081351230426
43667CB00017B/2797